THE STANDARD EDITION OF
THE COMPLETE PSYCHOLOGICAL WORKS
OF SIGMUND FREUD

VOLUME XVIII

Sigmund Freud in 1922

Max Halberstadt

THE STANDARD EDITION OF THE
COMPLETE PSYCHOLOGICAL WORKS OF

Sigmund Freud

VOLUME XVIII
(1920–1922)

BEYOND THE PLEASURE PRINCIPLE

GROUP PSYCHOLOGY

and

OTHER WORKS

TRANSLATED FROM THE GERMAN
UNDER THE GENERAL EDITORSHIP OF
James Strachey

IN COLLABORATION WITH
Anna Freud

ASSISTED BY
Alix Strachey and Alan Tyson

VINTAGE
THE HOGARTH PRESS
AND THE INSTITUTE OF PSYCHO-ANALYSIS

Published by Vintage 2001

5 7 9 10 8 6 4

Translation and editorial matter
© The Institute of Psycho-Analysis 1955

First published in Great Britain in 1955
by The Hogarth Press

Vintage
Random House, 20 Vauxhall Bridge Road,
London SW1V 2SA

www.vintage-books.co.uk

Addresses for companies within The Random House Group Limited can be found at:
www.randomhouse.co.uk/offices.htm

A CIP catalogue record for this book
is available from the British Library

ISBN 9780099426738

The Random House Group Limited makes every effort to ensure that the papers used in
its books are made from trees that have been legally sourced from well-managed and
credibly certified forests. Our paper procurement policy can be found at:
www.randomhouse.co.uk/paper.htm

Printed and bound in Denmark by
Nørhaven Paperback A/S, Viborg

CONTENTS

TWO ENCYCLOPAEDIA ARTICLES (1923 [1922])

SHORTER WRITINGS (1920–1922)

BEYOND THE PLEASURE PRINCIPLE
(1920)

EDITOR'S NOTE

JENSEITS DES LUSTPRINZIPS

(a) GERMAN EDITIONS:

1920   Leipzig, Vienna and Zurich: Internationaler Psycho-
          analytischer Verlag. Pp. 60.
1921   2nd ed. Same publishers. Pp. 64.
1923   3rd ed. Same publishers. Pp. 94.
1925   *G.S.*, **6**, 191–257.
1931   *Theoretische Schriften*, 178–247.
1940   *G.W.*, **13**, 3–69.

(b) ENGLISH TRANSLATIONS:

Beyond the Pleasure Principle

1922   London and Vienna: International Psycho-Analytical
          Press. Pp. viii + 90. (Tr. C. J. M. Hubback; Pref.
          Ernest Jones.)
1924   New York: Boni and Liveright.
1942   London: Hogarth Press and Institute of Psycho-Analy-
          sis. (Re-issue of above.)
1950   Same Publishers. Pp. vi + 97. (Tr. J. Strachey.)

Freud made a number of additions in the second edition, but
subsequent alterations were negligible. The present translation
is a somewhat modifield version of the one published in 1950.

As is shown by his correspondence, Freud had begun working
on a first draft of *Beyond the Pleasure Principle* in March, 1919,
and he reported the draft as finished in the following May.
During the same month he was completing his paper on 'The
Uncanny' (1919*h*), which includes a paragraph setting out
much of the gist of the present work in a few sentences. In this
paragraph he refers to the 'compulsion to repeat' as a phenomenon exhibited in the behaviour of children and in psycho-
analytic treatment; he suggests that this compulsion is something derived from the most intimate nature of the instincts;
and he declares that it is powerful enough to disregard the

pleasure principle. There is, however, no allusion to the 'death
instincts'. He adds that he has already completed a detailed
exposition of the subject. The paper on 'The Uncanny' containing this summary was published in the autumn of 1919.
But Freud held back *Beyond the Pleasure Principle* for another
year. In the early part of 1920 he was once more at work on it,
and now, for the first time apparently, there is a reference to
the 'death instincts' in a letter to Eitingon of February 20. He
was still revising the work in May and June and it was finally
completed by the middle of July, 1920. On September 9, he gave
an address to the International Psycho-Analytical Congress
at The Hague, with the title 'Supplements to the Theory of
Dreams' (*Ergänzungen zur Traumlehre*), in which he announced
the approaching publication of the book; it was issued soon
afterwards. An 'author's abstract' of the address appeared in
Int. Z. Psychoanal., 6 (1920), 397–8. (A translation of this was published in *Int. J. Psycho-Anal.*, 1, 354.) It does not seem certain
that this abstract was in fact by Freud himself, but it may be of
interest to reprint it here (in a new translation).

'Supplements to the Theory of Dreams'

'The speaker dealt in his brief remarks with three points
touching upon the theory of dreams. The first two of these were
concerned with the thesis that dreams are wish-fulfilments and
brought forward some necessary modifications of it. The third
point related to material which brought complete confirmation
of his rejection of the alleged "prospective" purposes of dreams.[1]

'The speaker explained that, alongside the familiar wishful
dreams and the anxiety dreams which could easily be included
in the theory, there were grounds for recognizing the existence
of a third category, to which he gave the name of "punishment
dreams". If we took into account the justifiable assumption of
the existence of a special self-observing and critical agency in
the ego (the ego ideal, the censor, conscience), these punishment dreams, too, should be subsumed under the theory of
wish-fulfilment; for they would represent the fulfilment of a
wish on the part of this critical agency. Such dreams, he said,
had approximately the same relation to ordinary wishful dreams

---

[1] [See *The Interpretation of Dreams*, 1900a, VI (I), *Stadarnd Ed.*, 5,
506–7 n.]

as the symptoms of obsessional neurosis, which arise from re-action formation, had to those of hysteria.

'Another class of dreams, however, seemed to the speaker to present a more serious exception to the rule that dreams are wish-fulfilments. These were the so-called "traumatic" dreams. They occur in patients suffering from accidents, but they also occur during psycho-analyses of neurotics and bring back to them forgotten traumas of childhood. In connection with the problem of fitting these dreams into the theory of wish-fulfil-ment, the speaker referred to a work shortly to be published under the title of *Beyond the Pleasure Principle*.

'The third point of the speaker's communication related to an investigation that had not yet been published, by Dr. Varen-donck of Ghent. This author had succeeded in bringing under his conscious observation the production of unconscious phan-tasies on an extensive scale in a half-sleeping state—a process which he described as "autistic thinking". It appeared from this enquiry that looking ahead at the possibilities of the next day, preparing attempts at solutions and adaptations, etc., lay wholly within the range of this preconscious activity, which also created latent dream-thoughts, and, as the speaker had always maintained, had nothing to do with the dream-work.'[1]

In the series of Freud's metapsychological writings, *Beyond the Pleasure Principle* may be regarded as introducing the final phase of his views. He had already drawn attention to the 'compulsion to repeat' as a clinical phenomenon, but here he attributes to it the characteristics of an instinct; here too for the first time he brings forward the new dichotomy between Eros and the death instincts which found its full elaboration in *The Ego and the Id* (1923b). In *Beyond the Pleasure Principle*, too, we can see signs of the new picture of the anatomical structure of the mind which was to dominate all Freud's later writings. Finally, the problem of destructiveness, which played an ever more prominent part in his theoretical works, makes its first explicit appearance. The derivation of various elements in the present discussion from his earlier metapsychological works— such as 'The Two Principles of Mental Functioning' (1911b),

[1] A preface by Freud to this book of Varendonck's will be found later in this Volume.

'Narcissism' (1914c) and 'Instincts and their Vicissitudes' (1915c)—will be obvious. But what is particularly remarkable is the closeness with which some of the earlier sections of the present work follow the 'Project for a Scientific Psychology' (1950a), drafted by Freud twenty-five years earlier, in 1895.

Extracts from the earlier (1922) translation of this work were included in Rickman's *General Selection from the Works of Sigmund Freud* (1937, 162–194).

BEYOND THE PLEASURE
PRINCIPLE

I

IN the theory of psycho-analysis we have no hesitation in assuming that the course taken by mental events is automatically regulated by the pleasure principle. We believe, that is to say, that the course of those events is invariably set in motion by an unpleasurable tension, and that it takes a direction such that its final outcome coincides with a lowering of that tension—that is, with an avoidance of unpleasure or a production of pleasure. In taking that course into account in our consideration of the mental processes which are the subject of our study, we are introducing an 'economic' point of view into our work; and if, in describing those processes, we try to estimate this 'economic' factor in addition to the 'topographical' and 'dynamic' ones, we shall, I think, be giving the most complete description of them of which we can at present conceive, and one which deserves to be distinguished by the term 'metapsychological'.[1]

It is of no concern to us in this connection to enquire how far, with this hypothesis of the pleasure principle, we have approached or adopted any particular, historically established, philosophical system. We have arrived at these speculative assumptions in an attempt to describe and to account for the facts of daily observation in our field of study. Priority and originality are not among the aims that psycho-analytic work sets itself; and the impressions that underlie the hypothesis of the pleasure principle are so obvious that they can scarcely be overlooked. On the other hand we would readily express our gratitude to any philosophical or psychological theory which was able to inform us of the meaning of the feelings of pleasure and unpleasure which act so imperatively upon us. But on this point we are, alas, offered nothing to our purpose. This is the most obscure and inaccessible region of the mind, and, since we cannot avoid contact with it, the least rigid hypothesis, it seems to me, will be the best. We have decided to relate

[1] [See Section IV of 'The Unconscious' (1915e).]

7

pleasure and unpleasure to the quantity of excitation that is present in the mind but is not in any way 'bound'; [1] and to relate them in such a manner that unpleasure corresponds to an *increase* in the quantity of excitation and pleasure to a *diminution*. What we are implying by this is not a simple relation between the strength of the feelings of pleasure and unpleasure and the corresponding modifications in the quantity of excitation; least of all—in view of all we have been taught by psychophysiology—are we suggesting any directly proportional ratio: the factor that determines the feeling is probably the amount of increase or diminution in the quantity of excitation *in a given period of time*. Experiment might possibly play a part here; but it is not advisable for us analysts to go into the problem further so long as our way is not pointed by quite definite observations. [2]

We cannot, however, remain indifferent to the discovery that an investigator of such penetration as G. T. Fechner held a view on the subject of pleasure and unpleasure which coincides in all essentials with the one that has been forced upon us by psycho-analytic work. Fechner's statement is to be found contained in a small work, *Einige Ideen zur Schöpfungs- und Entwicklungsgeschichte der Organismen*, 1873 (Part XI, Supplement, 94), and reads as follows: 'In so far as conscious impulses always have some relation to pleasure or unpleasure, pleasure and unpleasure too can be regarded as having a psycho-physical relation to conditions of stability and instability. This provides a basis for a hypothesis into which I propose to enter in greater detail elsewhere. According to this hypothesis, every psychophysical motion rising above the threshold of consciousness is attended by pleasure in proportion as, beyond a certain limit, it approximates to complete stability, and is attended by unpleasure in proportion as, beyond a certain limit, it deviates from complete stability; while between the two limits, which may be described as qualitative thresholds of pleasure and

---

[1] [The concepts of 'quantity' and of 'bound' excitation, which run through the whole of Freud's writings, found what is perhaps their most detailed discussion in the early 'Project' (1950a [1895]). See in particular the long discussion of the term 'bound' near the end of Section 1 of Part III of that work. See also p. 34 f. below.]

[2] [This point is again mentioned below on p. 63 and further developed in 'The Economic Problem of Masochism' (1924c).]

unpleasure, there is a certain margin of aesthetic indifference. . . .' [1]

The facts which have caused us to believe in the dominance
of the pleasure principle in mental life also find expression in
the hypothesis that the mental apparatus endeavours to keep
the quantity of excitation present in it as low as possible or at
least to keep it constant. This latter hypothesis is only another
way of stating the pleasure principle; for if the work of the
mental apparatus is directed towards keeping the quantity of
excitation low, then anything that is calculated to increase that
quantity is bound to be felt as adverse to the functioning of the
apparatus, that is as unpleasurable. The pleasure principle
follows from the principle of constancy: actually the latter
principle was inferred from the facts which forced us to adopt
the pleasure principle.[2] Moreover, a more detailed discussion
will show that the tendency which we thus attribute to the
mental apparatus is subsumed as a special case under Fechner's
principle of the 'tendency towards stability', to which he has
brought the feelings of pleasure and unpleasure into relation.

It must be pointed out, however, that strictly speaking it is
incorrect to talk of the dominance of the pleasure principle over
the course of mental processes. If such a dominance existed,
the immense majority of our mental processes would have to be
accompanied by pleasure or to lead to pleasure, whereas
universal experience completely contradicts any such conclusion. The most that can be said, therefore, is that there exists
in the mind a strong *tendency* towards the pleasure principle, but
that that tendency is opposed by certain other forces or circumstances, so that the final outcome cannot always be in harmony

---

[1] [Cf. 'Project', end of Section 8 of Part I.—'Aesthetic' is here used in
the old sense of 'relating to sensation or perception'.]

[2] [The 'principle of constancy' dates back to the very beginning of
Freud's psychological studies. The first published discussion of it of any
length was by Breuer (in semi-physiological terms) towards the end of
Section 2(A) of his theoretical part of the *Studies on Hysteria* (Breuer and
Freud, 1895). He there defines it as 'the tendency to keep intracerebral
excitation constant'. In the same passage he attributes this principle to
Freud and there in fact exist one or two earlier very brief references to
it by Freud himself, though these were not published until after his
death. (See Freud, 1941a [1892] and Breuer and Freud, 1940 [1892].)
The subject is also discussed at length at the beginning of Freud's
'Project', under the name of 'neuronic inertia'.]

with the tendency towards pleasure. We may compare what Fechner (1873, 90) remarks on a similar point: 'Since however a tendency towards an aim does not imply that the aim is attained, and since in general the aim is attainable only by approxima-tions. . . .'

If we turn now to the question of what circumstances are able to prevent the pleasure principle from being carried into effect, we find ourselves once more on secure and well-trodden ground and, in framing our answer, we have at our disposal a rich fund of analytic experience.

The first example of the pleasure principle being inhibited in this way is a familiar one which occurs with regularity. We know that the pleasure principle is proper to a *primary* method of working on the part of the mental apparatus, but that, from the point of view of the self-preservation of the organism among the difficulties of the external world, it is from the very outset inefficient and even highly dangerous. Under the influence of the ego's instincts of self-preservation, the pleasure principle is replaced by the *reality principle*.[1] This latter principle does not abandon the intention of ultimately obtaining pleasure, but it nevertheless demands and carries into effect the postponement of satisfaction, the abandonment of a number of possibilities of gaining satisfaction and the temporary toleration of unpleasure as a step on the long indirect road to pleasure. The pleasure principle long persists, however, as the method of working em-ployed by the sexual instincts, which are so hard to 'educate', and, starting from those instincts, or in the ego itself, it often succeeds in overcoming the reality principle, to the detriment of the organism as a whole.

There can be no doubt, however, that the replacement of the pleasure principle by the reality principle can only be made responsible for a small number, and by no means the most intense, of unpleasurable experiences. Another occasion of the release of unpleasure, which occurs with no less regularity, is to be found in the conflicts and dissensions that take place in the mental apparatus while the ego is passing through its develop-ment into more highly composite organizations. Almost all the energy with which the apparatus is filled arises from its innate instinctual impulses. But these are not all allowed to reach

[1] [See 'Formulations on the Two Principles of Mental Functioning', Freud 1911*b*.]

the same phases of development. In the course of things it happens again and again that individual instincts or parts of instincts turn out to be incompatible in their aims or demands with the remaining ones, which are able to combine into the inclusive unity of the ego. The former are then split off from this unity by the process of repression, held back at lower levels of psychical development and cut off, to begin with, from the possibility of satisfaction. If they succeed subsequently, as can so easily happen with repressed sexual instincts, in struggling through, by roundabout paths, to a direct or to a substitutive satisfaction, that event, which would in other cases have been an opportunity for pleasure, is felt by the ego as unpleasure. As a consequence of the old conflict which ended in repression, a new breach has occurred in the pleasure principle at the very time when certain instincts were endeavouring, in accordance with the principle, to obtain fresh pleasure. The details of the process by which repression turns a possibility of pleasure into a source of unpleasure are not yet clearly understood or cannot be clearly represented; but there is no doubt that all neurotic unpleasure is of that kind—pleasure that cannot be felt as such.[1]

The two sources of unpleasure which I have just indicated are very far from covering the majority of our unpleasurable experiences. But as regards the remainder it can be asserted with some show of justification that their presence does not contradict the dominance of the pleasure principle. Most of the unpleasure that we experience is *perceptual* unpleasure. It may be perception of pressure by unsatisfied instincts; or it may be external perception which is either distressing in itself or which excites unpleasurable expectations in the mental apparatus—that is, which is recognized by it as a 'danger'. The reaction to these instinctual demands and threats of danger, a reaction which constitutes the proper activity of the mental apparatus, can then be directed in a correct manner by the pleasure principle or the reality principle by which the former is modified. This does not seem to necessitate any far-reaching limitation of the pleasure principle. Nevertheless the investigation of the mental reaction to external danger is precisely in a position to produce new material and raise fresh questions bearing upon our present problem.

[1] [*Footnote added* 1925:] No doubt the essential point is that pleasure and unpleasure, being conscious feelings, are attached to the ego.

II

A CONDITION has long been known and described which occurs after severe mechanical concussions, railway disasters and other accidents involving a risk to life; it has been given the name of 'traumatic neurosis'. The terrible war which has just ended gave rise to a great number of illnesses of this kind, but it at least put an end to the temptation to attribute the cause of the disorder to organic lesions of the nervous system brought about by mechanical force.[1] The symptomatic picture presented by traumatic neurosis approaches that of hysteria in the wealth of its similar motor symptoms, but surpasses it as a rule in its strongly marked signs of subjective ailment (in which it resembles hypochondria or melancholia) as well as in the evidence it gives of a far more comprehensive general enfeeblement and disturbance of the mental capacities. No complete explanation has yet been reached either of war neuroses or of the traumatic neuroses of peace. In the case of the war neuroses, the fact that the same symptoms sometimes came about without the intervention of any gross mechanical force seemed at once enlightening and bewildering. In the case of the ordinary traumatic neuroses two characteristics emerge prominently: first, that the chief weight in their causation seems to rest upon the factor of surprise, of fright; and secondly, that a wound or injury inflicted simultaneously works as a rule *against* the development of a neurosis. 'Fright', 'fear' and 'anxiety'[2] are improperly used as synonymous expressions; they are in fact capable of clear distinction in their relation to danger. 'Anxiety' describes a particular state of expecting the danger or preparing for it, even though it may be an unknown one. 'Fear' requires a definite object of which to be afraid. 'Fright', however, is the name we give to the state a person gets into when he has run into danger without being prepared for it; it emphasizes the factor of surprise. I do not believe anxiety can produce a traumatic neuro-

---

[1] Cf. the discussion on the psycho-analysis of war neuroses by Freud, Ferenczi, Abraham, Simmel and Jones (1919) [to which Freud provided the introduction (1919d). See also his posthumously published 'Report on the Electrical Treatment of War Neuroses' (1955c [1920]).]

[2] [In German, *'Schreck'*, *'Furcht'* and *'Angst'*.]

sis. There is something about anxiety that protects its subject against fright and so against fright-neuroses. We shall return to this point later [p. 31 f.].[1]

The study of dreams may be considered the most trustworthy method of investigating deep mental processes. Now dreams occurring in traumatic neuroses have the characteristic of repeatedly bringing the patient back into the situation of his accident, a situation from which he wakes up in another fright. This astonishes people far too little. They think the fact that the traumatic experience is constantly forcing itself upon the patient even in his sleep is a proof of the strength of that experience: the patient is, as one might say, fixated to his trauma. Fixations to the experience which started the illness have long been familiar to us in hysteria. Breuer and Freud declared in 1893 [2] that 'hysterics suffer mainly from reminiscences'. In the war neuroses, too, observers like Ferenczi and Simmel have been able to explain certain motor symptoms by fixation to the moment at which the trauma occurred.

I am not aware, however, that patients suffering from traumatic neurosis are much occupied in their waking lives with memories of their accident. Perhaps they are more concerned with *not* thinking of it. Anyone who accepts it as something self-evident that their dreams should put them back at night into the situation that caused them to fall ill has misunderstood the nature of dreams. It would be more in harmony with their nature if they showed the patient pictures from his healthy past or of the cure for which he hopes. If we are not to be shaken in our belief in the wish-fulfilling tenor of dreams by the dreams of traumatic neurotics, we still have one resource open to us: we may argue that the function of dreaming, like so much else, is upset in this condition and diverted from its purposes, or we

[1] [Freud is very far indeed from always carrying out the distinction he makes here. More often than not he uses the word '*Angst*' to denote a state of fear without any reference to the future. It seems not unlikely that in this passage he is beginning to adumbrate the distinction drawn in *Inhibitions, Symptoms and Anxiety* (1926*d*) between anxiety as a reaction to a traumatic situation—probably equivalent to what is here called *Schreck*—and anxiety as a warning signal of the approach of such an event. See also his use of the phrase 'preparedness for anxiety' on p. 31.]

[2] ['On the Psychical Mechanism of Hysterical Phenomena', end of Section I.]

may be driven to reflect on the mysterious masochistic trends of the ego.[1]

At this point I propose to leave the dark and dismal subject of the traumatic neurosis and pass on to examine the method of working employed by the mental apparatus in one of its earliest *normal* activities—I mean in children's play.

The different theories of children's play have only recently been summarized and discussed from the psycho-analytic point of view by Pfeifer (1919), to whose paper I would refer my readers. These theories attempt to discover the motives which lead children to play, but they fail to bring into the foreground the *economic* motive, the consideration of the yield of pleasure involved. Without wishing to include the whole field covered by these phenomena, I have been able, through a chance opportunity which presented itself, to throw some light upon the first game played by a little boy of one and a half and invented by himself. It was more than a mere fleeting observation, for I lived under the same roof as the child and his parents for some weeks, and it was some time before I discovered the meaning of the puzzling activity which he constantly repeated.

The child was not at all precocious in his intellectual development. At the age of one and a half he could say only a few comprehensible words; he could also make use of a number of sounds which expressed a meaning intelligible to those around him. He was, however, on good terms with his parents and their one servant-girl, and tributes were paid to his being a 'good boy'. He did not disturb his parents at night, he conscientiously obeyed orders not to touch certain things or go into certain rooms, and above all he never cried when his mother left him for a few hours. At the same time, he was greatly attached to his mother, who had not only fed him herself but had also looked after him without any outside help. This good little boy, however, had an occasional disturbing habit of taking any small objects he could get hold of and throwing them away from him into a corner, under the bed, and so on, so that hunting for his toys and picking them up was often quite a business. As he did this he gave vent to a loud, long-drawn-out 'o-o-o-o', accompanied by an expression of interest and satisfaction. His mother

[1] [The last 15 words of this sentence were added in 1921. For all this see *The Interpretation of Dreams* (1900*a*), *Standard Ed.*, 5, 550 ff.]

and the writer of the present account were agreed in thinking
that this was not a mere interjection but represented the German word '*fort*' ['gone']. I eventually realized that it was a
game and that the only use he made of any of his toys was to
play 'gone' with them. One day I made an observation which
confirmed my view. The child had a wooden reel with a piece
of string tied round it. It never occurred to him to pull it along
the floor behind him, for instance, and play at its being a car-
riage. What he did was to hold the reel by the string and very
skilfully throw it over the edge of his curtained cot, so that it
disappeared into it, at the same time uttering his expressive
'o-o-o-o'. He then pulled the reel out of the cot again by the
string and hailed its reappearance with a joyful '*da*' ['there'].
This, then, was the complete game—disappearance and return.
As a rule one only witnessed its first act, which was repeated
untiringly as a game in itself, though there is no doubt that the
greater pleasure was attached to the second act.[1]

The interpretation of the game then became obvious. It
was related to the child's great cultural achievement—the instinctual renunciation (that is, the renunciation of instinctual
satisfaction) which he had made in allowing his mother to go
away without protesting. He compensated himself for this, as it
were, by himself staging the disappearance and return of the
objects within his reach. It is of course a matter of indifference
from the point of view of judging the effective nature of the
game whether the child invented it himself or took it over on
some outside suggestion. Our interest is directed to another
point. The child cannot possibly have felt his mother's departure as something agreeable or even indifferent. How then does
his repetition of this distressing experience as a game fit in with
the pleasure principle? It may perhaps be said in reply that her
departure had to be enacted as a necessary preliminary to her joyful return, and that it was in the latter that lay the true purpose

---

[1] A further observation subsequently confirmed this interpretation
fully. One day the child's mother had been away for several hours and
on her return was met with the words 'Baby o-o-o-o!' which was at first
incomprehensible. It soon turned out, however, that during this long
period of solitude the child had found a method of making *himself* disappear. He had discovered his reflection in a full-length mirror which
did not quite reach to the ground, so that by crouching down he could
make his mirror-image 'gone'. [A further reference to this story will be
found in *The Interpretation of Dreams*, Standard Ed., **5**, 461*n*.]

of the game. But against this must be counted the observed fact that the first act, that of departure, was staged as a game in itself and far more frequently than the episode in its entirety, with its pleasurable ending.

No certain decision can be reached from the analysis of a single case like this. On an unprejudiced view one gets an impression that the child turned his experience into a game from another motive. At the outset he was in a *passive* situation—he was overpowered by the experience; but, by repeating it, unpleasurable though it was, as a game, he took on an *active* part. These efforts might be put down to an instinct for mastery that was acting independently of whether the memory was in itself pleasurable or not. But still another interpretation may be attempted. Throwing away the object so that it was 'gone' might satisfy an impulse of the child's, which was suppressed in his actual life, to revenge himself on his mother for going away from him. In that case it would have a defiant meaning: 'All right, then, go away! I don't need you. I'm sending you away myself.' A year later, the same boy whom I had observed at his first game used to take a toy, if he was angry with it, and throw it on the floor, exclaiming: 'Go to the fwont!' He had heard at that time that his absent father was 'at the front', and was far from regretting his absence; on the contrary he made it quite clear that he had no desire to be disturbed in his sole possession of his mother.[1] We know of other children who liked to express similar hostile impulses by throwing away objects instead of persons.[2] We are therefore left in doubt as to whether the impulse to work over in the mind some overpowering experience so as to make oneself master of it can find expression as a primary event, and independently of the pleasure principle. For, in the case we have been discussing, the child may, after all, only have been able to repeat his unpleasant experience in play because the repetition carried along with it a yield of pleasure of another sort but none the less a direct one.

Nor shall we be helped in our hesitation between these two views by further considering children's play. It is clear that in

---

[1] When this child was five and three-quarters, his mother died. Now that she was really 'gone' ('o-o-o'), the little boy showed no signs of grief. It is true that in the interval a second child had been born and had roused him to violent jealousy.

[2] Cf. my note on a childhood memory of Goethe's (1917b).

their play children repeat everything that has made a great impression on them in real life, and that in doing so they abreact the strength of the impression and, as one might put it, make themselves master of the situation. But on the other hand it is obvious that all their play is influenced by a wish that dominates them the whole time—the wish to be grown-up and to be able to do what grown-up people do. It can also be observed that the unpleasurable nature of an experience does not always unsuit it for play. If the doctor looks down a child's throat or carries out some small operation on him, we may be quite sure that these frightening experiences will be the subject of the next game; but we must not in that connection overlook the fact that there is a yield of pleasure from another source. As the child passes over from the passivity of the experience to the activity of the game, he hands on the disagreeable experience to one of his playmates and in this way revenges himself on a substitute.

Nevertheless, it emerges from this discussion that there is no need to assume the existence of a special imitative instinct in order to provide a motive for play. Finally, a reminder may be added that the artistic play and artistic imitation carried out by adults, which, unlike children's, are aimed at an audience, do not spare the spectators (for instance, in tragedy) the most painful experiences and can yet be felt by them as highly enjoyable.[1] This is convincing proof that, even under the dominance of the pleasure principle, there are ways and means enough of making what is in itself unpleasurable into a subject to be recollected and worked over in the mind. The consideration of these cases and situations, which have a yield of pleasure as their final outcome, should be undertaken by some system of aesthetics with an economic approach to its subject-matter. They are of no use for *our* purposes, since they presuppose the existence and dominance of the pleasure principle; they give no evidence of the operation of tendencies *beyond* the pleasure principle, that is, of tendencies more primitive than it and independent of it.

[1] [Freud had made a tentative study of this point in his posthumously published paper on 'Psychopathic Characters on the Stage' (1942*a*) which was probably written in 1905 or 1906.]

III

TWENTY-FIVE years of intense work have had as their result
that the immediate aims of psycho-analytic technique are quite
other to-day than they were at the outset. At first the analysing
physician could do no more than discover the unconscious
material that was concealed from the patient, put it together,
and, at the right moment, communicate it to him. Psycho-
analysis was then first and foremost an art of interpreting.
Since this did not solve the therapeutic problem, a further aim
quickly came in view: to oblige the patient to confirm the
analyst's construction from his own memory. In that endeavour
the chief emphasis lay upon the patient's resistances: the art
consisted now in uncovering these as quickly as possible, in
pointing them out to the patient and in inducing him by human
influence—this was where suggestion operating as 'transference'
played its part—to abandon his resistances.

But it became ever clearer that the aim which had been set
up—the aim that what was unconscious should become conscious—is not completely attainable by that method. The
patient cannot remember the whole of what is repressed in him,
and what he cannot remember may be precisely the essential
part of it. Thus he acquires no sense of conviction of the cor-
rectness of the construction that has been communicated to
him. He is obliged to *repeat* the repressed material as a contemporary experience instead of, as the physician would prefer
to see, *remembering* it as something belonging to the past.[1] These
reproductions, which emerge with such unwished-for exacti-
tude, always have as their subject some portion of infantile
sexual life—of the Oedipus complex, that is, and its derivatives;
and they are invariably acted out in the sphere of the transference, of the patient's relation to the physician. When things
have reached this stage, it may be said that the earlier neurosis
has now been replaced by a fresh, 'transference neurosis'. It has

[1] See my paper on 'Recollecting, Repeating and Working Through'
(1914*g*). [An early reference will be found in this same paper to the
'compulsion to repeat', which is one of the principle topics discussed in
the present work. (See also the Editor's Note above, p. 5.)—The term
'transference neurosis' in the special sense in which it is used a few lines
lower down also appears in that paper.]

been the physician's endeavour to keep this transference neurosis within the narrowest limits: to force as much as possible into the channel of memory and to allow as little as possible to emerge as repetition. The ratio between what is remembered and what is reproduced varies from case to case. The physician cannot as a rule spare his patient this phase of the treatment. He must get him to re-experience some portion of his forgotten life, but must see to it, on the other hand, that the patient retains some degree of aloofness, which will enable him, in spite of everything, to recognize that what appears to be reality is in fact only a reflection of a forgotten past. If this can be successfully achieved, the patient's sense of conviction is won, together with the therapeutic success that is dependent on it.

In order to make it easier to understand this 'compulsion to repeat', which emerges during the psycho-analytic treatment of neurotics, we must above all get rid of the mistaken notion that what we are dealing with in our struggle against resistances is resistance on the part of the *unconscious*. The unconscious— that is to say, the 'repressed'—offers no resistance whatever to the efforts of the treatment. Indeed, it itself has no other endeavour than to break through the pressure weighing down on it and force its way either to consciousness or to a discharge through some real action. Resistance during treatment arises from the same higher strata and systems of the mind which originally carried out repression. But the fact that, as we know from experience, the motives of the resistances, and indeed the resistances themselves, are unconscious at first during the treatment, is a hint to us that we should correct a shortcoming in our terminology. We shall avoid a lack of clarity if we make our contrast not between the conscious and the unconscious but between the coherent *ego* [1] and the *repressed*. It is certain that much of the ego is itself unconscious, and notably what we may describe as its nucleus; only a small part of it is covered by the term 'preconscious'. [2] Having replaced a purely descriptive

[1] [The view of the ego as a coherent structure performing certain functions seem to go back to Freud's 'Project'. See, for instance Section 14 of Part I of that work (Freud 1950a). The subject was taken up and developed in *The Ego and the Id*, 1923b. Cf. in particular the end of Chapter I and Chapter II.

[2] [In its present form this sentence dates from 1921. In the first edition (1920) it ran: 'It may be that much of the ego is itself unconscious; only a part of it, probably, is covered by the term "preconscious".']

terminology by one which is systematic or dynamic, we can say that the patient's resistance arises from his ego,[1] and we then at once perceive that the compulsion to repeat must be ascribed to the unconscious repressed. It seems probable that the compulsion can only express itself after the work of treatment has gone half-way to meet it and has loosened the repression.[2]

There is no doubt that the resistance of the conscious and unconscious ego operates under the sway of the pleasure principle: it seeks to avoid the unpleasure which would be produced by the liberation of the repressed. *Our* efforts, on the other hand, are directed towards procuring the toleration of that unpleasure by an appeal to the reality principle. But how is the compulsion to repeat—the manifestation of the power of the repressed—related to the pleasure principle? It is clear that the greater part of what is re-experienced under the compulsion to repeat must cause the ego unpleasure, since it brings to light activities of repressed instinctual impulses. That, however, is unpleasure of a kind we have already considered and does not contradict the pleasure principle: unpleasure for one system and simultaneously satisfaction for the other.[3] But we come now to a new and remarkable fact, namely that the compulsion to repeat also recalls from the past experiences which include no possibility of pleasure, and which can never, even long ago, have brought satisfaction even to instinctual impulses which have since been repressed.

The early efflorescence of infantile sexual life is doomed to extinction because its wishes are incompatible with reality and with the inadequate stage of development which the child has reached. That efflorescence comes to an end in the most distressing circumstances and to the accompaniment of the most painful feelings. Loss of love and failure leave behind them a permanent injury to self-regard in the form of a narcissistic scar, which in my opinion, as well as in Marcinowski's (1918), contributes more than anything to the 'sense of inferiority'

[1] [A fuller and somewhat different account of the sources of resistance will be found in Chap. XI of *Inhibitions, Symptoms and Anxiety* (1926d).]

[2] [*Footnote added* 1923:] I have argued elsewhere [1923c] that what thus comes to the help of the compulsion to repeat is the factor of 'suggestion' in the treatment—that is, the patient's submissiveness to the physician, which has its roots deep in his unconscious parental complex.

[3] [Cf. Freud's allegorical use of the fairy tale of the 'Three Wishes' at the beginning of Lecture XIV of his *Introductory Lectures* (1916–17).]

which is so common in neurotics. The child's sexual researches, on which limits are imposed by his physical development, lead to no satisfactory conclusion; hence such later complaints as 'I can't accomplish anything; I can't succeed in anything'. The tie of affection, which binds the child as a rule to the parent of the opposite sex, succumbs to disappointment, to a vain expectation of satisfaction or to jealousy over the birth of a new baby—unmistakable proof of the infidelity of the object of the child's affections. His own attempt to make a baby himself, carried out with tragic seriousness, fails shamefully. The lessening amount of affection he receives, the increasing demands of education, hard words and an occasional punishment—these show him at last the full extent to which he has been scorned. These are a few typical and constantly recurring instances of the ways in which the love characteristic of the age of childhood is brought to a conclusion.

Patients repeat all of these unwanted situations and painful emotions in the transference and revive them with the greatest ingenuity. They seek to bring about the interruption of the treatment while it is still incomplete; they contrive once more to feel themselves scorned, to oblige the physician to speak severely to them and treat them coldly; they discover appropriate objects for their jealousy; instead of the passionately desired baby of their childhood, they produce a plan or a promise of some grand present—which turns out as a rule to be no less unreal. None of these things can have produced pleasure in the past, and it might be supposed that they would cause less unpleasure to-day if they emerged as memories or dreams instead of taking the form of fresh experiences. They are of course the activities of instincts intended to lead to satisfaction; but no lesson has been learnt from the old experience of these activities having led instead only to unpleasure.[1] In spite of that, they are repeated, under pressure of a compulsion.

What psycho-analysis reveals in the transference phenomena of neurotics can also be observed in the lives of some normal people. The impression they give is of being pursued by a malignant fate or possessed by some 'daemonic' power; but psychoanalysis has always taken the view that their fate is for the most part arranged by themselves and determined by early infantile influences. The compulsion which is here in evidence differs in

[1] [This sentence was added in 1921.]

no way from the compulsion to repeat which we have found in neurotics, even though the people we are now considering have never shown any signs of dealing with a neurotic conflict by producing symptoms. Thus we have come across people all of whose human relationships have the same outcome: such as the benefactor who is abandoned in anger after a time by each of his *protégés*, however much they may otherwise differ from one another, and who thus seems doomed to taste all the bitterness of ingratitude; or the man whose friendships all end in betrayal by his friend; or the man who time after time in the course of his life raises someone else into a position of great private or public authority and then, after a certain interval, himself upsets that authority and replaces him by a new one; or, again, the lover each of whose love affairs with a woman passes through the same phases and reaches the same conclusion. This 'perpetual recurrence of the same thing' causes us no astonishment when it relates to *active* behaviour on the part of the person concerned and when we can discern in him an essential character-trait which always remains the same and which is compelled to find expression in a repetition of the same experiences. We are much more impressed by cases where the subject appears to have a *passive* experience, over which he has no influence, but in which he meets with a repetition of the same fatality. There is the case, for instance, of the woman who married three successive husbands each of whom fell ill soon afterwards and had to be nursed by her on their death-beds.[1] The most moving poetic picture of a fate such as this is given by Tasso in his romantic epic *Gerusalemme Liberata*. Its hero, Tancred, unwittingly kills his beloved Clorinda in a duel while she is disguised in the armour of an enemy knight. After her burial he makes his way into a strange magic forest which strikes the Crusaders' army with terror. He slashes with his sword at a tall tree; but blood streams from the cut and the voice of Clorinda, whose soul is imprisoned in the tree, is heard complaining that he has wounded his beloved once again.

If we take into account observations such as these, based upon behaviour in the transference and upon the life-histories of men and women, we shall find courage to assume that there really does exist in the mind a compulsion to repeat which overrides the pleasure principle. Now too we shall be inclined to

[1] Cf. the apt remarks on this subject by C. G. Jung (1909).

relate to this compulsion the dreams which occur in traumatic neuroses and the impulse which leads children to play.

But it is to be noted that only in rare instances can we observe the pure effects of the compulsion to repeat, unsupported by other motives. In the case of children's play we have already laid stress on the other ways in which the emergence of the compulsion may be interpreted; the compulsion to repeat and instinctual satisfaction which is immediately pleasurable seem to converge here into an intimate partnership. The phenomena of transference are obviously exploited by the resistance which the ego maintains in its pertinacious insistence upon repression; the compulsion to repeat, which the treatment tries to bring into its service is, as it were, drawn over by the ego to *its* side (clinging as the ego does to the pleasure principle).[1] A great deal of what might be described as the compulsion of destiny seems intelligible on a rational basis; so that we are under no necessity to call in a new and mysterious motive force to explain it.

The least dubious instance [of such a motive force] is perhaps that of traumatic dreams. But on maturer reflection we shall be forced to admit that even in the other instances the whole ground is not covered by the operation of the familiar motive forces. Enough is left unexplained to justify the hypothesis of a compulsion to repeat—something that seems more primitive, more elementary, more instinctual than the pleasure principle which it over-rides. But if a compulsion to repeat *does* operate in the mind, we should be glad to know something about it, to learn what function it corresponds to, under what conditions it can emerge and what its relation is to the pleasure principle —to which, after all, we have hitherto ascribed dominance over the course of the processes of excitation in mental life.

[1] [Before 1923 the last clause read: 'the compulsion to repeat is as it were called to its help by the ego, clinging as it does to the pleasure principle.']

IV

WHAT follows is speculation, often far-fetched speculation, which the reader will consider or dismiss according to his individual predilection. It is further an attempt to follow out an idea consistently, out of curiosity to see where it will lead.

Psycho-analytic speculation takes as its point of departure the impression, derived from examining unconscious processes, that consciousness may be, not the most universal attribute of mental processes, but only a particular function of them. Speaking in metapsychological terms, it asserts that consciousness is a function of a particular system which it describes as *Cs.*[1] What consciousness yields consists essentially of perceptions of excitations coming from the external world and of feelings of pleasure and unpleasure which can only arise from within the mental apparatus; it is therefore possible to assign to the system *Pcpt.-Cs.*[2] a position in space. It must lie on the borderline between outside and inside; it must be turned towards the external world and must envelop the other psychical systems. It will be seen that there is nothing daringly new in these assumptions; we have merely adopted the views on localization held by cerebral anatomy, which locates the 'seat' of consciousness in the cerebral cortex—the outermost, enveloping layer of the central organ. Cerebral anatomy has no need to consider why, speaking anatomically, consciousness should be lodged on the surface of the brain instead of being safely housed somewhere in its inmost interior. Perhaps *we* shall be more successful in accounting for this situation in the case of our system *Pcpt.-Cs.*

Consciousness is not the only distinctive character which we ascribe to the processes in that system. On the basis of impressions derived from our psycho-analytic experience, we assume that all excitatory processes that occur in the *other* systems leave

[1] [See Freud, *The Interpretation of Dreams* (1900a), *Standard Ed.*, 5, 610 ff., and 'The Unconscious' (1915e), Section II.]

[2] [The system *Pcpt.* (the perceptual system) was first described by Freud in *The Interpretation of Dreams*, *Standard Ed.*, 5, 536 ff. In a later paper (1917d) he argued that the system *Pcpt.* coincided with the system *Cs.*]

24

permanent traces behind in them which form the foundation of memory. Such memory-traces, then, have nothing to do with the fact of becoming conscious; indeed they are often most powerful and most enduring when the process which left them behind was one which never entered consciousness. We find it hard to believe, however, that permanent traces of excitation such as these are also left in the system *Pcpt.-Cs.* If they remained constantly conscious, they would very soon set limits to the system's aptitude for receiving fresh excitations.[1] If, on the other hand, they were unconscious, we should be faced with the problem of explaining the existence of unconscious processes in a system whose functioning was otherwise accompanied by the phenomenon of consciousness. We should, so to say, have altered nothing and gained nothing by our hypothesis relegating the process of becoming conscious to a special system. Though this consideration is not absolutely conclusive, it nevertheless leads us to suspect that becoming conscious and leaving behind a memory-trace are processes incompatible with each other within one and the same system. Thus we should be able to say that the excitatory process becomes conscious in the system *Cs.* but leaves no permanent trace behind there; but that the excitation is transmitted to the systems lying next within and that it is in *them* that its traces are left. I followed these same lines in the schematic picture which I included in the speculative section of my *Interpretation of Dreams.*[2] It must be borne in mind that little enough is known from other sources of the origin of consciousness; when, therefore, we lay down the proposition that *consciousness arises instead of a memory-trace*, the assertion deserves consideration, at all events on the ground of its being framed in fairly precise terms.

If this is so, then, the system *Cs.* is characterized by the peculiarity that in it (in contrast to what happens in the other psychical systems) excitatory processes do not leave behind any permanent change in its elements but expire, as it were, in the phenomenon of becoming conscious. An exception of this sort

[1] What follows is based throughout on Breuer's views in [the second section of his theoretical contribution to] *Studies on Hysteria* (Breuer and Freud, 1895). [Freud himself discussed the subject in *The Interpretation of Dreams, Standard Ed.*, 5, 538 and it had previously been fully considered in his 'Project' of 1895 (1950a), Part I, Section 3. He returned to the topic later in his paper on the 'Mystic Writing-Pad' (1925a).]

[2] [*Standard Ed.*, 5, 538.]

to the general rule requires to be explained by some factor that applies exclusively to that one system. Such a factor, which is absent in the other systems, might well be the exposed situation of the system *Cs.*, immediately abutting as it does on the external world.

Let us picture a living organism in its most simplified possible form as an undifferentiated vesicle of a substance that is susceptible to stimulation. Then the surface turned towards the external world will from its very situation be differentiated and will serve as an organ for receiving stimuli. Indeed embryology, in its capacity as a recapitulation of developmental history, actually shows us that the central nervous system originates from the ectoderm; the grey matter of the cortex remains a derivative of the primitive superficial layer of the organism and may have inherited some of its essential properties. It would be easy to suppose, then, that as a result of the ceaseless impact of external stimuli on the surface of the vesicle, its substance to a certain depth may have become permanently modified, so that excitatory processes run a different course in it from what they run in the deeper layers. A crust would thus be formed which would at last have been so thoroughly 'baked through' by stimulation that it would present the most favourable possible conditions for the reception of stimuli and become incapable of any further modification. In terms of the system *Cs.*, this would mean that its elements could undergo no further permanent modification from the passage of excitation, because they had already been modified in the respect in question to the greatest possible extent: now, however, they would have become capable of giving rise to consciousness. Various ideas may be formed which cannot at present be verified as to the nature of this modification of the substance and of the excitatory process. It may be supposed that, in passing from one element to another, an excitation has to overcome a resistance, and that the diminution of resistance thus effected is what lays down a permanent trace of the excitation, that is, a facilitation. In the system *Cs.*, then, resistance of this kind to passage from one element to another would no longer exist.[1] This picture can be brought into relation with Breuer's distinction between quiescent (or bound) and mobile cathectic energy in the elements

[1] [This passage is foreshadowed in the later half of Section 3 of Part I of the 'Project'.]

of the psychical systems;[1] the elements of the system *Cs.* would carry no bound energy but only energy capable of free discharge. It seems best, however, to express oneself as cautiously as possible on these points. None the less, this speculation will have enabled us to bring the origin of consciousness into some sort of connection with the situation of the system *Cs.* and with the peculiarities that must be ascribed to the excitatory processes taking place in it.

But we have more to say of the living vesicle with its receptive cortical layer. This little fragment of living substance is suspended in the middle of an external world charged with the most powerful energies; and it would be killed by the stimulation emanating from these if it were not provided with a protective shield against stimuli. It acquires the shield in this way: its outermost surface ceases to have the structure proper to living matter, becomes to some degree inorganic and thenceforward functions as a special envelope or membrane resistant to stimuli. In consequence, the energies of the external world are able to pass into the next underlying layers, which have remained living, with only a fragment of their original intensity; and these layers can devote themselves, behind the protective shield, to the reception of the amounts of stimulus which have been allowed through it. By its death, the outer layer has saved all the deeper ones from a similar fate—unless, that is to say, stimuli reach it which are so strong that they break through the protective shield. *Protection against* stimuli is an almost more important function for the living organism than *reception of* stimuli. The protective shield is supplied with its own store of energy and must above all endeavour to preserve the special modes of transformation of energy operating in it against the effects threatened by the enormous energies at work in the external world—effects which tend towards a levelling out of them and hence towards destruction. The main purpose of the *reception* of stimuli is to discover the direction and nature of the external stimuli; and for that it is enough to take small specimens of the external world, to sample it in small quantities. In highly developed organisms the receptive cortical layer of the former vesicle has long been withdrawn into the depths of

[1] Breuer and Freud, 1895. [See Section 2 of Breuer's theoretical contribution, and in particular the footnote at the beginning of that section. Cf. also footnote 1 on p. 8 above.]

the interior of the body, though portions of it have been left behind on the surface immediately beneath the general shield against stimuli. These are the sense organs, which consist essentially of apparatus for the reception of certain specific effects of stimulation, but which also include special arrangements for further protection against excessive amounts of stimulation and for excluding unsuitable kinds of stimuli.[1] It is characteristic of them that they deal only with very small quantities of external stimulation and only take in *samples* of the external world. They may perhaps be compared with feelers which are all the time making tentative advances towards the external world and then drawing back from it.

At this point I shall venture to touch for a moment upon a subject which would merit the most exhaustive treatment. As a result of certain psycho-analytic discoveries, we are to-day in a position to embark on a discussion of the Kantian theorem that time and space are 'necessary forms of thought'. We have learnt that unconscious mental processes are in themselves 'timeless'.[2] This means in the first place that they are not ordered temporally, that time does not change them in any way and that the idea of time cannot be applied to them. These are negative characteristics which can only be clearly understood if a comparison is made with *conscious* mental processes. On the other hand, our abstract idea of time seems to be wholly derived from the method of working of the system *Pcpt.-Cs.* and to correspond to a perception on its own part of that method of working. This mode of functioning may perhaps constitute another way of providing a shield against stimuli. I know that these remarks must sound very obscure, but I must limit myself to these hints.[3]

We have pointed out how the living vesicle is provided with a shield against stimuli from the external world; and we had previously shown that the cortical layer next to that shield must be differentiated as an organ for receiving stimuli from without. This sensitive cortex, however, which is later to become the system *Cs.*, also receives excitations from *within*. The situation of the system between the outside and the inside and the differ-

----

[1] [Cf. 'Project', Part I, Sections 5 and 9.]

[2] [See Section V of 'The Unconscious' (1915*e*).]

[3] [Freud recurs to the origin of the idea of time at the end of his paper on 'The Mystic Writing-Pad' (1925*a*). The same paper contains a further discussion of the 'shield against stimuli'.]

ence between the conditions governing the reception of excitations in the two cases have a decisive effect on the functioning of the system and of the whole mental apparatus. Towards the outside it is shielded against stimuli, and the amounts of excitation impinging on it have only a reduced effect. Towards the inside there can be no such shield; [1] the excitations in the deeper layers extend into the system directly and in undiminished amount, in so far as certain of their characteristics give rise to feelings in the pleasure-unpleasure series. The excitations coming from within are, however, in their intensity and in other, qualitative, respects—in their amplitude, perhaps—more commensurate with the system's method of working than the stimuli which stream in from the external world. [2] This state of things produces two definite results. First, the feelings of pleasure and unpleasure (which are an index to what is happening in the interior of the apparatus) predominate over all external stimuli. And secondly, a particular way is adopted of dealing with any internal excitations which produce too great an increase of unpleasure: there is a tendency to treat them as though they were acting, not from the inside, but from the outside, so that it may be possible to bring the shield against stimuli into operation as a means of defence against them. This is the origin of *projection*, which is destined to play such a large part in the causation of pathological processes.

I have an impression that these last considerations have brought us to a better understanding of the dominance of the pleasure principle; but no light has yet been thrown on the cases that contradict that dominance. Let us therefore go a step further. We describe as 'traumatic' any excitations from outside which are powerful enough to break through the protective shield. It seems to me that the concept of trauma necessarily implies a connection of this kind with a breach in an otherwise efficacious barrier against stimuli. Such an event as an external trauma is bound to provoke a disturbance on a large scale in the functioning of the organism's energy and to set in motion every possible defensive measure. At the same time, the pleasure principle is for the moment put out of action. There is no longer any possibility of preventing the mental apparatus from being flooded with large amounts of stimulus, and another

---

[1] [Cf. 'Project', beginning of Section 10 of Part I.]
[2] [Cf. 'Project', later part of Section 4 of Part I.]

problem arises instead—the problem of mastering the amounts of stimulus which have broken in and of binding them, in the psychical sense, so that they can then be disposed of.

The specific unpleasure of physical pain is probably the result of the protective shield having been broken through in a limited area. There is then a continuous stream of excitations from the part of the periphery concerned to the central apparatus of the mind, such as could normally arise only from *within* the apparatus.[1] And how shall we expect the mind to react to this invasion? Cathectic energy is summoned from all sides to provide sufficiently high cathexes of energy in the environs of the breach. An 'anticathexis' on a grand scale is set up, for whose benefit all the other psychical systems are impoverished, so that the remaining psychical functions are extensively paralysed or reduced. We must endeavour to draw a lesson from examples such as this and use them as a basis for our metapsychological speculations. From the present case, then, we infer that a system which is itself highly cathected is capable of taking up an additional stream of fresh inflowing energy and of converting it into quiescent cathexis, that is of binding it psychically. The higher the system's own quiescent cathexis, the greater seems to be its binding force; conversely, therefore, the lower its cathexis, the less capacity will it have for taking up inflowing energy[2] and the more violent must be the consequences of such a breach in the protective shield against stimuli. To this view it cannot be justly objected that the increase of cathexis round the breach can be explained far more simply as the direct result of the inflowing masses of excitation. If that were so, the mental apparatus would merely receive an increase in its cathexes of energy, and the paralysing character of pain and the impoverishment of all the other systems would remain unexplained. Nor do the very violent phenomena of discharge to which pain gives rise affect our explanation, for they occur in a reflex manner—that is, they follow without the intervention of the mental apparatus. The indefiniteness of all our discussions on what we describe as metapsychology is of course due to the fact that we know nothing of the nature of the excitatory process that takes place in the elements of the

[1] Cf. 'Instincts and their Vicissitudes' (1915c), [and 'Project', Part I, Sections 6].

[2] [Cf. the 'principle of the insusceptibility to excitation of uncathected systems' in a footnote near the end of Freud, 1917d.]

psychical systems, and that we do not feel justified in framing any hypothesis on the subject. We are consequently operating all the time with a large unknown factor, which we are obliged to carry over into every new formula. It may be reasonably supposed that this excitatory process can be carried out with energies that vary *quantitatively*; it may also seem probable that it has more than one *quality* (in the nature of amplitude, for instance). As a new factor we have taken into consideration Breuer's hypothesis that charges of energy occur in two forms [see pp. 20–1]; so that we have to distinguish between two kinds of cathexis of the psychical systems or their elements—a freely flowing cathexis that presses on towards discharge and a quiescent cathexis. We may perhaps suspect that the binding of the energy that streams into the mental apparatus consists in its change from a freely flowing into a quiescent state.

We may, I think, tentatively venture to regard the common traumatic neurosis as a consequence of an extensive breach being made in the protective shield against stimuli. This would seem to reinstate the old, naive theory of shock, in apparent contrast to the later and psychologically more ambitious theory which attributes aetiological importance not to the effects of mechanical violence but to fright and the threat to life. These opposing views are not, however, irreconcilable; nor is the psycho-analytic view of the traumatic neurosis identical with the shock theory in its crudest form. The latter regards the essence of the shock as being the direct damage to the molecular structure or even to the histological structure of the elements of the nervous system; whereas what *we* seek to understand are the effects produced on the organ of the mind by the breach in the shield against stimuli and by the problems that follow in its train. And we still attribute importance to the element of fright. It is caused by lack of any preparedness for anxiety,[1] including lack of hypercathexis of the systems that would be the first to receive the stimulus. Owing to their low cathexis those systems are not in a good position for binding the inflowing amounts of excitation and the consequences of the breach in the protective shield follow all the more easily. It will be seen, then, that preparedness for anxiety and the hypercathexis of the receptive systems constitute the last line of defence of the shield against stimuli. In the case of quite a number of traumas, the

[1] [Cf. the note on p. 13 above.]

difference between systems that are unprepared and systems that are well prepared through being hypercathected may be a decisive factor in determining the outcome; though where the strength of a trauma exceeds a certain limit this factor will no doubt cease to carry weight. The fulfilment of wishes is, as we know, brought about in a hallucinatory manner by dreams, and under the dominance of the pleasure principle this has become their function. But it is not in the service of that principle that the dreams of patients suffering from traumatic neuroses lead them back with such regularity to the situation in which the trauma occurred. We may assume, rather, that dreams are here helping to carry out another task, which must be accomplished before the dominance of the pleasure principle can even begin. These dreams are endeavouring to master the stimulus retrospectively, by developing the anxiety whose omission was the cause of the traumatic neurosis. They thus afford us a view of a function of the mental apparatus which, though it does not contradict the pleasure principle, is nevertheless independent of it and seems to be more primitive than the purpose of gaining pleasure and avoiding unpleasure.

This would seem to be the place, then, at which to admit for the first time an exception to the proposition that dreams are fulfilments of wishes. Anxiety dreams, as I have shown repeatedly and in detail, offer no such exception. Nor do 'punishment dreams', for they merely replace the forbidden wish-fulfilment by the appropriate punishment for it; that is to say, they fulfil the wish of the sense of guilt which is the reaction to the repudiated impulse.[1] But it is impossible to classify as wish-fulfilments the dreams we have been discussing which occur in traumatic neuroses, or the dreams during psycho-analyses which bring to memory the psychical traumas of childhood. They arise, rather, in obedience to the compulsion to repeat, though it is true that in analysis that compulsion is supported by the wish (which is encouraged by 'suggestion')[2] to conjure up what has been forgotten and repressed. Thus it would seem that the function of dreams, which consists in

---

[1] [See *The Interpretation of Dreams* (1900a), *Standard Ed.*, 5, 557, and Section 9 of Freud's 'Remarks on the Theory and Practice of Dream-Interpretation' (1923c).]

[2] [The clause in brackets was substituted in 1923 for the words 'which is not unconscious' which appeared in the earlier editions.]

setting aside any motives that might interrupt sleep, by fulfilling the wishes of the disturbing impulses, is not their *original* function. It would not be possible for them to perform that function until the whole of mental life had accepted the dominance of the pleasure principle. If there is a 'beyond the pleasure principle', it is only consistent to grant that there was also a time before the purpose of dreams was the fulfilment of wishes. This would imply no denial of their later function. But if once this general rule has been broken, a further question arises. May not dreams which, with a view to the psychical binding of traumatic impressions, obey the compulsion to repeat—may not such dreams occur *outside* analysis as well? And the reply can only be a decided affirmative.

I have argued elsewhere [1] that 'war neuroses' (in so far as that term implies something more than a reference to the circumstances of the illness's onset) may very well be traumatic neuroses which have been facilitated by a conflict in the ego. The fact to which I have referred on page 6, that a gross physical injury caused simultaneously by the trauma diminishes the chances that a neurosis will develop, becomes intelligible if one bears in mind two facts which have been stressed by psycho-analytic research: firstly, that mechanical agitation must be recognized as one of the sources of sexual excitation,[2] and secondly, that painful and feverish illnesses exercise a powerful effect, so long as they last, on the distribution of libido. Thus, on the one hand, the mechanical violence of the trauma would liberate a quantity of sexual excitation which, owing to the lack of preparation for anxiety, would have a traumatic effect; but, on the other hand, the simultaneous physical injury, by calling for a narcissistic hypercathexis of the injured organ,[3] would bind the excess of excitation. It is also well known, though the libido theory has not yet made sufficient use of the fact, that such severe disorders in the distribution of libido as melancholia are temporarily brought to an end by intercurrent organic illness, and indeed that even a fully developed condition of dementia praecox is capable of a temporary remission in these same circumstances.

[1] See my introduction (1919*d*) to *Psycho-Analysis and the War Neuroses.*
[2] Cf. my remarks elsewhere (*Three Essays* [*Standard Ed.*, 7, 201–2]) on the effect of swinging and railway-travel.
[3] See my paper on narcissism (1914*c*) [Beginning of Section II].

V

THE fact that the cortical layer which receives stimuli is without any protective shield against excitations from within must have as its result that these latter transmissions of stimulus have a preponderance in economic importance and often occasion economic disturbances comparable with traumatic neuroses. The most abundant sources of this internal excitation are what are described as the organism's 'instincts'—the representatives of all the forces originating in the interior of the body and transmitted to the mental apparatus—at once the most important and the most obscure element of psychological research.

It will perhaps not be thought too rash to suppose that the impulses arising from the instincts do not belong to the type of *bound* nervous processes but of *freely mobile* processes which press towards discharge. The best part of what we know of these processes is derived from our study of the dream-work. We there discovered that the processes in the unconscious systems were fundamentally different from those in the preconscious (or conscious) systems. In the unconscious, cathexes can easily be completely transferred, displaced and condensed. Such treatment, however, could produce only invalid results if it were applied to preconscious material; and this accounts for the familiar peculiarities exhibited by manifest dreams after the preconscious residues of the preceding day have been worked over in accordance with the laws operating in the unconscious. I described the type of process found in the unconscious as the 'primary' psychical process, in contradistinction to the 'secondary' process which is the one obtaining in our normal waking life. Since all instinctual impulses have the unconscious systems as their point of impact, it is hardly an innovation to say that they obey the primary process. Again, it is easy to identify the primary psychical process with Breuer's freely mobile cathexis and the secondary process with changes in his bound or tonic cathexis.[1] If so, it would be the task of the higher strata of the mental apparatus to bind the instinctual excitation reaching

[1] Cf. my *Interpretation of Dreams*, Chapter VII [*Standard Ed.*, 5, 588 ff. Cf. also Breuer and Freud, 1895 (Section 2 of Breuer's theoretical contribution)].

the primary process. A failure to effect this binding would provoke a disturbance analogous to a traumatic neurosis; and only after the binding has been accomplished would it be possible for the dominance of the pleasure principle (and of its modification, the reality principle) to proceed unhindered. Till then the other task of the mental apparatus, the task of mastering or binding excitations, would have precedence—not, indeed, in *opposition* to the pleasure principle, but independently of it and to some extent in disregard of it.

The manifestations of a compulsion to repeat (which we have described as occurring in the early activities of infantile mental life as well as among the events of psycho-analytic treatment) exhibit to a high degree an instinctual[1] character and, when they act in opposition to the pleasure principle, give the appearance of some 'daemonic' force at work. In the case of children's play we seemed to see that children repeat unpleasurable experiences for the additional reason that they can master a powerful impression far more thoroughly by being active than they could by merely experiencing it passively. Each fresh repetition seems to strengthen the mastery they are in search of. Nor can children have their *pleasurable* experiences repeated often enough, and they are inexorable in their insistence that the repetition shall be an identical one. This character trait disappears later on. If a joke is heard for a second time it produces almost no effect; a theatrical production never creates so great an impression the second time as the first; indeed, it is hardly possible to persuade an adult who has very much enjoyed reading a book to re-read it immediately. Novelty is always the condition of enjoyment. But children will never tire of asking an adult to repeat a game that he has shown them or played with them, till he is too exhausted to go on. And if a child has been told a nice story, he will insist on hearing it over and over again rather than a new one; and he will remorselessly stipulate that the repetition shall be an identical one and will correct any alterations of which the narrator may be guilty—though they may actually have been made in the hope of gaining fresh approval.[2]

[1] ['*Triebhaft*' here and at the beginning of the next paragraph. The word '*Trieb*' bears much more of a feeling of urgency than the English 'instinct'.]

[2] [Cf. some remarks on this towards the end of the sixth section of Chapter VII of Freud's book on jokes (1905c).]

None of this contradicts the pleasure principle; repetition, the re-experiencing of something identical, is clearly in itself a source of pleasure. In the case of a person in analysis, on the contrary, the compulsion to repeat the events of his childhood in the transference evidently disregards the pleasure principle in every way. The patient behaves in a purely infantile fashion and thus shows us that the repressed memory-traces of his primaeval experiences are not present in him in a bound state and are indeed in a sense incapable of obeying the secondary process. It is to this fact of not being bound, moreover, that they owe their capacity for forming, in conjunction with the residues of the previous day, a wishful phantasy that emerges in a dream. This same compulsion to repeat frequently meets us as an obstacle to our treatment when at the end of an analysis we try to induce the patient to detach himself completely from his physician. It may be presumed, too, that when people unfamiliar with analysis feel an obscure fear—a dread of rousing something that, so they feel, is better left sleeping—what they are afraid of at bottom is the emergence of this compulsion with its hint of possession by some 'daemonic' power.

But how is the predicate of being 'instinctual' [1] related to the compulsion to repeat? At this point we cannot escape a suspicion that we may have come upon the track of a universal attribute of instincts and perhaps of organic life in general which has not hitherto been clearly recognized or at least not explicitly stressed. [2] *It seems, then, that an instinct is an urge inherent in organic life to restore an earlier state of things* which the living entity has been obliged to abandon under the pressure of external disturbing forces; that is, it is a kind of organic elasticity, or, to put it another way, the expression of the inertia inherent in organic life. [3]

This view of instincts strikes us as strange because we have become used to see in them a factor impelling towards change and development, whereas we are now asked to recognize in them the precise contrary—an expression of the *conservative* nature of living substance. On the other hand we soon call to mind examples from animal life which seem to confirm the

---

[1] [See the last footnote but one.]

[2] [The last six words were added in 1921.]

[3] I have no doubt that similar notions as to the nature of 'instincts' have already been put forward repeatedly.

view that instincts are historically determined. Certain fishes, for instance, undertake laborious migrations at spawning-time in order to deposit their spawn in particular waters far removed from their customary haunts. In the opinion of many biologists what they are doing is merely to seek out the localities in which their species formerly resided but which in the course of time they have exchanged for others. The same explanation is believed to apply to the migratory flights of birds of passage— but we are quickly relieved of the necessity for seeking for further examples by the reflection that the most impressive proofs of there being an organic compulsion to repeat lie in the phenomena of heredity and the facts of embryology. We see how the germ of a living animal is obliged in the course of its development to recapitulate (even if only in a transient and abbreviated fashion) the structures of all the forms from which it is sprung, instead of proceeding quickly by the shortest path to its final shape. This behaviour is only to a very slight degree attributable to mechanical causes, and the historical explanation cannot accordingly be neglected. So too the power of regenerating a lost organ by growing afresh a precisely similar one extends far up into the animal kingdom.

We shall be met by the plausible objection that it may very well be that, in addition to the conservative instincts which impel towards repetition, there may be others which push forward towards progress and the production of new forms. This argument must certainly not be overlooked, and it will be taken into account at a later stage.[1] But for the moment it is tempting to pursue to its logical conclusion the hypothesis that all instincts tend towards the restoration of an earlier state of things. The outcome may give an impression of mysticism or of sham profundity; but we can feel quite innocent of having had any such purpose in view. We seek only for the sober results of research or of reflection based on it; and we have no wish to find in those results any quality other than certainty.[2]

Let us suppose, then, that all the organic instincts are conservative, are acquired historically and tend towards the

---

[1] [The last half of this sentence was added in 1921.]

[2] [*Footnote added* 1925:] The reader should not overlook the fact that what follows is the development of an extreme line of thought. Later on, when account is taken of the sexual instincts, it will be found that the necessary limitations and corrections are applied to it.

restoration of an earlier state of things. It follows that the phenomena of organic development must be attributed to external disturbing and diverting influences. The elementary living entity would from its very beginning have had no wish to change; if conditions remained the same, it would do no more than constantly repeat the same course of life. In the last resort, what has left its mark on the development of organisms must be the history of the earth we live in and of its relation to the sun. Every modification which is thus imposed upon the course of the organism's life is accepted by the conservative organic instincts and stored up for further repetition. Those instincts are therefore bound to give a deceptive appearance of being forces tending towards change and progress, whilst in fact they are merely seeking to reach an ancient goal by paths alike old and new. Moreover it is possible to specify this final goal of all organic striving. It would be in contradiction to the conservative nature of the instincts if the goal of life were a state of things which had never yet been attained. On the contrary, it must be an *old* state of things, an initial state from which the living entity has at one time or other departed and to which it is striving to return by the circuitous paths along which its development leads. If we are to take it as a truth that knows no exception that everything living dies for *internal* reasons— becomes inorganic once again—then we shall be compelled to say that '*the aim of all life is death*' and, looking backwards, that '*inanimate things existed before living ones*'.

The attributes of life were at some time evoked in inanimate matter by the action of a force of whose nature we can form no conception. It may perhaps have been a process similar in type to that which later caused the development of consciousness in a particular stratum of living matter. The tension which then arose in what had hitherto been an inanimate substance endeavoured to cancel itself out. In this way the first instinct came into being: the instinct to return to the inanimate state. It was still an easy matter at that time for a living substance to die; the course of its life was probably only a brief one, whose direction was determined by the chemical structure of the young life. For a long time, perhaps, living substance was thus being constantly created afresh and easily dying, till decisive external influences altered in such a way as to oblige the still surviving substance to diverge ever more widely from its original course of life and to make ever more complicated *détours* before reaching its aim of death. These circuitous paths to death, faithfully kept to by the conservative instincts, would thus present us to-day with the picture of the phenomena of life. If we firmly maintain the exclusively conservative nature of instincts, we cannot arrive at any other notions as to the origin and aim of life.

The implications in regard to the great groups of instincts which, as we believe, lie behind the phenomena of life in organisms must appear no less bewildering. The hypothesis of self-preservative instincts, such as we attribute to all living beings, stands in marked opposition to the idea that instinctual life as a whole serves to bring about death. Seen in this light, the theoretical importance of the instincts of self-preservation, of self-assertion and of mastery greatly diminishes. They are component instincts whose function it is to assure that the organism shall follow its own path to death, and to ward off any possible ways of returning to inorganic existence other than those which are immanent in the organism itself. We have no longer to reckon with the organism's puzzling determination (so hard to fit into any context) to maintain its own existence in the face of every obstacle. What we are left with is the fact that the organism wishes to die only in its own fashion. Thus these guardians of life, too, were originally the myrmidons of death. Hence arises the paradoxical situation that the living organism struggles most energetically against events (dangers, in fact) which might help it to attain its life's aim rapidly—by a kind of short-circuit. Such behaviour is, however, precisely what characterizes purely instinctual as contrasted with intelligent efforts.[1]

But let us pause for a moment and reflect. It cannot be so. The sexual instincts, to which the theory of the neuroses gives a quite special place, appear under a very different aspect.

The external pressure which provokes a constantly increasing extent of development has not imposed itself upon *every* organism. Many have succeeded in remaining up to the present time at their lowly level. Many, though not all, such creatures, which must resemble the earliest stages of the higher animals

---

[1] [In the editions before 1925 the following footnote appeared at this point. 'A correction of this extreme view of the self-preservative instincts follows.']

and plants, are, indeed, living to-day. In the same way, the whole
path of development to natural death is not trodden by *all* the
elementary entities which compose the complicated body of one
of the higher organisms. Some of them, the germ-cells, probably
retain the original structure of living matter and, after a certain
time, with their full complement of inherited and freshly
acquired instinctual dispositions, separate themselves from the
organism as a whole. These two characteristics may be precisely
what enables them to have an independent existence. Under
favourable conditions, they begin to develop—that is, to repeat
the performance to which they owe their existence; and in the
end once again one portion of their substance pursues its
development to a finish, while another portion harks back once
again as a fresh residual germ to the beginning of the process
of development. These germ-cells, therefore, work against the
death of the living substance and succeed in winning for it
what we can only regard as potential immortality, though that
may mean no more than a lengthening of the road to death.
We must regard as in the highest degree significant the fact
that this function of the germ-cell is reinforced, or only made
possible, if it coalesces with another cell similar to itself and yet
differing from it.

The instincts which watch over the destinies of these elementary organisms that survive the whole individual, which provide
them with a safe shelter while they are defenceless against the
stimuli of the external world, which bring about their meeting
with other germ-cells, and so on—these constitute the group of
the sexual instincts. They are conservative in the same sense
as the other instincts in that they bring back earlier states of
living substance; but they are conservative to a higher degree
in that they are peculiarly resistant to external influences; and
they are conservative too in another sense in that they preserve
life itself for a comparatively long period.[1] They are the true
life instincts. They operate against the purpose of the other
instincts, which leads, by reason of their function, to death; and
this fact indicates that there is an opposition between them and
the other instincts, an opposition whose importance was long
ago recognized by the theory of the neuroses. It is as though the

---

[1] [*Footnote added* 1923:] Yet it is to them alone that we can attribute
an internal impulse towards 'progress' and towards higher development!
(See below [pp. 42–3].)

life of the organism moved with a vacillating rhythm. One group of instincts rushes forward so as to reach the final aim of life as swiftly as possible; but when a particular stage in the advance has been reached, the other group jerks back to a certain point to make a fresh start and so prolong the journey. And even though it is certain that sexuality and the distinction between the sexes did not exist when life began, the possibility remains that the instincts which were later to be described as sexual may have been in operation from the very first, and it may not be true that it was only at a later time that they started upon their work of opposing the activities of the 'ego-instincts'.[1]

Let us now hark back for a moment ourselves and consider whether there is any basis at all for these speculations. Is it really the case that, *apart from the sexual instincts*,[2] there are no instincts that do not seek to restore an earlier state of things? that there are none that aim at a state of things which has never yet been attained? I know of no certain example from the organic world that would contradict the characterization I have thus proposed. There is unquestionably no universal instinct towards higher development observable in the animal or plant world, even though it is undeniable that development does in fact occur in that direction. But on the one hand it is often merely a matter of opinion when we declare that one stage of development is higher than another, and on the other hand biology teaches us that higher development in one respect is very frequently balanced or outweighed by involution in another. Moreover there are plenty of animal forms from whose early stages we can infer that their development has, on the contrary, assumed a retrograde character. Both higher development and involution might well be the consequences of adaptation to the pressure of external forces; and in both cases the part played by instincts might be limited to the retention (in the form of an internal source of pleasure) of an obligatory modification.[3]

[1] [*Footnote added* 1925:] It should be understood from the context that the term 'ego-instincts' is used here as a provisional description and derives from the earliest psycho-analytical terminology. [See below, pp. 50–1 and 61.]

[2] [These five words were italicized from 1921 onwards.]

[3] Ferenczi (1913, 137) has reached the same conclusion along different lines: 'If this thought is pursued to its logical conclusion, one must make oneself familiar with the idea of a tendency to perseveration or

It may be difficult, too, for many of us, to abandon the belief
that there is an instinct towards perfection at work in human
beings, which has brought them to their present high level of
intellectual achievement and ethical sublimation and which
may be expected to watch over their development into super-
men. I have no faith, however, in the existence of any such
internal instinct and I cannot see how this benevolent illusion
is to be preserved. The present development of human beings
requires, as it seems to me, no different explanation from that of
animals. What appears in a minority of human individuals as
an untiring impulsion towards further perfection can easily be
understood as a result of the instinctual repression upon which
is based all that is most precious in human civilization. The
repressed instinct never ceases to strive for complete satisfaction,
which would consist in the repetition of a primary experience
of satisfaction. No substitutive or reactive formations and no
sublimations will suffice to remove the repressed instinct's
persisting tension; and it is the difference in amount between
the pleasure of satisfaction which is *demanded* and that which is
actually *achieved* that provides the driving factor which will
permit of no halting at any position attained, but, in the poet's
words, '*ungebändigt immer vorwärts dringt*'.[1] The backward path
that leads to complete satisfaction is as a rule obstructed by
the resistances which maintain the repressions. So there is no
alternative but to advance in the direction in which growth is
still free—though with no prospect of bringing the process to
a conclusion or of being able to reach the goal. The processes
involved in the formation of a neurotic phobia, which is nothing
else than an attempt at flight from the satisfaction of an instinct,
present us with a model of the manner of origin of this sup-
posititious 'instinct towards perfection'—an instinct which cannot possibly be attributed to *every* human being. The *dynamic*
conditions for its development are, indeed, universally present;
but it is only in rare cases that the *economic* situation appears
to favour the production of the phenomenon.

 I will add only a word to suggest that the efforts of Eros to

regression dominating organic life as well, while the tendency to further
development, to adaptation, etc., would become active only as a result
of external stimuli.'

[1] ['Presses ever forward unsubdued.'] Mephistopheles in *Faust*, Part I
[Scene 4].

combine organic substances into ever larger unities probably provide a substitute for this 'instinct towards perfection' whose existence we cannot admit. The phenomena that are attributed to it seem capable of explanation by these efforts of Eros taken in conjunction with the results of repression.[1]

[1] [This paragraph, which was added in 1923, anticipates the account of Eros that is to follow in the next chapter, p. 50 ff.]

VI

THE upshot of our enquiry so far has been the drawing of a sharp distinction between the 'ego-instincts' and the sexual instincts, and the view that the former exercise pressure towards death and the latter towards a prolongation of life. But this conclusion is bound to be unsatisfactory in many respects even to ourselves. Moreover, it is actually only of the former group of instincts that we can predicate a conservative, or rather retrograde, character corresponding to a compulsion to repeat. For on our hypothesis the ego-instincts arise from the coming to life of inanimate matter and seek to restore the inanimate state; whereas as regards the sexual instincts, though it is true that they reproduce primitive states of the organism, what they are clearly aiming at by every possible means is the coalescence of two germ-cells which are differentiated in a particular way. If this union is not effected, the germ-cell dies along with all the other elements of the multicellular organism. It is only on this condition that the sexual function can prolong the cell's life and lend it the appearance of immortality. But what is the important event in the development of living substance which is being repeated in sexual reproduction, or in its fore-runner, the conjugation of two protista? [1] We cannot say; and we should consequently feel relieved if the whole structure of our argument turned out to be mistaken. The opposition between the ego or death instincts [2] and the sexual or life instincts would then cease to hold and the compulsion to repeat would no longer possess the importance we have ascribed to it.

Let us turn back, then, to one of the assumptions that we have already made, with the expectation that we shall be able to give it a categorical denial. We have drawn far-reaching conclusions from the hypothesis that all living substance is bound to die from internal causes. We made this assumption thus carelessly because it does not seem to us to *be* an assumption. We are accustomed to think that such is the fact, and we

[1] [In what follows Freud appears to use the terms 'protista' and 'protozoa' indifferently to signify unicellular organisms. The translation follows the original.]

[2] [The first published appearance of the term.]

44

are strengthened in our thought by the writings of our poets. Perhaps we have adopted the belief because there is some comfort in it. If we are to die ourselves, and first to lose in death those who are dearest to us, it is easier to submit to a remorseless law of nature, to the sublime *'Aνάγκη* [Necessity], than to a chance which might perhaps have been escaped. It may be, however, that this belief in the internal necessity of dying is only another of those illusions which we have created *'um die Schwere des Daseins zu ertragen'*.[1] It is certainly not a primaeval belief. The notion of 'natural death' is quite foreign to primitive races; they attribute every death that occurs among them to the influence of an enemy or of an evil spirit. We must therefore turn to biology in order to test the validity of the belief.

If we do so, we may be astonished to find how little agreement there is among biologists on the subject of natural death and in fact that the whole concept of death melts away under their hands. The fact that there is a fixed average duration of life at least among the higher animals naturally argues in favour of there being such a thing as death from natural causes. But this impression is countered when we consider that certain large animals and certain gigantic arboreal growths reach a very advanced age and one which cannot at present be computed. According to the large conception of Wilhelm Fliess [1906], all the phenomena of life exhibited by organism —and also, no doubt, their death—are linked with the completion of fixed periods, which express the dependence of two kinds of living substance (one male and the other female) upon the solar year. When we see, however, how easily and how extensively the influence of external forces is able to modify the date of the appearance of vital phenomena (especially in the plant world) —to precipitate them or hold them back—doubts must be cast upon the rigidity of Fliess's formulas or at least upon whether the laws laid down by him are the sole determining factors.

The greatest interest attaches from our point of view to the treatment given to the subject of the duration of life and the death of organisms in the writings of Weismann (1882, 1884, 1892, etc.) It was he who introduced the division of living substance into mortal and immortal parts. The mortal part is

[1] ['To bear the burden of existence.' (Schiller, *Die Braut von Messina*, I, 8.]

the body in the narrower sense—the 'soma'—which alone is subject to natural death. The germ-cells, on the other hand, are potentially immortal, in so far as they are able, under certain favourable conditions, to develop into a new individual, or, in other words, to surround themselves with a new soma. (Weismann, 1884.)

What strikes us in this is the unexpected analogy with our own view, which was arrived at along such a different path. Weismann, regarding living substance morphologically, sees in it one portion which is destined to die—the soma, the body apart from the substance concerned with sex and inheritance—and an immortal portion—the germ-plasm, which is concerned with the survival of the species, with reproduction. We, on the other hand, dealing not with the living substance but with the forces operating in it, have been led to distinguish two kinds of instincts: those which seek to lead what is living to death, and others, the sexual instincts, which are perpetually attempting and achieving a renewal of life. This sounds like a dynamic corollary to Weismann's morphological theory.

But the appearance of a significant correspondence is dissipated as soon as we discover Weismann's views on the problem of death. For he only relates the distinction between the mortal soma and the immortal germ-plasm to *multicellular* organisms; in unicellular organisms the individual and the reproductive cell are still one and the same (Weismann, 1882, 38). Thus he considers that unicellular organisms are potentially immortal, and that death only makes its appearance with the multicellular metazoa. It is true that this death of the higher organisms is a natural one, a death from internal causes; but it is not founded on any primal characteristic of living substance (Weismann, 1884, 84) and cannot be regarded as an absolute necessity with its basis in the very nature of life (Weismann, 1882, 33). Death is rather a matter of expediency, a manifestation of adaptation to the external conditions of life; for, when once the cells of the body have been divided into soma and germ-plasm, an unlimited duration of individual life would become a quite pointless luxury. When this differentiation had been made in the multicellular organisms, death became possible and expedient. Since then, the soma of the higher organisms has died at fixed periods for internal reasons, while the protista have remained immortal. It is not the case, on the other hand, that reproduction was only introduced at the same time as death. On the contrary, it is a primal characteristic of living matter, like growth (from which it originated), and life has been continuous from its first beginning upon earth. (Weismann, 1884, 84 f.)

It will be seen at once that to concede in this way that higher organisms have a natural death is of very little help to us. For if death is a *late* acquisition of organisms, then there can be no question of there having been death instincts from the very beginning of life on this earth. Multicellular organisms may die for internal reasons, owing to defective differentiation or to imperfections in their metabolism, but the matter is of no interest from the point of view of our problem. An account of the origin of death such as this is moreover far less at variance with our habitual modes of thought than the strange assumption of 'death instincts'.

The discussion which followed upon Weismann's suggestions led, so far as I can see, to no conclusive results in any direction.[1] Some writers returned to the views of Goette (1883), who regarded death as a direct result of reproduction. Hartmann (1906, 29) does not regard the appearance of a 'dead body'—a dead portion of the living substance—as the criterion of death, but defines death as 'the termination of individual development'. In this sense protozoa too are mortal; in their case death always coincides with reproduction, but is to some extent obscured by it, since the whole substance of the parent animal may be transmitted directly into the young offspring.

Soon afterwards research was directed to the experimental testing on unicellular organisms of the alleged immortality of living substance. An American biologist, Woodruff, experimenting with a ciliate infusorian, the 'slipper-animalcule', which reproduces by fission into two individuals, persisted until the 3029th generation (at which point he broke off the experiment), isolating one of the part-products on each occasion and placing it in fresh water. This remote descendent of the first slipper-animalcule was just as lively as its ancestor and showed no signs of ageing or degeneration. Thus, in so far as figures of this kind prove anything, the immortality of the protista seemed to be experimentally demonstrable.[2]

Other experimenters arrived at different results. Maupas,

[1] Cf. Hartmann (1906), Lipschütz (1914) and Doflein (1919).
[2] For this and what follows see Lipschütz (1914, 26 and 52 ff.).

Calkins and others, in contrast to Woodruff, found that after a certain number of divisions these infusoria become weaker, diminish in size, suffer the loss of some part of their organization and eventually die, unless certain recuperative measures are applied to them. If this is so, protozoa would appear to die after a phase of senescence exactly like the higher animals—thus completely contradicting Weismann's assertion that death is a late acquisition of living organisms.

From the aggregate of these experiments two facts emerge which seem to offer us a firm footing.

First: If two of the animalculae, at the moment before they show signs of senescence, are able to coalesce with each other, that is to 'conjugate' (soon after which they once more separate), they are saved from growing old and become 're-juvenated'. Conjugation is no doubt the fore-runner of the sexual reproduction of higher creatures; it is as yet unconnected with propagation and is limited to the mixing of the substances of the two individuals. (Weismann's 'amphimixis'.) The re-cuperative effects of conjugation can, however, be replaced by certain stimulating agents, by alterations in the composition of the fluid which provides their nourishment, by raising their temperature or by shaking them. We are reminded of the celebrated experiment made by J. Loeb, in which, by means of certain chemical stimuli, he induced segmentation in sea-urchins' eggs—a process which can normally occur only after fertilization.

Secondly: It is probable nevertheless that infusoria die a natural death as a result of their own vital processes. For the contradiction between Woodruff's findings and the others is due to his having provided each generation with fresh nutrient fluid. If he omitted to do so, he observed the same signs of senescence as the other experimenters. He concluded that the animalculae were injured by the products of metabolism which they ex-truded into the surrounding fluid. He was then able to prove conclusively that it was only the products of its *own* metabolism which had fatal results for the particular kind of animalcule. For the same animalculae which inevitably perished if they were crowded together in their own nutrient fluid flourished in a solution which was over-saturated with the waste products of a distantly related species. An infusorian, therefore, if it is left to itself, dies a natural death owing to its incomplete voidance of the products of its own metabolism. (It may be that the same incapacity is the ultimate cause of the death of all higher animals as well.)

At this point the question may well arise in our minds whether any object whatever is served by trying to solve the problem of natural death from a study of the protozoa. The primitive organization of these creatures may conceal from our eyes important conditions which, though in fact present in them too, only become *visible* in higher animals where they are able to find morphological expression. And if we abandon the morphological point of view and adopt the dynamic one, it becomes a matter of complete indifference to us whether natural death can be shown to occur in protozoa or not. The substance which is later recognized as being immortal has not yet become separated in them from the mortal one. The instinctual forces which seek to conduct life into death may also be operating in protozoa from the first, and yet their effects may be so completely concealed by the life-preserving forces that it may be very hard to find any direct evidence of their presence. We have seen, moreover, that the observations made by biologists allow us to assume that internal processes of this kind leading to death do occur also in protista. But even if protista turned out to be immortal in Weismann's sense, his assertion that death is a late acquisition would apply only to its *manifest* phenomena and would not make impossible the assumption of processes *tending* towards it.

Thus our expectation that biology would flatly contradict the recognition of death instincts has not been fulfilled. We are at liberty to continue concerning ourselves with their possibility, if we have other reasons for doing so. The striking similarity between Weismann's distinction of soma and germ-plasm and our separation of the death instincts from the life instincts persists and retains its significance.

We may pause for a moment over this pre-eminently dualistic view of instinctual life. According to E. Hering's theory, two kinds of processes are constantly at work in living substance, operating in contrary directions, one constructive or assimilatory and the other destructive or dissimilatory. May we venture to recognize in these two directions taken by the vital processes the activity of our two instinctual impulses, the life instincts and the death instincts? There is something else, at any rate, that we cannot remain blind to. We have unwittingly steered our course into the harbour of Schopenhauer's philosophy. For him death is the 'true result and to that extent the purpose of life',[1] while the sexual instinct is the embodiment of the will to live.

Let us make a bold attempt at another step forward. It is generally considered that the union of a number of cells into a vital association—the multicellular character of organisms—has become a means of prolonging their life. One cell helps to preserve the life of another, and the community of cells can survive even if individual cells have to die. We have already heard that conjugation, too, the temporary coalescence of two unicellular organisms, has a life-preserving and rejuvenating effect on both of them. Accordingly, we might attempt to apply the libido theory which has been arrived at in psycho-analysis to the mutual relationship of cells. We might suppose that the life instincts or sexual instincts which are active in each cell take the other cells as their object, that they partly neutralize the death instincts (that is, the processes set up by them) in those cells and thus preserve their life; while the other cells do the same for *them*, and still others sacrifice themselves in the performance of this libidinal function. The germ-cells themselves would behave in a completely 'narcissistic' fashion—to use the phrase that we are accustomed to use in the theory of the neuroses to describe a whole individual who retains his libido in his ego and pays none of it out in object-cathexes. The germ-cells require their libido, the activity of their life instincts, for themselves, as a reserve against their later momentous constructive activity. (The cells of the malignant neoplasms which destroy the organism should also perhaps be described as narcissistic in this same sense: pathology is prepared to regard their germs as innate and to ascribe embryonic attributes to them.)[2] In this way the libido of our sexual instincts would coincide with the Eros of the poets and philosophers which holds all living things together.

Here then is an opportunity for looking back over the slow development of our libido theory. In the first instance the analysis of the transference neuroses forced upon our notice the opposition between the 'sexual instincts', which are directed towards an object, and certain other instincts, with which we were very insufficiently acquainted and which we described

[1] Schopenhauer (1851; *Sämtliche Werke*, ed. Hübscher, 1938, 5, 236).
[2] [This sentence was added in 1921.]

provisionally as the 'ego-instincts'.[1] A foremost place among
these was necessarily given to the instincts serving the self-
preservation of the individual. It was impossible to say what
other distinctions were to be drawn among them. No knowledge would have been more valuable as a foundation for
true psychological science than an approximate grasp of the
common characteristics and possible distinctive features of the
instincts. But in no region of psychology were we groping more
in the dark. Everyone assumed the existence of as many instincts
or 'basic instincts' as he chose, and juggled with them like the
ancient Greek natural philosophers with their four elements—
earth, air, fire and water. Psycho-analysis, which could not
escape making *some* assumption about the instincts, kept at first
to the popular division of instincts typified in the phrase 'hunger
and love'. At least there was nothing arbitrary in this; and by
its help the analysis of the psychoneuroses was carried forward
quite a distance. The concept of 'sexuality', and at the same
time of the sexual instinct, had, it is true, to be extended so as
to cover many things which could not be classed under the
reproductive function; and this caused no little hubbub in an
austere, respectable or merely hypocritical world.

The next step was taken when psycho-analysis felt its way
closer towards the psychological ego, which it had first come to
know only as a repressive, censoring agency, capable of erecting
protective structures and reactive formations. Critical and far-
seeing minds had, it is true, long since objected to the concept
of libido being restricted to the energy of the sexual instincts
directed towards an object. But they failed to explain how they
had arrived at their better knowledge or to derive from it
anything of which analysis could make use. Advancing more
cautiously, psycho-analysis observed the regularity with which
libido is withdrawn from the object and directed on to the ego
(the process of introversion); and, by studying the libidinal
development of children in its earliest phases, came to the conclusion that the ego is the true and original reservoir of libido,[2]

---

[1] [So, for instance, in the account of this opposition given in Freud's
paper on psychogenic disturbances of vision (1910*i*).]

[2] [This idea was fully stated by Freud in his paper on narcissism
(1914*c*), Section I. See, however, his later footnote, near the beginning
of Chapter III of *The Ego and the Id* (1923*b*), in which he corrects this
statement and describes the *id* as 'the great reservoir of libido'.]

and that it is only from that reservoir that libido is extended on to objects. The ego now found its position among sexual objects and was at once given the foremost place among them. Libido which was in this way lodged in the ego was described as 'narcissistic'.[1] This narcissistic libido was of course also a manifestation of the force of the sexual instinct in the analytical sense of those words, and it had necessarily to be identified with the 'self-preservative instincts' whose existence had been recognized from the first. Thus the original opposition between the ego-instincts and the sexual instincts proved to be inadequate. A portion of the ego-instincts was seen to be libidinal; sexual instincts—probably alongside others—operated in the ego. Nevertheless we are justified in saying that the old formula which lays it down that psychoneuroses are based on a conflict between ego-instincts and sexual instincts contains nothing that we need reject to-day. It is merely that the distinction between the two kinds of instinct, which was originally regarded as in some sort of way *qualitative*, must now be characterized differently—namely as being *topographical*. And in particular it is still true that the transference neuroses, the essential subject of psycho-analytic study, are the result of a conflict between the ego and the libidinal cathexis of objects.

But it is all the more necessary for us to lay stress upon the libidinal character of the self-preservative instincts now that we are venturing upon the further step of recognizing the sexual instinct as Eros, the preserver of all things, and of deriving the narcissistic libido of the ego from the stores of libido by means of which the cells of the soma are attached to one another. But we now find ourselves suddenly faced by another question. If the self-preservative instincts too are of a libidinal nature, are there perhaps no other instincts whatever but the libidinal ones? At all events there are none other visible. But in that case we shall after all be driven to agree with the critics who suspected from the first that psycho-analysis explains *everything* by sexuality, or with innovators like Jung who, making a hasty judgement, have used the word 'libido' to mean instinctual force in general. Must not this be so?

It was not our *intention* at all events to produce such a result. Our argument had as its point of departure a sharp distinction between ego-instincts, which we equated with death instincts,

[1] See my paper on narcissism (1914c) [Section I].

and sexual instincts, which we equated with life instincts. (We were prepared at one stage [p. 39] to include the so-called self-preservative instincts of the ego among the death instincts; but we subsequently [p. 52] corrected ourselves on this point and withdrew it.) Our views have from the very first been *dualistic*, and to-day they are even more definitely dualistic than before—now that we describe the opposition as being, not between ego-instincts and sexual instincts but between life instincts and death instincts. Jung's libido theory is on the contrary *monistic*; the fact that he has called his one instinctual force 'libido' is bound to cause confusion, but need not affect us otherwise.[1] We suspect that instincts other than those of self-preservation operate in the ego, and it ought to be possible for us to point to them. Unfortunately, however, the analysis of the ego has made so little headway that it is very difficult for us to do so. It is possible, indeed, that the libidinal instincts in the ego may be linked in a peculiar manner[2] with these other ego-instincts which are still strange to us. Even before we had any clear understanding of narcissism, psycho-analysts had a suspicion that the 'ego-instincts' had libidinal components attached to them. But these are very uncertain possibilities, to which our opponents will pay very little attention. The difficulty remains that psycho-analysis has not enabled us hitherto to point to any [ego-] instincts other than the libidinal ones. That, however, is no reason for our falling in with the conclusion that no others in fact exist.

In the obscurity that reigns at present in the theory of the instincts, it would be unwise to reject any idea that promises to throw light on it. We started out from the great opposition between the life and death instincts. Now object-love itself presents us with a second example of a similar polarity—that between love (or affection) and hate (or aggressiveness). If only we could succeed in relating these two polarities to each other and in deriving one from the other! From the very first we recognized the presence of a sadistic component in the sexual instinct.[3] As we know, it can make itself independent and can, in the form of a perversion, dominate an individual's entire

[1] [The two preceding sentences were added in 1921.]

[2] [In the first edition only: '—by instinctual "confluence", to borrow a term used by Adler [1908]—'.]

[3] This was already so in the first edition of *Three Essays on the Theory of Sexuality* in 1905 [*Standard Ed.*, **7**, 157 ff.].

sexual activity. It also emerges as a predominant component
instinct in one of the 'pregenital organizations', as I have
named them. But how can the sadistic instinct, whose aim it is
to injure the object, be derived from Eros, the preserver of life?
Is it not plausible to suppose that this sadism is in fact a death
instinct which, under the influence of the narcissistic libido, has
been forced away from the ego and has consequently only
emerged in relation to the object? It now enters the service of
the sexual function. During the oral stage of organization of the
libido, the act of obtaining erotic mastery over an object coincides with that object's destruction; later, the sadistic instinct
separates off, and finally, at the stage of genital primacy, it takes
on, for the purposes of reproduction, the function of overpowering the sexual object to the extent necessary for carrying out the
sexual act. It might indeed be said that the sadism which has
been forced out of the ego has pointed the way for the libidinal
components of the sexual instinct, and that these follow after it
to the object. Wherever the original sadism has undergone no
mitigation or intermixture, we find the familiar ambivalence of
love and hate in erotic life.[1]

If such an assumption as this is permissible, then we have met
the demand that we should produce an example of a death
instinct—though, it is true, a displaced one. But this way of
looking at things is very far from being easy to grasp and creates
a positively mystical impression. It looks suspiciously as though
we were trying to find a way out of a highly embarrassing situation at any price. We may recall, however, that there is nothing
new in an assumption of this kind. We put one forward on an
earlier occasion, before there was any question of an embarrassing situation. Clinical observations led us at that time to the
view that masochism, the component instinct which is complementary to sadism, must be regarded as sadism that has been
turned round upon the subject's own ego.[2] But there is no
difference in principle between an instinct turning from an
object to the ego and its turning from the ego to an object—
which is the new point now under discussion. Masochism, the
turning round of the instinct upon the subject's own ego, would

---

[1] [This foreshadows Freud's discussion of instinctual 'fusion' in
Chap. IV of *The Ego and the Id* (1923b).]

[2] See my *Three Essays* (1905d) [*Standard Ed.*, 7, 158]; and 'Instincts
and their Vicissitudes' (1915c).

in that case be a return to an earlier phase of the instinct's history, a regression. The account that was formerly given of masochism requires emendation as being too sweeping in one respect: there *might* be such a thing as primary masochism— a possibility which I had contested at that time.[1]

Let us, however, return to the self-preservative sexual instincts. The experiments upon protista have already shown us that conjugation—that is, the coalescence of two individuals which separate soon afterwards without any subsequent cell-division occurring—has a strengthening and rejuvenating effect upon both of them.[2] In later generations they show no signs of degenerating and seem able to put up a longer resistance to the injurious effects of their own metabolism. This single observation may, I think, be taken as typical of the effect produced by sexual union as well. But how is it that the coalescence of two only slightly different cells can bring about this renewal of life? The experiment which replaces the conjugation of protozoa by the application of chemical or even of mechanical stimuli (cf. Lipschütz, 1914) enables us to give what is no doubt a conclusive reply to this question. The result is brought about by the influx of fresh amounts of stimulus. This tallies well with the hypothesis that the life process of the individual leads for internal reasons to an abolition of chemical tensions, that is to say, to death, whereas union with the living substance of a different individual increases those tensions, introducing what may be described as fresh 'vital differences' which must then be lived off. As regards this dissimilarity there must of course be one or more optima. The dominating tendency of mental life, and perhaps of nervous life in general, is the effort to reduce, to keep constant or to remove internal tension due to

[1] A considerable portion of these speculations have been anticipated by Sabina Spielrein (1912) in an instructive and interesting paper which, however, is unfortunately not entirely clear to me. She there describes the sadistic components of the sexual instinct as 'destructive'. A. Stärke (1914), again, has attempted to identify the concept of libido itself with the biological concept (assumed on theoretical grounds) of an impetus towards death. See also Rank (1907). All these discussions, like that in the text, give evidence of the demand for a clarification of the theory of the instincts such as has not yet been achieved.—[A later discussion of the destructive instinct by Freud himself occupies Chapter VI of *Civilization and its Discontents* (1930a).]

[2] See the account quoted above, p. 48 from Lipschütz (1914).

stimuli (the 'Nirvana principle', to borrow a term from Barbara Low [1920, 73])—a tendency which finds expression in the pleasure principle; [1] and our recognition of that fact is one of our strongest reasons for believing in the existence of death instincts.

But we still feel our line of thought appreciably hampered by the fact that we cannot ascribe to the sexual instinct the characteristic of a compulsion to repeat which first put us on the track of the death instincts. The sphere of embryonic developmental processes is no doubt extremely rich in such phenomena of repetition; the two germ-cells that are involved in sexual reproduction and their life history are themselves only repetitions of the beginnings of organic life. But the essence of the processes to which sexual life is directed is the coalescence of two cell-bodies. That alone is what guarantees the immortality of the living substance in the higher organisms.

In other words, we need more information on the origin of sexual reproduction and of the sexual instincts in general. This is a problem which is calculated to daunt an outsider and which the specialists themselves have not yet been able to solve. We shall therefore give only the briefest summary of whatever seems relevant to our line of thought from among the many discordant assertions and opinions.

One of these views deprives the problem of reproduction of its mysterious fascination by representing it as a part manifestation of growth. (Cf. multiplication by fission, sprouting or gemmation.) The origin of reproduction by sexually differentiated germ-cells might be pictured along sober Darwinian lines by supposing that the advantage of amphimixis, arrived at on some occasion by the chance conjugation of two protista, was retained and further exploited in later development.[2] On this view 'sex' would not be anything very ancient; and the extraordinarily violent instincts whose aim it is to bring about

[1] [Cf. p. 7 ff. The whole topic is further considered in 'The Economic Problem of Masochism' (1924c).]

[2] Though Weismann (1892) denies this advantage as well: 'In no case does fertilization correspond to a rejuvenescence or renewal of life, nor is its occurrence necessary in order that life may endure: it is merely an arrangement which renders possible the intermingling of two different hereditary tendencies.' [English translation, 1893, 231.] He nevertheless believes that an intermingling of this kind leads to an increase in the variability of the organism concerned.

sexual union would be repeating something that had once occurred by chance and had since become established as being advantageous.

The question arises here, as in the case of death [p. 49], whether we do right in ascribing to protista those characteristics alone which they actually exhibit, and whether it is correct to assume that forces and processes which become visible only in the higher organisms originated in those organisms for the first time. The view of sexuality we have just mentioned is of little help for our purposes. The objection may be raised against it that it postulates the existence of life instincts already operating in the simplest organisms; for otherwise conjugation, which works counter to the course of life and makes the task of ceasing to live more difficult, would not be retained and elaborated but would be avoided. If, therefore, we are not to abandon the hypothesis of death instincts, we must suppose them to be associated from the very first with life instincts. But it must be admitted that in that case we shall be working upon an equation with two unknown quantities.

Apart from this, science has so little to tell us about the origin of sexuality that we can liken the problem to a darkness into which not so much as a ray of a hypothesis has penetrated. In quite a different region, it is true, we *do* meet with such a hypothesis; but it is of so fantastic a kind—a myth rather than a scientific explanation—that I should not venture to produce it here, were it not that it fulfils precisely the one condition whose fulfilment we desire. For it traces the origin of an instinct to *a need to restore an earlier state of things*.

What I have in mind is, of course, the theory which Plato put into the mouth of Aristophanes in the *Symposium*, and which deals not only with the *origin* of the sexual instinct but also with the most important of its variations in relation to its object. 'The original human nature was not like the present, but different. In the first place, the sexes were originally three in number, not two as they are now; there was man, woman, and the union of the two. . . .' Everything about these primaeval men was double: they had four hands and four feet, two faces, two privy parts, and so on. Eventually Zeus decided to cut these men in two, 'like a sorb-apple which is halved for pickling'. After the division had been made, 'the two parts of man, each desiring his other half, came together, and threw their arms about one another eager to grow into one'.[1]

Shall we follow the hint given us by the poet-philosopher, and venture upon the hypothesis that living substance at the time of its coming to life was torn apart into small particles, which have ever since endeavoured to reunite through the sexual instincts? that these instincts, in which the chemical affinity of inanimate matter persisted, gradually succeeded, as they developed through the kingdom of the protista, in overcoming the difficulties put in the way of that endeavour by an environment charged with dangerous stimuli—stimuli which compelled them to form a protective cortical layer? that these splintered fragments of living substance in this way attained a multicellular condition and finally transferred the instinct for reuniting, in the most highly concentrated form, to the germ-cells?—But here, I think, the moment has come for breaking off.

[1] [Jowett's translation. *Footnote added* 1921:] I have to thank Professor Heinrich Gomperz, of Vienna, for the following discussion on the origin of the Platonic myth, which I give partly in his own words. It is to be remarked that what is essentially the same theory is already to be found in the Upanishads. For we find the following passage in the *Brihadâranyaka-upanishad*, 1, 4, 3 [Max-Müller's translation, 2, 85 f.], where the origin of the world from the Atman (the Self or Ego) is described: 'But he felt no delight. Therefore a man who is lonely feels no delight. He wished for a second. He was so large as man and wife together. He then made this his Self to fall in two, and then arose husband and wife. Therefore Yagñavalkya said: "We two are thus (each of us) like half a shell." Therefore the void which was there, is filled by the wife.'

The *Brihadâranyaka-upanishad* is the most ancient of all the Upanishads, and no competent authority dates it later than about the year 800 B.C. In contradiction to the prevailing opinion, I should hesitate to give an unqualified denial to the possibility of Plato's myth being derived, even if it were only indirectly, from the Indian source, since a similar possibility cannot be excluded in the case of the doctrine of transmigration. But even if a derivation of this kind (through the Pythagoreans in the first instance) were established, the significance of the coincidence between the two trains of thought would scarcely be diminished. For Plato would not have adopted a story of this kind which had somehow reached him through some oriental tradition—to say nothing of giving it so important a place—unless it had struck him as containing an element of truth.

In a paper devoted to a systematic examination of this line of thought before the time of Plato, Ziegler (1913) traces it back to Babylonian origins.

[Freud had already alluded to Plato's myth in his *Three Essays, Standard Ed.*, 7, 136.]

Not, however, without the addition of a few words of critical reflection. It may be asked whether and how far I am myself convinced of the truth of the hypotheses that have been set out in these pages. My answer would be that I am not convinced myself and that I do not seek to persuade other people to believe in them. Or, more precisely, that I do not know how far I believe in them. There is no reason, as it seems to me, why the emotional factor of conviction should enter into this question at all. It is surely possible to throw oneself into a line of thought and to follow it wherever it leads out of simple scientific curiosity, or, if the reader prefers, as an *advocatus diaboli*, who is not on that account himself sold to the devil. I do not dispute the fact that the third step in the theory of the instincts, which I have taken here, cannot lay claim to the same degree of certainty as the two earlier ones—the extension of the concept of sexuality and the hypothesis of narcissism. These two innovations were a direct translation of observation into theory and were no more open to sources of error than is inevitable in all such cases. It is true that my assertion of the regressive character of instincts also rests upon observed material—namely on the facts of the compulsion to repeat. It may be, however, that I have over-estimated their significance. And in any case it is impossible to pursue an idea of this kind except by repeatedly combining factual material with what is purely speculative and thus diverging widely from empirical observation. The more frequently this is done in the course of constructing a theory, the more untrustworthy, as we know, must be the final result. But the degree of uncertainty is not assignable. One may have made a lucky hit or one may have gone shamefully astray. I do not think a large part is played by what is called 'intuition' in work of this kind. From what I have seen of intuition, it seems to me to be the product of a kind of intellectual impartiality. Unfortunately, however, people are seldom impartial where ultimate things, the great problems of science and life, are concerned. Each of us is governed in such cases by deep-rooted internal prejudices, into whose hands our speculation unwittingly plays. Since we have such good grounds for being distrustful, our attitude towards the results of our own deliberations cannot well be other than one of cool benevolence. I hasten to add, however, that self-criticism such as this is far from binding one to any special tolerance towards dissentient opinions. It is perfectly legitimate to reject remorselessly theories which are contradicted by the very first steps in the analysis of observed facts, while yet being aware at the same time that the validity of one's own theory is only a provisional one.

We need not feel greatly disturbed in judging our speculation upon the life and death instincts by the fact that so many bewildering and obscure processes occur in it—such as one instinct being driven out by another or an instinct turning from the ego to an object, and so on. This is merely due to our being obliged to operate with the scientific terms, that is to say with the figurative language, peculiar to psychology (or, more precisely, to depth psychology). We could not otherwise describe the processes in question at all, and indeed we could not have become aware of them. The deficiencies in our description would probably vanish if we were already in a position to replace the psychological terms by physiological or chemical ones. It is true that they too are only part of a figurative language; but it is one with which we have long been familiar and which is perhaps a simpler one as well.

On the other hand it should be made quite clear that the uncertainty of our speculation has been greatly increased by the necessity for borrowing from the science of biology. Biology is truly a land of unlimited possibilities. We may expect it to give us the most surprising information and we cannot guess what answers it will return in a few dozen years to the questions we have put to it. They may be of a kind which will blow away the whole of our artificial structure of hypotheses. If so, it may be asked why I have embarked upon such a line of thought as the present one, and in particular why I have decided to make it public. Well—I cannot deny that some of the analogies, correlations and connections which it contains seemed to me to deserve consideration.[1]

[1] I will add a few words to clarify our terminology, which has undergone some development in the course of the present work. We came to know what the 'sexual instincts' were from their relation to the sexes and to the reproductive function. We retained this name after we had been obliged by the findings of psycho-analysis to connect them less closely with reproduction. With the hypothesis of narcissistic libido and the extension of the concept of libido to the individual cells, the sexual instinct was transformed for us into Eros, which seeks to force together and hold together the portions of living substance. What are commonly called the sexual instincts are looked upon by us as the part of Eros

which is directed towards objects. Our speculations have suggested that Eros operates from the beginning of life and appears as a 'life instinct' in opposition to the 'death instinct' which was brought into being by the coming to life of inorganic substance. These speculations seek to solve the riddle of life by supposing that these two instincts were struggling with each other from the very first. [*Added* 1921:] It is not so easy, perhaps, to follow the transformations through which the concept of the 'ego-instincts' has passed. To begin with we applied that name to all the instinctual trends (of which we had no closer knowledge) which could be distinguished from the sexual instincts directed towards an object; and we opposed the ego-instincts to the sexual instincts of which the libido is the manifestation. Subsequently we came to closer grips with the analysis of the ego and recognized that a portion of the 'ego-instincts' is also of a libidinal character and has taken the subject's own ego as its object. These narcissistic self-preservative instincts had thenceforward to be counted among the libidinal sexual instincts. The opposition between the ego-instincts and the sexual instincts was transformed into one between the ego-instincts and the object-instincts, both of a libidinal nature. But in its place a fresh opposition appeared between the libidinal (ego- and object-) instincts and others, which must be presumed to be present in the ego and which may perhaps actually be observed in the destructive instincts. Our speculations have transformed this opposition into one between the life instincts (Eros) and the death instincts.

VII

IF it is really the case that seeking to restore an earlier state of things is such a universal characteristic of instincts, we need not be surprised that so many processes take place in mental life independently of the pleasure principle. This characteristic would be shared by all the component instincts and in their case would aim at returning once more to a particular stage in the course of development. These are matters over which the pleasure principle has as yet no control; but it does not follow that any of them are necessarily opposed to it, and we have still to solve the problem of the relation of the instinctual processes of repetition to the dominance of the pleasure principle.

We have found that one of the earliest and most important functions of the mental apparatus is to bind the instinctual impulses which impinge on it, to replace the primary process prevailing in them by the secondary process and convert their freely mobile cathectic energy into a mainly quiescent (tonic) cathexis. While this transformation is taking place no attention can be paid to the development of unpleasure; but this does not imply the suspension of the pleasure principle. On the contrary, the transformation occurs on *behalf* of the pleasure principle; the binding is a preparatory act which introduces and assures the dominance of the pleasure principle.

Let us make a sharper distinction than we have hitherto made between function and tendency. The pleasure principle, then, is a tendency operating in the service of a function whose business it is to free the mental apparatus entirely from excitation or to keep the amount of excitation in it constant or to keep it as low as possible. We cannot yet decide with certainty in favour of any of these ways of putting it; but it is clear that the function thus described would be concerned with the most universal endeavour of all living substance—namely to return to the quiescence of the inorganic world. We have all experienced how the greatest pleasure attainable by us, that of the sexual act, is associated with a momentary extinction of a highly intensified excitation. The binding of an instinctual impulse would be a preliminary function designed to prepare the excitation for its final elimination in the pleasure of discharge.

This raises the question of whether feelings of pleasure and unpleasure can be produced equally from bound and from unbound excitatory processes. And there seems to be no doubt whatever that the unbound or primary processes give rise to far more intense feelings in both directions than the bound or secondary ones. Moreover the primary processes are the earlier in time; at the beginning of mental life there are no others, and we may infer that if the pleasure principle had not already been operative in *them* it could never have been established for the later ones. We thus reach what is at bottom no very simple conclusion, namely that at the beginning of mental life the struggle for pleasure was far more intense than later but not so unrestricted: it had to submit to frequent interruptions. In later times the dominance of the pleasure principle is very much more secure, but it itself has no more escaped the process of taming than the other instincts in general. In any case, whatever it is that causes the appearance of feelings of pleasure and unpleasure in processes of excitation must be present in the secondary process just as it is in the primary one.

Here might be the starting-point for fresh investigations. Our consciousness communicates to us feelings from within not only of pleasure and unpleasure but also of a peculiar tension which in its turn can be either pleasurable or unpleasurable. Should the difference between these feelings enable us to distinguish between bound and unbound processes of energy? or is the feeling of tension to be related to the absolute magnitude, or perhaps to the level, of the cathexis, while the pleasure and unpleasure series indicates a change in the magnitude of the cathexis *within a given unit of time*? [1] Another striking fact is that the life instincts have so much more contact with our internal perception—emerging as breakers of the peace and constantly producing tensions whose release is felt as pleasure—while the death instincts seem to do their work unobtrusively. The pleasure principle seems actually to serve the death instincts. It is true that it keeps watch upon stimuli from without, which are regarded as dangers by both kinds of instincts; but it is more especially on guard against increases of stimulation from within, which would make the task of living more difficult. This in turn raises a host of other questions to which we can at

[1] [Cf. above, p. 8. These questions had already been touched on by Freud in his 'Project', e.g. in Part I, Section 8 and Part III, Section 1.]

present find no answer. We must be patient and await fresh methods and occasions of research. We must be ready, too, to abandon a path that we have followed for a time, if it seems to be leading to no good end. Only believers, who demand that science shall be a substitute for the catechism they have given up, will blame an investigator for developing or even transforming his views. We may take comfort, too, for the slow advances of our scientific knowledge in the words of the poet:

Was man nicht erfliegen kann, muss man erhinken.

.   .   .   .

Die Schrift sagt, es ist keine Sünde zu hinken.[1]

[1] ['What we cannot reach flying we must reach limping. . . . The Book tells us it is no sin to limp.' The last lines of 'Die beiden Gulden', a version by Rückert of one of the *Maqâmât* of al-Hariri. Freud also quoted these lines in a letter to Fliess of Oct. 20, 1895 (Freud 1950*a*, Letter 32).]

GROUP PSYCHOLOGY AND THE
ANALYSIS OF THE EGO
(1921)

EDITOR'S NOTE

MASSENPSYCHOLOGIE UND ICH-ANALYSE

(*a*) GERMAN EDITIONS:
1921 Leipzig, Vienna and Zurich: Internationaler Psycho-analytischer Verlag. Pp. iii + 140.
1923 2nd ed. Same publishers. Pp. iv + 120.
1925 *G.S.*, **6**, 261–349.
1931 *Theoretische Schriften*, 248–337.
1940 *G.W.*, **13**, 71–161.

(*b*) ENGLISH TRANSLATION:
Group Psychology and the Analysis of the Ego
1922 London and Vienna: International Psycho-Analytical Press. Pp. viii + 134. (Tr. J. Strachey.)
1940 London: Hogarth Press and Institute of Psycho-Analysis; New York: Liveright. (Re-issue of above.)

In the first German edition some of the paragraphs in the text were printed in small type. The English translator was instructed by Freud at the time to transfer these paragraphs to footnotes. The same transposition was carried out in all the later German editions except in the case mentioned on p. 95 below. Freud made some slight changes and additions in the later editions of the work. The present translation is a considerably altered version of the one published in 1922.

Freud's letters showed that the first 'simple idea' of an explanation of group psychology occurred to him during the spring of 1919. Nothing came of this at the time, but in February, 1920, he was working at the subject and he had written a first draft in August of the same year. It was not until February, 1921, however, that he began giving it its final form. The book was finished before the end of March, 1921, and published some three or four months later.

There is little direct connection between the present work and its close predecessor, *Beyond the Pleasure Principle* (1920g).

The trains of thought which Freud here takes up are more especially derived from the fourth essay in *Totem and Taboo* (1912–13) and his papers on narcissism (1914*c*) (the last paragraph of which raises in a highly condensed form many of the points discussed in the present work) and 'Mourning and Melancholia' (1917*e*). Freud also returns here to his early interest in hypnotism and suggestion, which dated from his studies with Charcot in 1885–6.

As is indicated by its title, the work is important in two different directions. On the one hand it explains the psychology of groups on the basis of changes in the psychology of the individual mind. And on the other hand it carries a stage further Freud's investigation of the anatomical structure of the mind which was already foreshadowed in *Beyond the Pleasure Principle* (1920*g*) and was to be more completely worked out in *The Ego and the Id* (1923*b*).

Extracts from the earlier (1922) translation of this work were included in Rickman's *General Selection from the Works of Sigmund Freud* (1937, 195–244).

GROUP PSYCHOLOGY AND THE ANALYSIS OF THE EGO

I

INTRODUCTION

THE contrast between individual psychology and social or group[1] psychology, which at a first glance may seem to be full of significance, loses a great deal of its sharpness when it is examined more closely. It is true that individual psychology is concerned with the individual man and explores the paths by which he seeks to find satisfaction for his instinctual impulses; but only rarely and under certain exceptional conditions is individual psychology in a position to disregard the relations of this individual to others. In the individual's mental life someone else is invariably involved, as a model, as an object, as a helper, as an opponent; and so from the very first individual psychology, in this extended but entirely justifiable sense of the words, is at the same time social psychology as well.

The relations of an individual to his parents and to his brothers and sisters, to the object of his love, and to his physician—in fact all the relations which have hitherto been the chief subject of psycho-analytic research—may claim to be considered as social phenomena; and in this respect they may be contrasted with certain other processes, described by us as 'narcissistic', in which the satisfaction of the instincts is partially or totally withdrawn from the influence of other people. The contrast between social and narcissistic—Bleuler [1912] would perhaps call them 'autistic'—mental acts therefore falls wholly within the domain of individual psychology, and is not well calculated to differentiate it from a social or group psychology.

---

[1] ['Group' is used throughout the translation of this work as equivalent to the rather more comprehensive German '*Masse*'. The author uses this latter word to render both McDougall's 'group', and also Le Bon's '*foule*', which would more naturally be translated 'crowd' in English. For the sake of uniformity, however, 'group' has been preferred in this case as well, and has been substituted for 'crowd' even in the extracts from the English translation of Le Bon.]

69

The individual in the relations which have already been mentioned—to his parents and to his brothers and sisters, to the person he is in love with, to his friend, and to his physician—comes under the influence of only a single person, or of a very small number of persons, each one of whom has become enormously important to him. Now in speaking of social or group psychology it has become usual to leave these relations on one side and to isolate as the subject of inquiry the influencing of an individual by a large number of people simultaneously, people with whom he is connected by something, though otherwise they may in many respects be strangers to him. Group psychology is therefore concerned with the individual man as a member of a race, of a nation, of a caste, of a profession, of an institution, or as a component part of a crowd of people who have been organized into a group at some particular time for some definite purpose. When once natural continuity has been severed in this way, if a breach is thus made between things which are by nature interconnected, it is easy to regard the phenomena that appear under these special conditions as being expressions of a special instinct that is not further reducible—the social instinct ('herd instinct', 'group mind'),[1] which does not come to light in any other situations. But we may perhaps venture to object that it seems difficult to attribute to the factor of number a significance so great as to make it capable by itself of arousing in our mental life a new instinct that is otherwise not brought into play. Our expectation is therefore directed towards two other possibilities: that the social instinct may not be a primitive one and insusceptible of dissection, and that it may be possible to discover the beginnings of its development in a narrower circle, such as that of the family.

Although group psychology is only in its infancy, it embraces an immense number of separate issues and offers to investigators countless problems which have hitherto not even been properly distinguished from one another. The mere classification of the different forms of group formation and the description of the mental phenomena produced by them require a great expenditure of observation and exposition, and have already given rise to a copious literature. Anyone who compares the narrow dimensions of this little book with the wide extent of group psycho-

---

[1] [These terms are in English in the original.]

logy will at once be able to guess that only a few points chosen from the whole material are to be dealt with here. And they will in fact only be a few questions with which the depth-psychology of psycho-analysis is specially concerned.

LE BON'S DESCRIPTION OF THE
GROUP MIND

INSTEAD of starting from a definition, it seems more useful to begin with some indication of the range of the phenomena under review, and to select from among them a few specially striking and characteristic facts to which our enquiry can be attached. We can achieve both of these aims by means of quotation from Le Bon's deservedly famous work *Psychologie des foules* [1895].

Let us make the matter clear once again. If a psychology, concerned with exploring the predispositions, the instinctual impulses, the motives and the aims of an individual man down to his actions and his relations with those who are nearest to him, had completely achieved its task, and had cleared up the whole of these matters with their interconnections, it would then suddenly find itself confronted by a new task which would lie before it unachieved. It would be obliged to explain the surprising fact that under a certain condition this individual, whom it had come to understand, thought, felt and acted in quite a different way from what would have been expected. And this condition is his insertion into a collection of people which has acquired the characteristic of a 'psychological group'. What, then, is a 'group'? How does it acquire the capacity for exercising such a decisive influence over the mental life of the individual? And what is the nature of the mental change which it forces upon the individual?

It is the task of a theoretical group psychology to answer these three questions. The best way of approaching them is evidently to start with the third. Observation of the changes in the individual's reactions is what provides group psychology with its material; for every attempt at an explanation must be preceded by a description of the thing that is to be explained.

I will now let Le Bon speak for himself. He says: 'The most striking peculiarity presented by a psychological group [1] is the

[1] [See footnote p. 69.—This and the following quotations are from the English translation.]

following. Whoever be the individuals that compose it, however like or unlike be their mode of life, their occupations, their
character, or their intelligence, the fact that they have been
transformed into a group puts them in possession of a sort of
collective mind which makes them feel, think, and act in a manner quite different from that in which each individual of them
would feel, think, and act were he in a state of isolation. There
are certain ideas and feelings which do not come into being, or
do not transform themselves into acts except in the case of
individuals forming a group. The psychological group is a provisional being formed of heterogeneous elements, which for a
moment are combined, exactly as the cells which constitute a
living body form by their reunion a new being which displays
characteristics very different from those possessed by each of
the cells singly.' (Trans. 1920, 29.)

We shall take the liberty of interrupting Le Bon's exposition
with glosses of our own, and shall accordingly insert an observation at this point. If the individuals in the group are combined
into a unity, there must surely be something to unite them, and
this bond might be precisely the thing that is characteristic of
a group. But Le Bon does not answer this question; he goes on
to consider the alteration which the individual undergoes when
in a group and describes it in terms which harmonize well with
the fundamental postulates of our own depth-psychology.

'It is easy to prove how much the individual forming part of
a group differs from the isolated individual, but it is less easy
to discover the causes of this difference.

'To obtain at any rate a glimpse of them it is necessary in
the first place to call to mind the truth established by modern
psychology, that unconscious phenomena play an altogether
preponderating part not only in organic life, but also in the
operations of the intelligence. The conscious life of the mind is
of small importance in comparison with its unconscious life.
The most subtle analyst, the most acute observer, is scarcely
successful in discovering more than a very small number of the
conscious [1] motives that determine his conduct. Our conscious
acts are the outcome of an unconscious substratum created in

---

[1] [As was pointed out in a footnote in the German edition of 1940,
the original French text reads '*inconscients*'. The English translation of
Le Bon has 'unconscious', but the German version, quoted by Freud,
has '*bewusster*' ('conscious').]

the mind mainly by hereditary influences. This substratum consists of the innumerable common characteristics handed down from generation to generation, which constitute the genius of a race. Behind the avowed causes of our acts there undoubtedly lie secret causes that we do not avow, but behind these secret causes there are many others more secret still, of which we ourselves are ignorant.[1] The greater part of our daily actions are the result of hidden motives which escape our observation.' (Ibid., 30.)

Le Bon thinks that the particular acquirements of individuals become obliterated in a group, and that in this way their distinctiveness vanishes. The racial unconscious emerges; what is heterogeneous is submerged in what is homogeneous. As we should say, the mental superstructure, the development of which in individuals shows such dissimilarities, is removed, and the unconscious foundations, which are similar in everyone, stand exposed to view.

In this way individuals in a group would come to show an average character. But Le Bon believes that they also display new characteristics which they have not previously possessed, and he seeks the reason for this in three different factors.

'The first is that the individual forming part of a group acquires, solely from numerical considerations, a sentiment of invincible power which allows him to yield to instincts which, had he been alone, he would perforce have kept under restraint. He will be the less disposed to check himself, from the consideration that, a group being anonymous and in consequence irresponsible, the sentiment of responsibility which always controls individuals disappears entirely.' (Ibid., 33.)

From our point of view we need not attribute so much importance to the appearance of new characteristics. For us it would be enough to say that in a group the individual is brought under conditions which allow him to throw off the repressions of his unconscious instinctual impulses. The apparently new characteristics which he then displays are in fact the manifestations of this unconscious, in which all that is evil in the human mind is contained as a predisposition. We can find no difficulty in understanding the disappearance of conscience or of a sense of responsibility in these circumstances. It has long been our

[1] [The English translation reads 'which we ourselves ignore'—a misunderstanding of the French word *ignorées*.]

contention that 'social anxiety' is the essence of what is called conscience.[1]

'The second cause, which is contagion, also intervenes to determine the manifestation in groups of their special characteristics, and at the same time the trend they are to take. Contagion is a phenomenon of which it is easy to establish the presence, but which it is not easy to explain. It must be classed among those phenomena of a hypnotic order, which we shall shortly study. In a group every sentiment and act is contagious, and contagious to such a degree that an individual readily sacrifices his personal interest to the collective interest. This is an aptitude very contrary to his nature, and of which a man is scarcely capable, except when he makes part of a group.' (Ibid., 33.)

We shall later on base an important conjecture upon this last statement.

'A third cause, and by far the most important, determines in the individuals of a group special characteristics which are quite contrary at times to those presented by the isolated individual. I allude to that suggestibility of which, moreover, the contagion mentioned above is only an effect.

'To understand this phenomenon it is necessary to bear in mind certain recent physiological discoveries. We know to-day that by various processes an individual may be brought into such a condition that, having entirely lost his conscious personality, he obeys all the suggestions of the operator who has deprived him of it, and commits acts in utter contradiction with his character and habits. The most careful investigations seem to prove that an individual immersed for some length of time in a group in action soon finds himself—either in consequence of the magnetic influence given out by the group, or from some other cause of which we are ignorant—in a special state, which much resembles the state of "fascination" in which the

[1] There is some difference between Le Bon's view and ours owing to his concept of the unconscious not quite coinciding with the one adopted by psycho-analysis. Le Bon's unconscious more especially contains the most deeply buried features of the racial mind, which as a matter of fact lies outside the scope of psycho-analysis. We do not fail to recognize, indeed, that the ego's nucleus, which comprises the 'archaic heritage' of the human mind, is unconscious; but in addition to this we distinguish the 'unconscious repressed', which arose from a portion of that heritage. This concept of the repressed is not to be found in Le Bon.

hypnotized individual finds himself in the hands of the hypnotizer. . . . The conscious personality has entirely vanished; will
and discernment are lost. All feelings and thoughts are bent in
the direction determined by the hypnotizer.

'Such also is approximately the state of the individual forming part of a psychological group. He is no longer conscious of
his acts. In his case, as in the case of the hypnotized subject, at
the same time that certain faculties are destroyed, others may
be brought to a high degree of exaltation. Under the influence
of a suggestion, he will undertake the accomplishment of certain
acts with irresistible impetuosity. This impetuosity is the more
irresistible in the case of groups than in that of the hypnotized
subject, from the fact that, the suggestion being the same for all
the individuals in the group, it gains in strength by reciprocity.'
(Ibid., 34.)

'We see, then, that the disappearance of the conscious personality, the predominance of the unconscious personality, the
turning by means of suggestion and contagion of feelings and
ideas in an identical direction, the tendency to immediately
transform the suggested ideas into acts; these, we see, are the
principal characteristics of the individual forming part of a
group. He is no longer himself, but has become an automaton
who has ceased to be guided by his will.' (Ibid., 35.)

I have quoted this passage so fully in order to make it quite
clear that Le Bon explains the condition of an individual in a
group as being actually hypnotic, and does not merely make a
comparison between the two states. We have no intention of
raising any objection at this point, but wish only to emphasize
the fact that the two last causes of an individual becoming
altered in a group (the contagion and the heightened suggestibility) are evidently not on a par, since the contagion seems
actually to be a manifestation of the suggestibility. Moreover
the effects of the two factors do not seem to be sharply differentiated in the text of Le Bon's remarks. We may perhaps best
interpret his statement if we connect the contagion with the
effects of the individual members of the group on one another, while we point to another source for those manifestations
of suggestion in the group which he regards as similar to the
phenomena of hypnotic influence. But to what source? We cannot avoid being struck with a sense of deficiency when we notice
that one of the chief elements of the comparison, namely the

person who is to replace the hypnotist in the case of the group, is not mentioned in Le Bon's exposition. But he nevertheless distinguishes between this influence of 'fascination' which remains plunged in obscurity and the contagious effect which the individuals exercise upon one another and by which the original suggestion is strengthened.

Here is yet another important consideration for helping us to understand the individual in a group: 'Moreover, by the mere fact that he forms part of an organized group, a man descends several rungs in the ladder of civilization. Isolated, he may be a cultivated individual; in a crowd, he is a barbarian— that is, a creature acting by instinct. He possesses the spontaneity, the violence, the ferocity, and also the enthusiasm and heroism of primitive beings.' (Ibid., 36.) Le Bon then dwells especially upon the lowering in intellectual ability which an individual experiences when he becomes merged in a group.[1]

Let us now leave the individual, and turn to the group mind, as it has been outlined by Le Bon. It shows not a single feature which a psycho-analyst would find any difficulty in placing or in deriving from its source. Le Bon himself shows us the way by pointing to its similarity with the mental life of primitive people and of children (ibid., 40).

A group is impulsive, changeable and irritable. It is led almost exclusively by the unconscious.[2] The impulses which a group obeys may according to circumstances be generous or cruel, heroic or cowardly, but they are always so imperious that no personal interest, not even that of self-preservation, can make itself felt (ibid., 41). Nothing about it is premeditated. Though it may desire things passionately, yet this is never so for long, for it is incapable of perseverance. It cannot tolerate any delay between its desire and the fulfilment of what it desires. It has a sense of omnipotence; the notion of impossibility disappears for the individual in a group.[3]

[1] Compare Schiller's couplet:
Jeder, sieht man ihn einzeln, ist leidlich klug und verständig;
    Sind sie in corpore, gleich wird euch ein Dummkopf daraus.
[Everyone, looked at alone, is passably shrewd and discerning;
    When they're *in corpore*, then straightway you'll find he's an ass.]
 [2] 'Unconscious' is used here correctly by Le Bon in the descriptive sense, where it does not mean only the 'repressed'.
 [3] Compare the third essay in my *Totem and Taboo* (1912–13) [*Standard Ed.*, 13, 85 ff.].

A group is extraordinarily credulous and open to influence, it has no critical faculty, and the improbable does not exist for it. It thinks in images, which call one another up by association (just as they arise with individuals in states of free imagination), and whose agreement with reality is never checked by any reasonable agency. The feelings of a group are always very simple and very exaggerated. So that a group knows neither doubt nor uncertainty.[1]

It goes directly to extremes; if a suspicion is expressed, it is instantly changed into an incontrovertible certainty; a trace of antipathy is turned into furious hatred (ibid., 56).[2]

Inclined as it itself is to all extremes, a group can only be excited by an excessive stimulus. Anyone who wishes to produce an effect upon it needs no logical adjustment in his arguments; he must paint in the most forcible colours, he must exaggerate, and he must repeat the same thing again and again.

Since a group is in no doubt as to what constitutes truth or error, and is conscious, moreover, of its own great strength, it is as intolerant as it is obedient to authority. It respects force and can only be slightly influenced by kindness, which it regards merely as a form of weakness. What it demands of its heroes is strength, or even violence. It wants to be ruled and oppressed

[1] In the interpretation of dreams, to which, indeed, we owe our best knowledge of unconscious mental life, we follow a technical rule of disregarding doubt and uncertainty in the narrative of the dream, and of treating every element of the manifest dream as being quite certain. We attribute doubt and uncertainty to the influence of the censorship to which the dream-work is subjected, and we assume that the primary dream-thoughts are not acquainted with doubt and uncertainty as critical processes. They may of course be present, like anything else, as part of the content of the day's residues which lead to the dream. (See *The Interpretation of Dreams* (1900a), *Standard Ed.*, 5, 516-7.)

[2] The same extreme and unmeasured intensification of every emotion is also a feature of the affective life of children, and it is present as well in dream life. Thanks to the isolation of the single emotions in the unconscious, a slight annoyance during the day will express itself in a dream as a wish for the offending person's death, or a breath of temptation may give the impetus to the portrayal in the dream of a criminal action. Hanns Sachs has made an appropriate remark on this point: 'If we look in our consciousness at something that has been told us by a dream about a contemporary (real) situation, we ought not to be surprised to find that the monster which we saw under the magnifying glass of analysis turns out to be a tiny infusorian.' (*The Interpretation of Dreams* (1900a), *Standard Ed.*, 5, 620.)

and to fear its masters. Fundamentally it is entirely conservative, and it has a deep aversion to all innovations and advances and an unbounded respect for tradition (ibid., 62).

In order to make a correct judgement upon the morals of groups, one must take into consideration the fact that when individuals come together in a group all their individual inhibitions fall away and all the cruel, brutal and destructive instincts, which lie dormant in individuals as relics of a primitive epoch, are stirred up to find free gratification. But under the influence of suggestion groups are also capable of high achievements in the shape of abnegation, unselfishness, and devotion to an ideal. While with isolated individuals personal interest is almost the only motive force, with groups it is very rarely prominent. It is possible to speak of an individual having his moral standards raised by a group (ibid., 65). Whereas the intellectual capacity of a group is always far below that of an individual, its ethical conduct may rise as high above his as it may sink deep below it.

Some other features in Le Bon's description show in a clear light how well justified is the identification of the group mind with the mind of primitive people. In groups the most contradictory ideas can exist side by side and tolerate each other, without any conflict arising from the logical contradiction between them. But this is also the case in the unconscious mental life of individuals, of children and of neurotics, as psycho-analysis has long pointed out.[1]

---

[1] In young children, for instance, ambivalent emotional attitudes towards those who are nearest to them exist side by side for a long time, without either of them interfering with the expression of the other and opposite one. If eventually a conflict breaks out between the two, it is often settled by the child making a change of object and displacing one of the ambivalent emotions on to a substitute. The history of the development of a neurosis in an adult will also show that a suppressed emotion may frequently persist for a long time in unconscious or even in conscious phantasies, the content of which naturally runs directly counter to some predominant tendency, and yet that this opposition does not result in any proceedings on the part of the ego against what it has repudiated. The phantasy is tolerated for quite a long time, until suddenly one day, usually as a result of an increase in the affective cathexis of the phantasy, a conflict breaks out between it and the ego with all the usual consequences. In the process of a child's development into a mature adult there is a more and more extensive integration of his personality, a co-ordination of the separate instinctual impulses and

A group, further, is subject to the truly magical power of words; they can evoke the most formidable tempests in the group mind, and are also capable of stilling them (ibid., 117). 'Reason and arguments are incapable of combating certain words and formulas. They are uttered with solemnity in the presence of groups, and as soon as they have been pronounced an expression of respect is visible on every countenance, and all heads are bowed. By many they are considered as natural forces or as supernatural powers.' (Ibid., 117). It is only necessary in this connection to remember the taboo upon names among primitive people and the magical powers which they ascribe to names and words.[1]

And, finally, groups have never thirsted after truth. They demand illusions, and cannot do without them. They constantly give what is unreal precedence over what is real; they are almost as strongly influenced by what is untrue as by what is true. They have an evident tendency not to distinguish between the two (ibid., 77).

We have pointed out that this predominance of the life of phantasy and of the illusion born of an unfulfilled wish is the ruling factor in the psychology of neuroses. We have found that what neurotics are guided by is not ordinary objective reality but psychological reality. A hysterical symptom is based upon phantasy instead of upon the repetition of real experience, and the sense of guilt in an obsessional neurosis is based upon the fact of an evil intention which was never carried out. Indeed, just as in dreams and in hypnosis, in the mental operations of a group the function for testing the reality of things falls into the background in comparison with the strength of wishful impulses with their affective cathexis.

What Le Bon says on the subject of leaders of groups is less

purposive trends which have grown up in him independently of one another. The analogous process in the domain of sexual life has long been known to us as the co-ordination of all the sexual instincts into a definitive genital organization. (*Three Essays on the Theory of Sexuality*, 1905*d* [*Standard Ed.*, **7**, 207].) Moreover, that the unification of the ego is liable to the same interferences as that of the libido is shown by numerous familiar instances, such as that of men of science who have preserved their faith in the Bible, and other similar cases.—[*Added* 1923:] The various possible ways in which the ego can later disintegrate form a special chapter in psychopathology.

[1] See *Totem and Taboo* (1912-13), *Standard Ed.*, **13**, 54-7.

exhaustive, and does not enable us to make out an underlying
principle so clearly. He thinks that as soon as living beings are
gathered together in certain numbers, no matter whether they
are a herd of animals or a collection of human beings, they place
themselves instinctively under the authority of a chief (ibid.,
134). A group is an obedient herd, which could never live
without a master. It has such a thirst for obedience that it
submits instinctively to anyone who appoints himself its master.

Although in this way the needs of a group carry it half-way
to meet the leader, yet he too must fit in with it in his personal
qualities. He must himself be held in fascination by a strong
faith (in an idea) in order to awaken the group's faith; he must
possess a strong and imposing will, which the group, which has
no will of its own, can accept from him. Le Bon then discusses
the different kinds of leaders, and the means by which they
work upon the group. On the whole he believes that the leaders
make themselves felt by means of the ideas in which they themselves are fanatical believers.

Moreover, he ascribes both to the ideas and to the leaders a
mysterious and irresistible power, which he calls 'prestige'.
Prestige is a sort of domination exercised over us by an individual, a work or an idea. It entirely paralyses our critical
faculty, and fills us with wonderment and respect. It would
seem to arouse a feeling like that of 'fascination' in hypnosis
(ibid., 148). He distinguishes between acquired or artificial and
personal prestige. The former is attached to persons in virtue of
their name, fortune and reputation, and to opinions, works of
art, etc., in virtue of tradition. Since in every case it harks back
to the past, it cannot be of much help to us in understanding
this puzzling influence. Personal prestige is attached to a few
people, who become leaders by means of it, and it has the effect
of making everyone obey them as though by the operation of
some magnetic magic. All prestige, however, is also dependent
upon success, and is lost in the event of failure (ibid., 159).

Le Bon does not give the impression of having succeeded in
bringing the function of the leader and the importance of prestige completely into harmony with his brilliantly executed picture of the group mind.

III

OTHER ACCOUNTS OF COLLECTIVE
MENTAL LIFE

WE have made use of Le Bon's description by way of introduction, because it fits in so well with our own psychology in the emphasis which it lays upon unconscious mental life. But we must now add that as a matter of fact none of that author's statements bring forward anything new. Everything that he says to the detriment and depreciation of the manifestations of the group mind had already been said by others before him with equal distinctness and equal hostility, and has been repeated in unison by thinkers, statesmen and writers since the earliest periods of literature.[1] The two theses which comprise the most important of Le Bon's opinions, those touching upon the collective inhibition of intellectual functioning and the heightening of affectivity in groups, had been formulated shortly before by Sighele.[2] At bottom, all that is left over as being peculiar to Le Bon are the two notions of the unconscious and of the comparison with the mental life of primitive people, and even these had naturally often been alluded to before him.

But, what is more, the description and estimate of the group mind as they have been given by Le Bon and the rest have not by any means been left undisputed. There is no doubt that all the phenomena of the group mind which have just been mentioned have been correctly observed, but it is also possible to distinguish other manifestations of group formation, which operate in a precisely opposite sense, and from which a much higher opinion of the group mind must necessarily follow.

Le Bon himself was prepared to admit that in certain circumstances the morals of a group can be higher than those of the individuals that compose it, and that only collectivities are capable of a high degree of unselfishness and devotion. 'While with isolated individuals personal interest is almost the only motive force, with groups it is very rarely prominent.' (Le Bon, trans. 1920, 65.) Other writers adduce the fact that it is only society

[1] See Kraškovič (1915), particularly the bibliography.
[2] See Moede (1915).

82

which prescribes any ethical standards at all for the individual, while he as a rule fails in one way or another to come up to its high demands. Or they point out that in exceptional circumstances there may arise in communities the phenomenon of enthusiasm, which has made the most splendid group achievements possible.

As regards intellectual work it remains a fact, indeed, that great decisions in the realm of thought and momentous discoveries and solutions of problems are only possible to an individual working in solitude. But even the group mind is capable of creative genius in the field of intelligence, as is shown above all by language itself, as well as by folk-song, folklore and the like. It remains an open question, moreover, how much the individual thinker or writer owes to the stimulation of the group in which he lives, and whether he does more than perfect a mental work in which the others have had a simultaneous share.

In face of these completely contradictory accounts, it looks as though the work of group psychology were bound to come to an ineffectual end. But it is easy to find a more hopeful escape from the dilemma. A number of very different structures have probably been merged under the term 'group' and may require to be distinguished. The assertions of Sighele, Le Bon and the rest relate to groups of a short-lived character, which some passing interest has hastily agglomerated out of various sorts of individuals. The characteristics of revolutionary groups, and especially those of the great French Revolution, have unmistakably influenced their descriptions. The opposite opinions owe their origin to the consideration of those stable groups or associations in which mankind pass their lives, and which are embodied in the institutions of society. Groups of the first kind stand in the same sort of relation to those of the second as a high but choppy sea to a ground swell.

McDougall, in his book on *The Group Mind* (1920a), starts out from the same contradiction that has just been mentioned, and finds a solution for it in the factor of organization. In the simplest case, he says, the 'group' possesses no organization at all or one scarcely deserving the name. He describes a group of this kind as a 'crowd'. But he admits that a crowd of human beings can hardly come together without possessing at all events the rudiments of an organization, and that precisely in these simple groups some fundamental facts of collective psychology can be observed with special ease (McDougall, 1920*a*, 22). Before the members of a random crowd of people can constitute something like a group in the psychological sense, a condition has to be fulfilled: these individuals must have something in common with one another, a common interest in an object, a similar emotional bias in some situation or other, and ('consequently', I should like to interpolate) 'some degree of reciprocal influence' (ibid., 23). The higher the degree of 'this mental homogeneity', the more readily do the individuals form a psychological group, and the more striking are the manifestations of a group mind.

The most remarkable and also the most important result of the formation of a group is the 'exaltation or intensification of emotion' produced in every member of it (ibid., 24). In McDougall's opinion men's emotions are stirred in a group to a pitch that they seldom or never attain under other conditions; and it is a pleasurable experience for those who are concerned, to surrender themselves so unreservedly to their passions and thus to become merged in the group and to lose the sense of the limits of their individuality. The manner in which individuals are thus carried away by a common impulse is explained by McDougall by means of what he calls the 'principle of direct induction of emotion by way of the primitive sympathetic response' (ibid., 25), that is, by means of the emotional contagion with which we are already familiar. The fact is that the perception of the signs of an affective state is calculated automatically to arouse the same affect in the person who perceives them. The greater the number of people in whom the same affect can be simultaneously observed, the stronger does this automatic compulsion grow. The individual loses his power of criticism, and lets himself slip into the same affect. But in so doing he increases the excitement of the other people, who had produced this result in him, and thus the affective charge of the individuals becomes intensified by mutual interaction. Something is unmistakably at work in the nature of a compulsion to do the same as the others, to remain in harmony with the many. The cruder and simpler emotional impulses are the more apt to spread through a group in this way (ibid., 39).

This mechanism for the intensification of affect is favoured by some other influences which emanate from groups. A group impresses the individual as being an unlimited power and an insurmountable peril. For the moment it replaces the whole of human society, which is the wielder of authority, whose punishments the individual fears, and for whose sake he has submitted to so many inhibitions. It is clearly perilous for him to put himself in opposition to it, and it will be safer to follow the example of those around him and perhaps even 'hunt with the pack'. In obedience to the new authority he may put his former 'conscience' out of action, and so surrender to the attraction of the increased pleasure that is certainly obtained from the removal of inhibitions. On the whole, therefore, it is not so remarkable that we should see an individual in a group doing or approving things which he would have avoided in the normal conditions of life; and in this way we may even hope to clear up a little of the obscurity which is so often covered by the enigmatic word 'suggestion'.

McDougall does not dispute the thesis as to the collective inhibition of intelligence in groups (ibid., 41). He says that the minds of lower intelligence bring down those of a higher order to their own level. The latter are obstructed in their activity, because in general an intensification of affect creates unfavourable conditions for sound intellectual work, and further because the individuals are intimidated by the group and their mental activity is not free, and because there is a lowering in each individual of his sense of responsibility for his own performances.

The judgement with which McDougall sums up the psychological behaviour of a simple 'unorganized' group is no more friendly than that of Le Bon. Such a group 'is excessively emotional, impulsive, violent, fickle, inconsistent, irresolute and extreme in action, displaying only the coarser emotions and the less refined sentiments; extremely suggestible, careless in deliberation, hasty in judgement, incapable of any but the simpler and imperfect forms of reasoning; easily swayed and led, lacking in self-consciousness, devoid of self-respect and of sense of responsibility, and apt to be carried away by the consciousness of its own force, so that it tends to produce all the manifestations we have learnt to expect of any irresponsible and absolute power. Hence its behaviour is like that of an unruly child or an untutored passionate savage in a strange situation, rather than like that of its average member; and in the worst cases it is like that of a wild beast, rather than like that of human beings.' (Ibid., 45.)

Since McDougall contrasts the behaviour of a highly organized group with what has just been described, we shall be particularly interested to learn in what this organization consists, and by what factors it is produced. The author enumerates five 'principal conditions' for raising collective mental life to a higher level.

The first and fundamental condition is that there should be some degree of continuity of existence in the group. This may be either material or formal: material, if the same individuals persist in the group for some time; and formal, if there is developed within the group a system of fixed positions which are occupied by a succession of individuals.

The second condition is that in the individual member of the group some definite idea should be formed of the nature, composition, functions and capacities of the group, so that from this he may develop an emotional relation to the group as a whole.

The third is that the group should be brought into interaction (perhaps in the form of rivalry) with other groups similar to it but differing from it in many respects.

The fourth is that the group should possess traditions, customs and habits, and especially such as determine the relations of its members to one another.

The fifth is that the group should have a definite structure, expressed in the specialization and differentiation of the functions of its constituents.

According to McDougall, if these conditions are fulfilled, the psychological disadvantages of group formations are removed. The collective lowering of intellectual ability is avoided by withdrawing the performance of intellectual tasks from the group and reserving them for individual members of it.

It seems to us that the condition which McDougall designates as the 'organization' of a group can with more justification be described in another way. The problem consists in how to procure for the group precisely those features which were characteristic of the individual and which are extinguished in him by the formation of the group. For the individual, outside the primitive group, possessed his own continuity, his self-consciousness, his traditions and customs, his own particular functions and position, and he kept apart from his rivals. Owing to his entry into an 'unorganized' group he had lost this distinctiveness for a time. If we thus recognize that the aim is to equip the group with the attributes of the individual, we shall be reminded of a valuable remark of Trotter's,[1] to the effect that the tendency towards the formation of groups is biologically a continuation of the multicellular character of all the higher organisms.[2]

[1] *Instincts of the Herd in Peace and War* (1916). [See below, p. 118 ff.]

[2] [*Footnote added* 1923:] I differ from what is in other respects an understanding and shrewd criticism by Hans Kelsen (1922) [of the present work] when he says that to provide the 'group mind' with an organization of this kind signifies a hypostasis of it—that is to say, implies an attribution to it of independence of the mental processes in the individual.

SUGGESTION AND LIBIDO

WE started from the fundamental fact that an individual in a group is subjected through its influence to what is often a profound alteration in his mental activity. His liability to affect becomes extraordinarily intensified, while his intellectual ability is markedly reduced, both processes being evidently in the direction of an approximation to the other individuals in the group; and this result can only be reached by the removal of those inhibitions upon his instincts which are peculiar to each individual, and by his resigning those expressions of his inclinations which are especially his own. We have heard that these often unwelcome consequences are to some extent at least prevented by a higher 'organization' of the group; but this does not contradict the fundamental fact of group psychology—the two theses as to the intensification of the affects and the inhibition of the intellect in primitive groups. Our interest is now directed to discovering the psychological explanation of this mental change which is experienced by the individual in a group.

It is clear that rational factors (such as the intimidation of the individual which has already been mentioned, that is, the action of his instinct of self-preservation) do not cover the observable phenomena. Beyond this what we are offered as an explanation by authorities on sociology and group psychology is always the same, even though it is given various names, and that is— the magic word 'suggestion'. Tarde [1890] calls it 'imitation'; but we cannot help agreeing with a writer who protests that imitation comes under the concept of suggestion, and is in fact one of its results (Brugeilles, 1913). Le Bon traces back all the puzzling features of social phenomena to two factors: the mutual suggestion of individuals and the prestige of leaders. But prestige, again, is only recognizable by its capacity for evoking suggestion. McDougall for a moment gives us an impression that his principle of 'primitive induction of emotion' might enable us to do without the assumption of suggestion. But on further consideration we are forced to perceive that this principle makes no more than the familiar assertions about 'imitation' or 'contagion', except for a decided stress upon the emotional factor. There is no doubt that something exists in us which, when we become aware of signs of an emotion in someone else, tends to make us fall into the same emotion; but how often do we not successfully oppose it, resist the emotion, and react in quite an opposite way? Why, therefore, do we invariably give way to this contagion when we are in a group? Once more we should have to say that what compels us to obey this tendency is imitation, and what induces the emotion in us is the group's suggestive influence. Moreover, quite apart from this, McDougall does not enable us to evade suggestion; we hear from him as well as from other writers that groups are distinguished by their special suggestibility.

We shall therefore be prepared for the statement that suggestion (or more correctly suggestibility) is actually an irreducible, primitive phenomenon, a fundamental fact in the mental life of man. Such, too, was the opinion of Bernheim, of whose astonishing arts I was a witness in the year 1889. But I can remember even then feeling a muffled hostility to this tyranny of suggestion. When a patient who showed himself unamenable was met with the shout: 'What are you doing? *Vous vous contre-suggestionnez!*', I said to myself that this was an evident injustice and an act of violence. For the man certainly had a right to counter-suggestions if people were trying to subdue him with suggestions. Later on my resistance took the direction of protesting against the view that suggestion, which explained everything, was itself to be exempt from explanation.[1] Thinking of it, I repeated the old conundrum:[2]

> Christoph trug Christum,
> Christus trug die ganze Welt,
> Sag' wo hat Christoph
> Damals hin den Fuss gestellt?

> Christophorus Christum, sed Christus sustulit orbem:
> Constiterit pedibus dic ubi Christophorus?[3]

Now that I once more approach the riddle of suggestion after

[1] [See, for instance, some remarks in Freud's case history of 'Little Hans' (1909b), *Standard Ed.*, **10**, 102.]

[2] Konrad Richter, 'Der deutsche S. Christoph.'

[3] [Literally: 'Christopher bore Christ; Christ bore the whole world; Say, where did Christopher then put his foot?']

having kept away from it for some thirty years, I find there is no change in the situation. (There is one exception to be made to this statement, and one which bears witness precisely to the influence of psycho-analysis.) I notice that particular efforts are being made to formulate the concept of suggestion correctly, that is, to fix the conventional use of the name (e.g. McDougall, 1920*b*). And this is by no means superfluous, for the word is acquiring a more and more extended use and a looser and looser meaning [in German], and will soon come to designate any sort of influence whatever, just as it does in English, where 'to suggest' and 'suggestion' correspond to our *nahelegen* and *Anregung*. But there has been no explanation of the nature of suggestion, that is, of the conditions under which influence without adequate logical foundation takes place. I should not avoid the task of supporting this statement by an analysis of the literature of the last thirty years, if I were not aware that an exhaustive enquiry is being undertaken close at hand which has in view the fulfilment of this very task.[1]

Instead of this I shall make an attempt at using the concept of *libido* for the purpose of throwing light upon group psychology, a concept which has done us such good service in the study of psychoneuroses.

Libido is an expression taken from the theory of the emotions. We call by that name the energy, regarded as a quantitative magnitude (though not at present actually measurable), of those instincts which have to do with all that may be comprised under the word 'love'. The nucleus of what we mean by love naturally consists (and this is what is commonly called love, and what the poets sing of) in sexual love with sexual union as its aim. But we do not separate from this—what in any case has a share in the name 'love'—on the one hand, self-love, and on the other, love for parents and children, friendship and love for humanity in general, and also devotion to concrete objects and to abstract ideas. Our justification lies in the fact that psycho-analytic research has taught us that all these tendencies are an expression of the same instinctual impulses; in relations between the sexes these impulses force their way towards sexual union, but in other circumstances they are diverted from this aim or are prevented from reaching it, though always preserving enough of

[1] [*Footnote added* 1925:] This work has unfortunately not materialized.

their original nature to keep their identity recognizable (as in such features as the longing for proximity, and self-sacrifice).

We are of opinion, then, that language has carried out an entirely justifiable piece of unification in creating the word 'love' with its numerous uses, and that we cannot do better than take it as the basis of our scientific discussions and expositions as well. By coming to this decision, psycho-analysis has let loose a storm of indignation, as though it had been guilty of an act of outrageous innovation. Yet it has done nothing original in taking love in this 'wider' sense. In its origin, function, and relation to sexual love, the 'Eros' of the philosopher Plato coincides exactly with the love-force, the libido of psycho-analysis, as has been shown in detail by Nachansohn (1915) and Pfister (1921); and when the apostle Paul, in his famous epistle to the Corinthians, praises love above all else, he certainly understands it in the same 'wider' sense.[1] But this only shows that men do not always take their great thinkers seriously, even when they profess most to admire them.

Psycho-analysis, then, gives these love instincts the name of sexual instincts, *a potiori* and by reason of their origin. The majority of 'educated' people have regarded this nomenclature as an insult, and have taken their revenge by retorting upon psycho-analysis with the reproach of 'pan-sexualism'. Anyone who considers sex as something mortifying and humiliating to human nature is at liberty to make use of the more genteel expressions 'Eros' and 'erotic'. I might have done so myself from the first and thus have spared myself much opposition. But I did not want to, for I like to avoid concessions to faintheartedness. One can never tell where that road may lead one; one gives way first in words, and then little by little in substance too. I cannot see any merit in being ashamed of sex; the Greek word 'Eros', which is to soften the affront, is in the end nothing more than a translation of our German word *Liebe* [love]; and finally, he who knows how to wait need make no concessions.

We will try our fortune, then, with the supposition that love relationships (or, to use a more neutral expression, emotional ties) also constitute the essence of the group mind. Let us remember that the authorities make no mention of any such relations. What would correspond to them is evidently concealed

[1] 'Though I speak with the tongues of men and of angels, and have not charity [love], I am become as sounding brass, or a tinkling cymbal.'

behind the shelter, the screen, of suggestion. Our hypo-thesis finds support in the first instance from two passing thoughts. First, that a group is clearly held together by a power of some kind: and to what power could this feat be better ascribed than to Eros, which holds together everything in the world?[1] Secondly, that if an individual gives up his distinctive-ness in a group and lets its other members influence him by suggestion, it gives one the impression that he does it because he feels the need of being in harmony with them rather than in opposition to them—so that perhaps after all he does it *'ihnen zu Liebe'*.[2]

[1] [See above, p. 50.]

[2] [An idiom meaning 'for their sake'. Literally: 'for love of them'.—A line of thought similar to that expressed in the last three paragraphs will be found in the almost contemporary Preface to the Fourth Edition of Freud's *Three Essays* (1905d), *Standard Ed.*, 7, 134.]

TWO ARTIFICIAL GROUPS: THE CHURCH AND THE ARMY

WE may recall from what we know of the morphology of groups that it is possible to distinguish very different kinds of groups and opposing lines in their development. There are very fleeting groups and extremely lasting ones; homogeneous ones, made up of the same sorts of individuals, and unhomogeneous ones; natural groups, and artificial ones, requiring an external force to keep them together; primitive groups, and highly organized ones with a definite structure. But for reasons which remain to be explained we should like to lay particular stress upon a distinction to which writers on the subject have been inclined to give too little attention; I refer to that between leaderless groups and those with leaders. And, in complete opposition to the usual practice, we shall not choose a relatively simple group formation as our point of departure, but shall begin with highly organized, lasting and artificial groups. The most interesting example of such structures are Churches—communities of believers—and armies.

A Church and an army are artificial groups—that is, a certain external force is employed to prevent them from disintegrating [1] and to check alterations in their structure. As a rule a person is not consulted, or is given no choice, as to whether he wants to enter such a group; any attempt at leaving it is usually met with persecution or with severe punishment, or has quite definite conditions attached to it. It is quite outside our present interest to enquire why these associations need such special safeguards. We are only attracted by one circumstance, namely that certain facts, which are far more concealed in other cases, can be observed very clearly in those highly organized groups which are protected from dissolution in the manner that has been mentioned.

In a Church (and we may with advantage take the Catholic Church as a type) as well as in an army, however different the

[1] [*Footnote added* 1923:] In groups, the attributes 'stable' and 'artificial' seem to coincide or at least to be intimately connected.

two may be in other respects, the same illusion holds good of
there being a head—in the Catholic Church Christ, in an army
its Commander-in-Chief—who loves all the individuals in the
group with an equal love. Everything depends upon this
illusion; if it were to be dropped, then both Church and army
would dissolve, so far as the external force permitted them to.
This equal love was expressly enunciated by Christ: 'Inasmuch
as ye have done it unto one of the least of these my brethren,
ye have done it unto me.' He stands to the individual members
of the group of believers in the relation of a kind elder brother;
he is their substitute father. All the demands that are made
upon the individual are derived from this love of Christ's. A
democratic strain runs through the Church, for the very reason
that before Christ everyone is equal, and that everyone has an
equal share in his love. It is not without a deep reason that the
similarity between the Christian community and a family is
invoked, and that believers call themselves brothers in Christ,
that is, brothers through the love which Christ has for them.
There is no doubt that the tie which unites each individual
with Christ is also the cause of the tie which unites them with
one another. The like holds good of an army. The Commander-
in-Chief is a father who loves all soldiers equally, and for that
reason they are comrades among themselves. The army differs
structurally from the Church in being built up of a series of
such groups. Every captain is, as it were, the Commander-in-
Chief and the father of his company, and so is every non-
commissioned officer of his section. It is true that a similar
hierarchy has been constructed in the Church, but it does not
play the same part in it economically; [1] for more knowledge and
care about individuals may be attributed to Christ than to a
human Commander-in-Chief.

An objection will justly be raised against this conception of
the libidinal structure of an army on the ground that no place
has been found in it for such ideas as those of one's country, of
national glory, etc., which are of such importance in holding an
army together. The answer is that that is a different instance of
a group tie, and no longer such a simple one; for the examples
of great generals, like Caesar, Wallenstein, or Napoleon, show
that such ideas are not indispensable to the existence of an army.

[1] [i.e. in the quantitative distribution of the psychical forces involved.]

We shall presently touch upon the possibility of a leading idea being substituted for a leader and upon the relations between the two. The neglect of this libidinal factor in an army, even when it is not the only factor operative, seems to be not merely a theoretical omission but also a practical danger. Prussian militarism, which was just as unpsychological as German science, may have had to suffer the consequences of this in the [first] World War. We know that the war neuroses which ravaged the German army have been recognized as being a protest of the individual against the part he was expected to play in the army; and according to the communication of Simmel (1918), the hard treatment of the men by their superiors may be considered as foremost among the motive forces of the disease. If the importance of the libido's claims on this score had been better appreciated, the fantastic promises of the American President's Fourteen Points would probably not have been believed so easily, and the splendid instrument would not have broken in the hands of the German leaders.[1]

It is to be noticed that in these two artificial groups each individual is bound by libidinal ties on the one hand to the leader (Christ, the Commander-in-Chief) and on the other hand to the other members of the group. How these two ties are related to each other, whether they are of the same kind and the same value, and how they are to be described psychologically— these questions must be reserved for subsequent enquiry. But we shall venture even now upon a mild reproach against earlier writers for not having sufficiently appreciated the importance of the leader in the psychology of the group, while our own choice of this as a first subject for investigation has brought us into a more favourable position. It would appear as though we were on the right road towards an explanation of the principal phenomenon of group psychology—the individual's lack of free-dom in a group. If each individual is bound in two directions by such an intense emotional tie, we shall find no difficulty in attributing to that circumstance the alteration and limitation which have been observed in his personality.

A hint to the same effect, that the essence of a group lies in

[1] [By Freud's wish this paragraph was printed as a footnote in the English translation of 1922. It appears in the text in all the German editions, however, both before and after that date. See Editor's Note, p. 67.]

the libidinal ties existing in it, is also to be found in the phenomenon of panic, which is best studied in military groups. A
panic arises if a group of that kind becomes disintegrated. Its
characteristics are that none of the orders given by superiors are
any longer listened to, and that each individual is only solicitous
on his own account, and without any consideration for the rest.
The mutual ties have ceased to exist, and a gigantic and sense-
less fear is set free. At this point, again, the objection will naturally be made that it is rather the other way round; and that the
fear has grown so great as to be able to disregard all ties and all
feelings of consideration for others. McDougall (1920a, 24) has
even made use of panic (though not of military panic) as a
typical instance of that intensification of emotion by contagion
('primary induction') on which he lays so much emphasis.
But nevertheless this rational method of explanation is here
quite inadequate. The very question that needs explanation is
why the fear has become so gigantic. The greatness of the danger
cannot be responsible, for the same army which now falls a
victim to panic may previously have faced equally great or
greater danger with complete success; it is of the very essence
of panic that it bears no relation to the danger that threatens,
and often breaks out on the most trivial occasions. If an
individual in panic fear begins to be solicitous only on his own
account, he bears witness in so doing to the fact that the
emotional ties, which have hitherto made the danger seem small
to him, have ceased to exist. Now that he is by himself in facing
the danger, he may surely think it greater. The fact is, therefore,
that panic fear presupposes a relaxation in the libidinal structure of the group and reacts to that relaxation in a justifiable
manner, and the contrary view—that the libidinal ties of the
group are destroyed owing to fear in the face of the danger—
can be refuted.

The contention that fear in a group is increased to enormous
proportions through induction (contagion) is not in the least
contradicted by these remarks. McDougall's view meets the case
entirely when the danger is a really great one and when the
group has no strong emotional ties—conditions which are
fulfilled, for instance, when a fire breaks out in a theatre or a
place of amusement. But the truly instructive case and the one
which can be best employed for our purposes is that mentioned
above, in which a body of troops breaks into a panic although

the danger has not increased beyond a degree that is usual and has often been previously faced. It is not to be expected that the usage of the word 'panic' should be clearly and unambiguously determined. Sometimes it is used to describe any collective fear, sometimes even fear in an individual when it exceeds all bounds, and often the name seems to be reserved for cases in which the outbreak of fear is not warranted by the occasion. If we take the word 'panic' in the sense of collective fear, we can establish a far-reaching analogy. Fear in an individual is provoked either by the greatness of a danger or by the cessation of emotional ties (libidinal cathexes); the latter is the case of neurotic fear or anxiety.[1] In just the same way panic arises either owing to an increase of the common danger or owing to the disappearance of the emotional ties which hold the group together; and the latter case is analogous to that of neurotic anxiety.[2]

Anyone who, like McDougall (1920a), describes a panic as one of the plainest functions of the 'group mind', arrives at the paradoxical position that this group mind does away with itself in one of its most striking manifestations. It is impossible to doubt that panic means the disintegration of a group; it involves the cessation of all the feelings of consideration which the members of the group otherwise show one another.

The typical occasion of the outbreak of a panic is very much as it is represented in Nestroy's parody of Hebbel's play about Judith and Holofernes. A soldier cries out: 'The general has lost his head!' and thereupon all the Assyrians take to flight. The loss of the leader in some sense or other, the birth of misgivings about him, brings on the outbreak of panic, though the danger remains the same; the mutual ties between the members of the group disappear, as a rule, at the same time as the tie with their leader. The group vanishes in dust, like a Prince Rupert's drop when its tail is broken off.

The dissolution of a religious group is not so easy to observe. A short time ago there came into my hands an English novel of Catholic origin, recommended by the Bishop of London, with

[1] See Lecture XXV of my *Introductory Lectures* (1916–17). [See also, however, *Inhibitions, Symptoms and Anxiety* (1926d).]

[2] Compare Béla von Felszeghy's interesting though somewhat over-imaginative paper 'Panik und Pankomplex' (1920).

the title *When It Was Dark*.[1] It gave a clever and, as it seems to me, a convincing picture of such a possibility and its consequences. The novel, which is supposed to relate to the present day, tells how a conspiracy of enemies of the person of Christ and of the Christian faith succeed in arranging for a sepulchre to be discovered in Jerusalem. In this sepulchre is an inscription, in which Joseph of Arimathaea confesses that for reasons of piety he secretly removed the body of Christ from its grave on the third day after its entombment and buried it in this spot. The resurrection of Christ and his divine nature are by this means disproved, and the result of this archaeological discovery is a convulsion in European civilization and an extraordinary increase in all crimes and acts of violence, which only ceases when the forgers' plot has been revealed.

The phenomenon which accompanies the dissolution that is here supposed to overtake a religious group is not fear, for which the occasion is wanting. Instead of it ruthless and hostile impulses towards other people make their appearance, which, owing to the equal love of Christ, they had previously been unable to do.[2] But even during the kingdom of Christ those people who do not belong to the community of believers, who do not love him, and whom he does not love, stand outside this tie. Therefore a religion, even if it calls itself the religion of love, must be hard and unloving to those who do not belong to it. Fundamentally indeed every religion is in this same way a religion of love for all those whom it embraces; while cruelty and intolerance towards those who do not belong to it are natural to every religion. However difficult we may find it personally, we ought not to reproach believers too severely on this account; people who are unbelieving or indifferent are much better off psychologically in this matter [of cruelty and intolerance]. If to-day that intolerance no longer shows itself so violent and cruel as in former centuries, we can scarcely conclude that there has been a softening in human manners. The cause is rather to be found in the undeniable weakening of religious feelings and the libidinal ties which depend upon

[1] [A book by 'Guy Thorne' (pseudonym of C. Ranger Gull) which enjoyed extremely large sales at the time of its publication in 1903.]

[2] Compare the explanation of similar phenomena after the abolition of the paternal authority of the sovereign given in Federn's *Die vaterlose Gesellschaft* (1919).

them. If another group tie takes the place of the religious one
—and the socialistic tie seems to be succeeding in doing so—
then there will be the same intolerance towards outsiders as in
the age of the Wars of Religion; and if differences between
scientific opinions could ever attain a similar significance for
groups, the same result would again be repeated with this new
motivation.

FURTHER PROBLEMS AND LINES
OF WORK

WE have hitherto considered two artificial groups and have found that both are dominated by emotional ties of two kinds. One of these, the tie with the leader, seems (at all events for these cases) to be more of a ruling factor than the other, which holds between the members of the group.

Now much else remains to be examined and described in the morphology of groups. We should have to start from the ascertained fact that a mere collection of people is not a group, so long as these ties have not been established in it; but we should have to admit that in any collection of people the tendency to form a psychological group may very easily come to the fore. We should have to give our attention to the different kinds of groups, more or less stable, that arise spontaneously, and to study the conditions of their origin and of their dissolution. We should above all be concerned with the distinction between groups which have a leader and leaderless groups. We should consider whether groups with leaders may not be the more primitive and complete, whether in the others an idea, an abstraction, may not take the place of the leader (a state of things to which religious groups, with their invisible head, form a transitional stage), and whether a common tendency, a wish in which a number of people can have a share, may not in the same way serve as a substitute. This abstraction, again, might be more or less completely embodied in the figure of what we might call a secondary leader, and interesting varieties would arise from the relation between the idea and the leader. The leader or the leading idea might also, so to speak, be negative; hatred against a particular person or institution might operate in just the same unifying way, and might call up the same kind of emotional ties as positive attachment. Then the question would also arise whether a leader is really indispensable to the essence of a group—and other questions besides.

But all these questions, which may, moreover, have been dealt with in part in the literature of group psychology, will not succeed in diverting our interest from the fundamental psychological problems that confront us in the structure of a group. And our attention will first be attracted by a consideration which promises to bring us in the most direct way to a proof that libidinal ties are what characterize a group.

Let us keep before our eyes the nature of the emotional relations which hold between men in general. According to Schopenhauer's famous simile of the freezing porcupines no one can tolerate a too intimate approach to his neighbour.[1]

The evidence of psycho-analysis shows that almost every intimate emotional relation between two people which lasts for some time—marriage, friendship, the relations between parents and children [2]—contains a sediment of feelings of aversion and hostility, which only escapes perception as a result of repression.[3] This is less disguised in the common wrangles between business partners or in the grumbles of a subordinate at his superior. The same thing happens when men come together in larger units. Every time two families become connected by a marriage, each of them thinks itself superior to or of better birth than the other. Of two neighbouring towns each is the other's most jealous rival; every little canton looks down upon the others with contempt. Closely related races keep one another at arm's length; the South German cannot endure the North German, the Englishman casts every kind of aspersion upon the Scot, the Spaniard despises the Portuguese.[4] We are no longer astonished that greater differences should lead to an almost insuperable repugnance, such as the Gallic people feel for the German, the Aryan for the Semite, and the white races for the coloured.

[1] 'A company of porcupines crowded themselves very close together one cold winter's day so as to profit by one another's warmth and so save themselves from being frozen to death. But soon they felt one another's quills, which induced them to separate again. And now, when the need for warmth brought them nearer together again, the second evil arose once more. So that they were driven backwards and forwards from one trouble to the other, until they had discovered a mean distance at which they could most tolerably exist.' (*Parerga und Paralipomena*, Part II, 31, 'Gleichnisse und Parabeln'.)

[2] Perhaps with the solitary exception of the relation of a mother to her son, which is based on narcissism, is not disturbed by subsequent rivalry, and is reinforced by a rudimentary attempt at sexual object-choice.

[3] [In the first German edition the last clause read 'which has first to be eliminated by repression'. It was emended in 1923.]

[4] ['The narcissism of minor differences', Chapter V of Freud, 1930a.]

When this hostility is directed against people who are otherwise loved we describe it as ambivalence of feeling; and we explain the fact, in what is probably far too rational a manner, by means of the numerous occasions for conflicts of interest which arise precisely in such intimate relations. In the undisguised antipathies and aversions which people feel towards strangers with whom they have to do we may recognize the expression of self-love—of narcissism. This self-love works for the preservation of the individual, and behaves as though the occurrence of any divergence from his own particular lines of development involved a criticism of them and a demand for their alteration. We do not know why such sensitiveness should have been directed to just these details of differentiation; but it is unmistakable that in this whole connection men give evidence of a readiness for hatred, an aggressiveness, the source of which is unknown, and to which one is tempted to ascribe an elementary character.[1]

But when a group is formed the whole of this intolerance vanishes, temporarily or permanently, within the group. So long as a group formation persists or so far as it extends, individuals in the group behave as though they were uniform, tolerate the peculiarities of its other members, equate themselves with them, and have no feeling of aversion towards them. Such a limitation of narcissism can, according to our theoretical views, only be produced by one factor, a libidinal tie with other people. Love for oneself knows only one barrier—love for others, love for objects.[2] The question will at once be raised whether community of interest in itself, without any addition of libido, must not necessarily lead to the toleration of other people and to considerateness for them. This objection may be met by the reply that nevertheless no lasting limitation of narcissism is effected in this way, since this tolerance does not persist longer than the immediate advantage gained from the other people's collaboration. But the practical importance of this discussion is less than might be supposed, for experience has

---

[1] In a recently published study, *Beyond the Pleasure Principle* [1920g, this volume, p. 53 ff.], I have attempted to connect the polarity of love and hatred with a hypothetical opposition between instincts of life and death, and to establish the sexual instincts as the purest examples of the former, the instincts of life.

[2] See my paper on narcissism (1914c).

shown that in cases of collaboration libidinal ties are regularly formed between the fellow-workers which prolong and solidify the relation between them to a point beyond what is merely profitable. The same thing occurs in men's social relations as has become familiar to psycho-analytic research in the course of the development of the individual libido. The libido attaches itself to the satisfaction of the great vital needs, and chooses as its first objects the people who have a share in that process.[1] And in the development of mankind as a whole, just as in individuals, love alone acts as the civilizing factor in the sense that it brings a change from egoism to altruism. And this is true both of sexual love for women, with all the obligations which it involves of not harming the things that are dear to women, and also of desexualized, sublimated homosexual love for other men, which springs from work in common.

If therefore in groups narcissistic self-love is subject to limitations which do not operate outside them, that is cogent evidence that the essence of a group formation consists in new kinds of libidinal ties among the members of the group.

Our interest now leads us on to the pressing question as to what may be the nature of these ties which exist in groups. In the psycho-analytic study of neuroses we have hitherto been occupied almost exclusively with ties with objects made by love instincts which still pursue directly sexual aims. In groups there can evidently be no question of sexual aims of that kind. We are concerned here with love instincts which have been diverted from their original aims, though they do not operate with less energy on that account. Now, within the range of the usual sexual object-cathexis, we have already observed phenomena which represent a diversion of the instinct from its sexual aim. We have described them as degrees of being in love, and have recognized that they involve a certain encroachment upon the ego. We shall now turn our attention more closely to these phenomena of being in love, in the firm expectation of finding in them conditions which can be transferred to the ties that exist in groups. But we should also like to know whether this kind of object-cathexis, as we know it in sexual life, represents the only manner of emotional tie with other people, or whether we must take other mechanisms of the

[1] [See Section 5 of the third of Freud's *Three Essays* (1905*d*), *Standard Ed.*, 7, 222.]

sort into account. As a matter of fact we learn from psycho-analysis that there do exist other mechanisms for emotional ties, the so-called *identifications*,[1] insufficiently-known processes and hard to describe, the investigation of which will for some time keep us away from the subject of group psychology.

[1] [Freud had discussed identification, though less fully, in Chapter IV of *The Interpretation of Dreams* (1900*a*), *Standard Ed.*, 4, 149–151, and 'Mourning and Melancholia' (1917*e*). The subject is already touched on in the Fliess correspondence, e.g. in Draft N of May 31, 1897 (Freud, 1950*a*).]

IDENTIFICATION

IDENTIFICATION is known to psycho-analysis as the earliest expression of an emotional tie with another person. It plays a part in the early history of the Oedipus complex. A little boy will exhibit a special interest in his father; he would like to grow like him and be like him, and take his place everywhere. We may say simply that he takes his father as his ideal. This behaviour has nothing to do with a passive or feminine attitude towards his father (and towards males in general); it is on the contrary typically masculine. It fits in very well with the Oedipus complex, for which it helps to prepare the way.

At the same time as this identification with his father, or a little later, the boy has begun to develop a true object-cathexis towards his mother according to the attachment [anaclitic] type.[1] He then exhibits, therefore, two psychologically distinct ties: a straightforward sexual object-cathexis towards his mother and an identification with his father which takes him as his model. The two subsist side by side for a time without any mutual influence or interference. In consequence of the irresistible advance towards a unification of mental life, they come together at last; and the normal Oedipus complex originates from their confluence. The little boy notices that his father stands in his way with his mother. His identification with his father then takes on a hostile colouring and becomes identical with the wish to replace his father in regard to his mother as well. Identification, in fact, is ambivalent from the very first; it can turn into an expression of tenderness as easily as into a wish for someone's removal. It behaves like a derivative of the first, *oral* phase of the organization of the libido, in which the object that we long for and prize is assimilated by eating and is in that way annihilated as such. The cannibal, as we know, has remained at this standpoint; he has a devouring affection for his enemies and only devours people of whom he is fond.[2]

[1] [See Section II of Freud's paper on narcissism (1914c).]

[2] See my *Three Essays* (1905d) [*Standard Ed.*, **7**, 198] and Abraham (1916).

The subsequent history of this identification with the father may easily be lost sight of. It may happen that the Oedipus complex becomes inverted, and that the father is taken as the object of a feminine attitude, an object from which the directly sexual instincts look for satisfaction; in that event the identification with the father has become the precursor of an object-tie with the father. The same holds good, with the necessary substitutions, of the baby daughter as well.[1]

It is easy to state in a formula the distinction between an identification with the father and the choice of the father as an object. In the first case one's father is what one would like to *be*, and in the second he is what one would like to *have*. The distinction, that is, depends upon whether the tie attaches to the subject or to the object of the ego. The former kind of tie is therefore already possible before any sexual object-choice has been made. It is much more difficult to give a clear metapsychological representation of the distinction. We can only see that identification endeavours to mould a person's own ego after the fashion of the one that has been taken as a model.

Let us disentangle identification as it occurs in the structure of a neurotic symptom from its rather complicated connections. Supposing that a little girl (and we will keep to her for the present) develops the same painful symptom as her mother—for instance, the same tormenting cough. This may come about in various ways. The identification may come from the Oedipus complex; in that case it signifies a hostile desire on the girl's part to take her mother's place, and the symptom expresses her object-love towards her father, and brings about a realization, under the influence of a sense of guilt, of her desire to take her mother's place: 'You wanted to be your mother, and now you *are*—anyhow so far as your sufferings are concerned.' This is the complete mechanism of the structure of a hysterical symptom. Or, on the other hand, the symptom may be the same as that of the person who is loved; so, for instance, Dora [2] imitated her father's cough. In that case we can only describe the state of things by saying *that identification has appeared instead of object-*

---

[1] [The 'complete' Oedipus complex, comprising both its 'positive' and its 'negative' forms, is discussed by Freud in Chapter III of *The Ego and the Id* (1923*b*).]

[2] In my 'Fragment of an Analysis of a Case of Hysteria' (1905*e*) [*Standard Ed.*, 7, 82–3].

choice, and that object-choice has regressed to identification. We have heard that identification is the earliest and original form of emotional tie; it often happens that under the conditions in which symptoms are constructed, that is, where there is repression and where the mechanisms of the unconscious are dominant, object-choice is turned back into identification—the ego assumes the characteristics of the object. It is noticeable that in these identifications the ego sometimes copies the person who is not loved and sometimes the one who is loved. It must also strike us that in both cases the identification is a partial and extremely limited one and only borrows a single trait from the person who is its object.

There is a third particularly frequent and important case of symptom formation, in which the identification leaves entirely out of account any object-relation to the person who is being copied. Supposing, for instance, that one of the girls in a boarding school has had a letter from someone with whom she is secretly in love which arouses her jealousy, and that she reacts to it with a fit of hysterics; then some of her friends who know about it will catch the fit, as we say, by mental infection. The mechanism is that of identification based upon the possibility or desire of putting oneself in the same situation. The other girls would like to have a secret love affair too, and under the influence of a sense of guilt they also accept the suffering involved in it. It would be wrong to suppose that they take on the symptom out of sympathy. On the contrary, the sympathy only arises out of the identification, and this is proved by the fact that infection or imitation of this kind takes place in circumstances where even less pre-existing sympathy is to be assumed than usually exists between friends in a girls' school. One ego has perceived a significant analogy with another upon one point —in our example upon openness to a similar emotion; an identification is thereupon constructed on this point, and, under the influence of the pathogenic situation, is displaced on to the symptom which the one ego has produced. The identification by means of the symptom has thus become the mark of a point of coincidence between the two egos which has to be kept repressed.

What we have learned from these three sources may be summarized as follows. First, identification is the original form of emotional tie with an object; secondly, in a regressive way it becomes a substitute for a libidinal object-tie, as it were by means of introjection of the object into the ego; and thirdly, it may arise with any new perception of a common quality shared with some other person who is not an object of the sexual instinct. The more important this common quality is, the more successful may this partial identification become, and it may thus represent the beginning of a new tie.

We already begin to divine that the mutual tie between members of a group is in the nature of an identification of this kind, based upon an important emotional common quality; and we may suspect that this common quality lies in the nature of the tie with the leader. Another suspicion may tell us that we are far from having exhausted the problem of identification, and that we are faced by the process which psychology calls 'empathy [*Einfühlung*]' and which plays the largest part in our understanding of what is inherently foreign to our ego in other people. But we shall here limit ourselves to the immediate emotional effects of identification, and shall leave on one side its significance for our intellectual life.

Psycho-analytic research, which has already occasionally attacked the more difficult problems of the psychoses, has also been able to exhibit identification to us in some other cases which are not immediately comprehensible. I shall treat two of these cases in detail as material for our further consideration.

The genesis of male homosexuality in a large class of cases is as follows.[1] A young man has been unusually long and intensely fixated upon his mother in the sense of the Oedipus complex. But at last, after the end of puberty, the time comes for exchanging his mother for some other sexual object. Things take a sudden turn: the young man does not abandon his mother, but identifies himself with her; he transforms himself into her, and now looks about for objects which can replace his ego for him, and on which he can bestow such love and care as he has experienced from his mother. This is a frequent process, which can be confirmed as often as one likes, and which is naturally quite independent of any hypothesis that may be made as to the organic driving force and the motives of the sudden transformation. A striking thing about this identification is its ample scale; it remoulds the ego in one of its important

---

[1] [See Chapter III of Freud's study on Leonardo (1910c). For other mechanisms of the genesis of homosexuality see pp. 158 f. and 231 f.]

features—in its sexual character—upon the model of what has hitherto been the object. In this process the object itself is renounced—whether entirely or in the sense of being preserved only in the unconscious is a question outside the present discussion. Identification with an object that is renounced or lost, as a substitute for that object—introjection of it into the ego—is indeed no longer a novelty to us. A process of the kind may sometimes be directly observed in small children. A short time ago an observation of this sort was published in the *Internationale Zeitschrift für Psychoanalyse*. A child who was unhappy over the loss of a kitten declared straight out that now he himself was the kitten, and accordingly crawled about on all fours, would not eat at table, etc.[1]

Another such instance of introjection of the object has been provided by the analysis of melancholia,[2] an affection which counts among the most notable of its exciting causes the real or emotional loss of a loved object. A leading characteristic of these cases is a cruel self-depreciation of the ego combined with relentless self-criticism and bitter self-reproaches. Analyses have shown that this disparagement and these reproaches apply at bottom to the object and represent the ego's revenge upon it. The shadow of the object has fallen upon the ego, as I have said elsewhere.[3] The introjection of the object is here unmistakably clear.

But these melancholias also show us something else, which may be of importance for our later discussions. They show us the ego divided, fallen apart into two pieces, one of which rages against the second. This second piece is the one which has been altered by introjection and which contains the lost object. But the piece which behaves so cruelly is not unknown to us either. It comprises the conscience, a critical agency within the ego, which even in normal times takes up a critical attitude towards the ego, though never so relentlessly and so unjustifiably. On previous occasions [4] we have been driven to the hypothesis that some such agency develops in our ego which may cut itself off

---

[1] Marcuszewicz (1920).

[2] [Freud habitually uses the term 'melancholia' for conditions which would now be described as 'depression'.]

[3] See 'Mourning and Melancholia' (1917e).

[4] In my paper on narcissism (1914c) and in 'Mourning and Melancholia' (1917e).

from the rest of the ego and come into conflict with it. We have called it the 'ego ideal', and by way of functions we have ascribed to it self-observation, the moral conscience, the censorship of dreams, and the chief influence in repression. We have said that it is the heir to the original narcissism in which the childish ego enjoyed self-sufficiency; it gradually gathers up from the influences of the environment the demands which that environment makes upon the ego and which the ego cannot always rise to; so that a man, when he cannot be satisfied with his ego itself, may nevertheless be able to find satisfaction in the ego ideal which has been differentiated out of the ego. In delusions of observation, as we have further shown, the disintegration of this agency has become patent, and has thus revealed its origin in the influence of superior powers, and above all of parents.[1] But we have not forgotten to add that the amount of distance between this ego ideal and the real ego is very variable from one individual to another, and that with many people this differentiation within the ego does not go further than with children.

But before we can employ this material for understanding the libidinal organization of groups, we must take into account some other examples of the mutual relations between the object and the ego.[2]

[1] Section III of my paper on narcissism.

[2] We are very well aware that we have not exhausted the nature of identification with these examples taken from pathology, and that we have consequently left part of the riddle of group formations untouched. A far more fundamental and comprehensive psychological analysis would have to intervene at this point. A path leads from identification by way of imitation to empathy, that is, to the comprehension of the mechanism by means of which we are enabled to take up any attitude at all towards another mental life. Moreover there is still much to be explained in the manifestations of existing identifications. These result among other things in a person limiting his aggressiveness towards those with whom he has identified himself, and in his sparing them and giving them help. The study of such identifications, like those, for instance, which lie at the root of clan feeling, led Robertson Smith (*Kinship and Marriage*, 1885) to the surprising discovery that they rest upon the acknowledgment of the possession of a common substance [by the members of the clan], and may even therefore be created by a meal eaten in common. This feature makes it possible to connect this kind of identification with the early history of the human family which I constructed in *Totem and Taboo*.

BEING IN LOVE AND HYPNOSIS

EVEN in its caprices the usage of language remains true to some kind of reality. Thus it gives the name of 'love' to a great many kinds of emotional relationship which we too group together theoretically as love; but then again it feels a doubt whether this love is real, true, actual love, and so hints at a whole scale of possibilities within the range of the phenomena of love. We shall have no difficulty in making the same discovery from our own observations.

In one class of cases being in love is nothing more than object-cathexis on the part of the sexual instincts with a view to directly sexual satisfaction, a cathexis which expires, moreover, when this aim has been reached; this is what is called common, sensual love. But, as we know, the libidinal situation rarely remains so simple. It was possible to calculate with certainty upon the revival of the need which had just expired; and this must no doubt have been the first motive for directing a lasting cathexis upon the sexual object and for 'loving' it in the passionless intervals as well.

To this must be added another factor derived from the very remarkable course of development which is pursued by the erotic life of man. In its first phase, which has usually come to an end by the time a child is five years old, he has found the first object for his love in one or other of his parents, and all of his sexual instincts with their demand for satisfaction have been united upon this object. The repression which then sets in compels him to renounce the greater number of these infantile sexual aims, and leaves behind a profound modification in his relation to his parents. The child still remains tied to his parents, but by instincts which must be described as being 'inhibited in their aim'. The emotions which he feels henceforward towards these objects of his love are characterized as 'affectionate'. It is well known that the earlier 'sensual' tendencies remain more or less strongly preserved in the unconscious, so that in a certain sense the whole of the original current continues to exist.[1]

[1] See my *Three Essays* (1905d) [*Standard Ed.*, 7, 200].

At puberty, as we know, there set in new and very strong impulsions towards directly sexual aims. In unfavourable cases they remain separate, in the form of a sensual current, from the 'affectionate' trends of feeling which persist. We then have before us a picture whose two aspects are typified with such delight by certain schools of literature. A man will show a sentimental enthusiasm for women whom he deeply respects but who do not excite him to sexual activities, and he will only be potent with other women whom he does not 'love' and thinks little of or even despises.[1] More often, however, the adolescent succeeds in bringing about a certain degree of synthesis between the unsensual, heavenly love and the sensual, earthly love, and his relation to his sexual object is characterized by the interaction of uninhibited instincts and of instincts inhibited in their aim. The depth to which anyone is in love, as contrasted with his purely sensual desire, may be measured by the size of the share taken by the aim-inhibited instincts of affection.

In connection with this question of being in love we have always been struck by the phenomenon of sexual overvaluation —the fact that the loved object enjoys a certain amount of freedom from criticism, and that all its characteristics are valued more highly than those of people who are not loved, or than its own were at a time when it itself was not loved. If the sensual impulsions are more or less effectively repressed or set aside, the illusion is produced that the object has come to be sensually loved on account of its spiritual merits, whereas on the contrary these merits may really only have been lent to it by its sensual charm.

The tendency which falsifies judgement in this respect is that of *idealization*. But now it is easier for us to find our bearings. We see that the object is being treated in the same way as our own ego, so that when we are in love a considerable amount of narcissistic libido overflows on to the object.[2] It is even obvious, in many forms of love-choice, that the object serves as a substitute for some unattained ego ideal of our own. We love it on account of the perfections which we have striven to reach for

[1] 'On the Universal Tendency to Debasement in the Sphere of Love' (1912d).

[2] [Cf. a passage towards the beginning of Part III of Freud's paper on narcissism (1914c).]

our own ego, and which we should now like to procure in this roundabout way as a means of satisfying our narcissism.

If the sexual overvaluation and the being in love increase even further, then the interpretation of the picture becomes still more unmistakable. The impulsions whose trend is towards directly sexual satisfaction may now be pushed into the background entirely, as regularly happens, for instance, with a young man's sentimental passion; the ego becomes more and more unassuming and modest, and the object more and more sublime and precious, until at last it gets possession of the entire self-love of the ego, whose self-sacrifice thus follows as a natural consequence. The object has, so to speak, consumed the ego. Traits of humility, of the limitation of narcissism, and of self-injury occur in every case of being in love; in the extreme case they are merely intensified, and as a result of the withdrawal of the sensual claims they remain in solitary supremacy.

This happens especially easily with love that is unhappy and cannot be satisfied; for in spite of everything each sexual satisfaction always involves a reduction in sexual overvaluation. Contemporaneously with this 'devotion' of the ego to the object, which is no longer to be distinguished from a sublimated devotion to an abstract idea, the functions allotted to the ego ideal entirely cease to operate. The criticism exercised by that agency is silent; everything that the object does and asks for is right and blameless. Conscience has no application to anything that is done for the sake of the object; in the blindness of love remorselessness is carried to the pitch of crime. The whole situation can be completely summarized in a formula: *The object has been put in the place of the ego ideal.*

It is now easy to define the difference between identification and such extreme developments of being in love as may be described as 'fascination' or 'bondage'.[1] In the former case the ego has enriched itself with the properties of the object, it has 'introjected' the object into itself, as Ferenczi [1909] expresses it. In the second case it is impoverished, it has surrendered itself to the object, it has substituted the object for its own most important constituent. Closer consideration soon makes it plain, however, that this kind of account creates an illusion of contradistinctions that have no real existence. Economically there is

[1] [The 'bondage' of love had been discussed by Freud in the early part of his paper on 'The Taboo of Virginity' (1918a).]

no question of impoverishment or enrichment; it is even possible to describe an extreme case of being in love as a state in
which the ego has introjected the object into itself. Another
distinction is perhaps better calculated to meet the essence of the
matter. In the case of identification the object has been lost or
given up; it is then set up again inside the ego, and the ego
makes a partial alteration in itself after the model of the lost
object. In the other case the object is retained, and there is a
hypercathexis of it by the ego and at the ego's expense. But here
again a difficulty presents itself. Is it quite certain that identification presupposes that object-cathexis has been given up?
Can there be no identification while the object is retained? And
before we embark upon a discussion of this delicate question,
the perception may already be beginning to dawn on us that
yet another alternative embraces the real essence of the matter,
namely, *whether the object is put in the place of the ego or of the ego
ideal*.

From being in love to hypnosis is evidently only a short step.
The respects in which the two agree are obvious. There is the
same humble subjection, the same compliance, the same absence
of criticism, towards the hypnotist as towards the loved object.[1]
There is the same sapping of the subject's own initiative; no
one can doubt that the hypnotist has stepped into the place of
the ego ideal. It is only that everything is even clearer and more
intense in hypnosis, so that it would be more to the point to
explain being in love by means of hypnosis than the other way
round. The hypnotist is the sole object, and no attention is paid
to any but him. The fact that the ego experiences in a dream-
like way whatever he may request or assert reminds us that we
omitted to mention among the functions of the ego ideal the
business of testing the reality of things.[2] No wonder that the ego
takes a perception for real if its reality is vouched for by the
mental agency which ordinarily discharges the duty of testing
the reality of things. The complete absence of impulsions which

[1] [This point had already been made in a footnote to the first of
Freud's *Three Essays* (1905d), *Standard Ed.*, 7, 150, and in his paper on
'Psychical Treatment' (1905b), ibid., 296.]

[2] Cf. Freud (1917d).—[*Added* 1923:] There seems, however, to be
some doubt whether the attribution of this function to the ego ideal is
justified. The point requires thorough discussion. [See the footnote at
the beginning of Chapter III of *The Ego and The Id* (1923b), where the
function is definitely attributed to the *ego*.]

are uninhibited in their sexual aims contributes further towards the extreme purity of the phenomena. The hypnotic relation is the unlimited devotion of someone in love, but with sexual satisfaction excluded; whereas in the actual case of being in love this kind of satisfaction is only temporarily kept back, and remains in the background as a possible aim at some later time.

But on the other hand we may also say that the hypnotic relation is (if the expression is permissible) a group formation with two members. Hypnosis is not a good object for comparison with a group formation, because it is truer to say that it is identical with it. Out of the complicated fabric of the group it isolates one element for us—the behaviour of the individual to the leader. Hypnosis is distinguished from a group formation by this limitation of number, just as it is distinguished from being in love by the absence of directly sexual trends. In this respect it occupies a middle position between the two.

It is interesting to see that it is precisely those sexual impulsions that are inhibited in their aims which achieve such lasting ties between people. But this can easily be understood from the fact that they are not capable of complete satisfaction, while sexual impulsions which are uninhibited in their aims suffer an extraordinary reduction through the discharge of energy every time the sexual aim is attained. It is the fate of sensual love to become extinguished when it is satisfied; for it to be able to last, it must from the beginning be mixed with purely affectionate components—with such, that is, as are inhibited in their aims— or it must itself undergo a transformation of this kind.

Hypnosis would solve the riddle of the libidinal constitution of groups for us straight away, if it were not that it itself exhibits some features which are not met by the rational explanation we have hitherto given of it as a state of being in love with the directly sexual trends excluded. There is still a great deal in it which we must recognize as unexplained and mysterious. It contains an additional element of paralysis derived from the relation between someone with superior power and someone who is without power and helpless—which may afford a transition to the hypnosis of fright which occurs in animals. The manner in which it is produced and its relationship to sleep are not clear; and the puzzling way in which some people are subject to it, while others resist it completely, points to some factor still unknown which is realized in it and which perhaps alone makes possible the purity of the attitudes of the libido which it exhibits. It is noticeable that, even when there is complete suggestive compliance in other respects, the moral conscience of the person hypnotized may show resistance. But this may be due to the fact that in hypnosis as it is usually practised some knowledge may be retained that what is happening is only a game, an untrue reproduction of another situation of far more importance to life.

But after the preceding discussions we are quite in a position to give the formula for the libidinal constitution of groups, or at least of such groups as we have hitherto considered—namely, those that have a leader and have not been able by means of too much 'organization' to acquire secondarily the characteristics of an individual. *A primary group of this kind is a number of individuals who have put one and the same object in the place of their ego ideal and have consequently identified themselves with one another in their ego.* This condition admits of graphic representation:

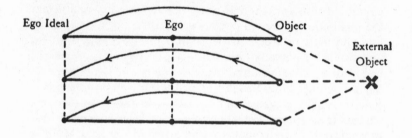

THE HERD INSTINCT

WE cannot for long enjoy the illusion that we have solved the riddle of the group with this formula. It is impossible to escape the immediate and disturbing recollection that all we have really done has been to shift the question on to the riddle of hypnosis, about which so many points have yet to be cleared up. And now another objection shows us our further path.

It might be said that the intense emotional ties which we observe in groups are quite sufficient to explain one of their characteristics—the lack of independence and initiative in their members, the similarity in the reactions of all of them, their reduction, so to speak, to the level of group individuals. But if we look at it as a whole, a group shows us more than this. Some of its features—the weakness of intellectual ability, the lack of emotional restraint, the incapacity for moderation and delay, the inclination to exceed every limit in the expression of emotion and to work it off completely in the form of action—these and similar features, which we find so impressively described in Le Bon, show an unmistakable picture of a regression of mental activity to an earlier stage such as we are not surprised to find among savages or children. A regression of this sort is in particular an essential characteristic of common groups, while, as we have heard, in organized and artificial groups it can to a large extent be checked.

We thus have an impression of a state in which an individual's private emotional impulses and intellectual acts are too weak to come to anything by themselves and are entirely dependent for this on being reinforced by being repeated in a similar way in the other members of the group. We are reminded of how many of these phenomena of dependence are part of the normal constitution of human society, of how little originality and personal courage are to be found in it, of how much every individual is ruled by those attitudes of the group mind which exhibit themselves in such forms as racial characteristics, class prejudices, public opinion, etc. The influence of suggestion becomes a greater riddle for us when we admit that it is not exercised only by the leader, but by every individual upon every other individual; and we must reproach ourselves with having unfairly emphasized the relation to the leader and with having kept the other factor of mutual suggestion too much in the background.

After this encouragement to modesty, we shall be inclined to listen to another voice, which promises us an explanation based upon simpler grounds. Such a one is to be found in Trotter's thoughtful book on the herd instinct (1916), concerning which my only regret is that it does not entirely escape the antipathies that were set loose by the recent great war.

Trotter derives the mental phenomena that are described as occurring in groups from a herd instinct ('gregariousness' [1]), which is innate in human beings just as in other species of animals. Biologically, he says, this gregariousness is an analogy to multicellularity and as it were a continuation of it. (In terms of the libido theory it is a further manifestation of the tendency which proceeds from the libido and which is felt by all living beings of the same kind, to combine in more and more comprehensive units.[2]) The individual feels incomplete if he is alone. The fear shown by small children would seem already to be an expression of this herd instinct. Opposition to the herd is as good as separation from it, and is therefore anxiously avoided. But the herd turns away from anything that is new or unusual. The herd instinct would appear to be something primary, something which cannot be split up.[3]

Trotter gives as the list of instincts which he considers as primary those of self-preservation, of nutrition, of sex, and of the herd. The last often comes into opposition with the others. The feelings of guilt and of duty are the peculiar possessions of a gregarious animal. Trotter also derives from the herd instinct the repressive forces which psycho-analysis has shown to exist in the ego, and from the same source accordingly the resistances which the physician comes up against in psycho-analytic treatment. Speech owes its importance to its aptitude for mutual understanding in the herd, and upon it the identification of the individuals with one another largely rests.

While Le Bon is principally concerned with typical transient

[1] [This word is in English in the original.]
[2] See *Beyond the Pleasure Principle* [this volume, p. 50].
[3] [The last five words are in English in the original.]

group formations, and McDougall with stable associations, Trotter has chosen as the centre of his interest the most generalized form of assemblage in which man, that ζῷον πολιτικόν,[1] passes his life, and he gives us its psychological basis. But Trotter is under no necessity of tracing back the herd instinct, for he characterizes it as primary and not further reducible. Boris Sidis's attempt, to which he refers, at tracing the herd instinct back to suggestibility is fortunately superfluous as far as he is concerned; it is an explanation of a familiar and unsatisfactory type, and the converse proposition—that suggestibility is a derivative of the herd instinct—would seem to me to throw far more light on the subject.

But Trotter's exposition is open, with even more justice than the others, to the objection that it takes too little account of the leader's part in a group, while we incline rather to the opposite judgement, that it is impossible to grasp the nature of a group if the leader is disregarded. The herd instinct leaves no room at all for the leader; he is merely thrown in along with the herd, almost by chance; it follows, too, that no path leads from this instinct to the need for a God; the herd is without a herdsman. But besides this, Trotter's exposition can be undermined psychologically; that is to say, it can be made at all events probable that the herd instinct is not irreducible, that it is not primary in the same sense as the instinct of self-preservation and the sexual instinct.

It is naturally no easy matter to trace the ontogenesis of the herd instinct. The fear which is shown by small children when they are left alone, and which Trotter claims as being already a manifestation of the instinct, nevertheless suggests more readily another interpretation. The fear relates to the child's mother, and later to other familiar people, and it is the expression of an unfulfilled desire, which the child does not yet know how to deal with in any way except by turning it into anxiety.[2] Nor is the child's fear when it is alone pacified by the sight of any haphazard 'member of the herd', but on the contrary it is brought into existence by the approach of a 'stranger' of this sort. Then for a long time nothing in the nature of herd instinct or group feeling is to be observed in children. Something like it

[1] ['Political animal' (Aristotle, *Politics*, 1252b).]
[2] See the remarks upon anxiety in my *Introductory Lectures* (1916–17), Lecture XXV.

first grows up, in a nursery containing many children, out of the children's relation to their parents, and it does so as a re-action to the initial envy with which the elder child receives the younger one. The elder child would certainly like to put his successor jealously aside, to keep it away from the parents, and to rob it of all its privileges; but in the face of the fact that this younger child (like all that come later) is loved by the parents as much as he himself is, and in consequence of the impossibility of his maintaining his hostile attitude without damaging him-self, he is forced into identifying himself with the other children. So there grows up in the troop of children a communal or group feeling, which is then further developed at school. The first demand made by this reaction-formation is for justice, for equal treatment for all. We all know how loudly and implacably this claim is put forward at school. If one cannot be the favourite oneself, at all events nobody else shall be the favourite. This transformation—the replacing of jealousy by a group feeling in the nursery and classroom—might be considered improbable, if the same process could not later on be observed again in other circumstances. We have only to think of the troop of women and girls, all of them in love in an enthusiastically senti-mental way, who crowd round a singer or pianist after his per-formance. It would certainly be easy for each of them to be jealous of the rest; but, in the face of their numbers and the consequent impossibility of their reaching the aim of their love, they renounce it, and, instead of pulling out one another's hair, they act as a united group, do homage to the hero of the occa-sion with their common actions, and would probably be glad to have a share of *his* flowing locks. Originally rivals, they have succeeded in identifying themselves with one another by means of a similar love for the same object. When, as is usual, an in-stinctual situation is capable of various outcomes, we shall not be surprised that the actual outcome is one which brings with it the possibility of a certain amount of satisfaction, whereas some other outcome, in itself more obvious, is passed over because the circumstances of life prevent its leading to any such satisfaction.

What appears later on in society in the shape of *Gemeingeist*, *esprit de corps*, 'group spirit', etc., does not belie its derivation from what was originally envy. No one must want to put him-self forward, every one must be the same and have the same.

Social justice means that we deny ourselves many things so that others may have to do without them as well, or, what is the same thing, may not be able to ask for them. This demand for equality is the root of social conscience and the sense of duty. It reveals itself unexpectedly in the syphilitic's dread of infecting other people, which psycho-analysis has taught us to understand. The dread exhibited by these poor wretches corresponds to their violent struggles against the unconscious wish to spread their infection on to other people; for why should they alone be infected and cut off from so much? why not other people as well? And the same germ is to be found in the apt story of the judgement of Solomon. If one woman's child is dead, the other shall not have a live one either. The bereaved woman is recognized by this wish.

Thus social feeling is based upon the reversal of what was first a hostile feeling into a positively-toned tie in the nature of an identification. So far as we have hitherto been able to follow the course of events, this reversal seems to occur under the influence of a common affectionate tie with a person outside the group. We do not ourselves regard our analysis of identification as exhaustive, but it is enough for our present purpose that we should revert to this one feature—its demand that equalization shall be consistently carried through. We have already heard in the discussion of the two artificial groups, Church and army, that their necessary precondition is that all their members should be loved in the same way by one person, the leader. Do not let us forget, however, that the demand for equality in a group applies only to its members and not to the leader. All the members must be equal to one another, but they all want to be ruled by one person. Many equals, who can identify themselves with one another, and a single person superior to them all—that is the situation that we find realized in groups which are capable of subsisting. Let us venture, then, to correct Trotter's pronouncement that man is a herd animal and assert that he is rather a horde animal, an individual creature in a horde led by a chief.

X

THE GROUP AND THE PRIMAL HORDE

In 1912 I took up a conjecture of Darwin's to the effect that the primitive form of human society was that of a horde ruled over despotically by a powerful male. I attempted to show that the fortunes of this horde have left indestructible traces upon the history of human descent; and, especially, that the development of totemism, which comprises in itself the beginnings of religion, morality, and social organization, is connected with the killing of the chief by violence and the transformation of the paternal horde into a community of brothers.[1] To be sure, this is only a hypothesis, like so many others with which archaeologists endeavour to lighten the darkness of prehistoric times—a 'Just-So Story', as it was amusingly called by a not unkind English critic;[2] but I think it is creditable to such a hypothesis if it proves able to bring coherence and understanding into more and more new regions.

Human groups exhibit once again the familiar picture of an individual of superior strength among a troop of equal companions, a picture which is also contained in our idea of the primal horde. The psychology of such a group, as we know it from the descriptions to which we have so often referred—the dwindling of the conscious individual personality, the focusing of thoughts and feelings into a common direction, the predominance of the affective side of the mind and of unconscious psychical life, the tendency to the immediate carrying out of intentions as they emerge—all this corresponds to a state of regression to a primitive mental activity, of just such a sort as we should be inclined to ascribe to the primal horde.[3]

[1] *Totem and Taboo* (1912–13) [Essay IV. Freud uses the term 'horde' to signify a relatively small collection of people.]

[2] [In the 1st edition only, the name 'Kroeger' appeared here. This was evidently a misprint for 'Kroeber'—incidentally the name of the well-known *American* anthropologist. But see the addendum on p. 128.]

[3] What we have just described in our general characterization of mankind must apply especially to the primal horde. The will of the individual was too weak; he did not venture upon action. No impulses whatever came into existence except collective ones; there was only a

Thus the group appears to us as a revival of the primal horde. Just as primitive man survives potentially in every individual, so the primal horde may arise once more out of any random collection; in so far as men are habitually under the sway of group formation we recognize in it the survival of the primal horde. We must conclude that the psychology of groups is the oldest human psychology; what we have isolated as individual psychology, by neglecting all traces of the group, has only since come into prominence out of the old group psychology, by a gradual process which may still, perhaps, be described as incomplete. We shall later venture upon an attempt at specifying the point of departure of this development. [See p. 135 ff.]

Further reflection will show us in what respect this statement requires correction. Individual psychology must, on the contrary, be just as old as group psychology, for from the first there were two kinds of psychologies, that of the individual members of the group and that of the father, chief, or leader. The members of the group were subject to ties just as we see them to-day, but the father of the primal horde was free. His intellectual acts were strong and independent even in isolation, and his will needed no reinforcement from others. Consistency leads us to assume that his ego had few libidinal ties; he loved no one but himself, or other people only in so far as they served his needs. To objects his ego gave away no more than was barely necessary.

He, at the very beginning of the history of mankind, was the 'superman' whom Nietzsche only expected from the future. Even to-day the members of a group stand in need of the illusion that they are equally and justly loved by their leader; but the leader himself need love no one else, he may be of a

common will, there were no single ones. An idea did not dare to turn itself into an act of will unless it felt itself reinforced by a perception of its general diffusion. This weakness of the idea is to be explained by the strength of the emotional tie which is shared by all the members of the horde; but the similarity in the circumstances of their life and the absence of any private property assist in determining the uniformity of their individual mental acts. As we may observe with children and soldiers, common activity is not excluded even in the excretory functions. The one great exception is provided by the sexual act, in which a third person is at best superfluous and in the extreme case is condemned to a state of painful expectancy. As to the reaction of the sexual need (for genital satisfaction) towards gregariousness, see below [p 140].

masterful nature, absolutely narcissistic, self-confident and independent. We know that love puts a check upon narcissism, and it would be possible to show how, by operating in this way, it became a factor of civilization.

The primal father of the horde was not yet immortal, as he later became by deification. If he died, he had to be replaced; his place was probably taken by a youngest son, who had up to then been a member of the group like any other. There must therefore be a possibility of transforming group psychology into individual psychology; a condition must be discovered under which such a transformation is easily accomplished, just as it is possible for bees in case of necessity to turn a larva into a queen instead of into a worker. One can imagine only one possibility: the primal father had prevented his sons from satisfying their directly sexual impulsions; he forced them into abstinence and consequently into the emotional ties with him and with one another which could arise out of those of their impulsions that were inhibited in their sexual aim. He forced them, so to speak, into group psychology. His sexual jealousy and intolerance became in the last resort the causes of group psychology.[1]

Whoever became his successor was also given the possibility of sexual satisfaction, and was by that means offered a way out of the conditions of group psychology. The fixation of the libido to woman and the possibility of satisfaction without any need for delay or accumulation made an end of the importance of those of his sexual impulsions that were inhibited in their aim, and allowed his narcissism always to rise to its full height. We shall return in a postscript [p. 137 ff.] to this connection between love and character formation.

We may further emphasize, as being specially instructive, the relation that holds between the contrivance by means of which an artificial group is held together and the constitution of the primal horde. We have seen that with an army and a Church this contrivance is the illusion that the leader loves all of the individuals equally and justly. But this is simply an idealistic remodelling of the state of affairs in the primal horde,

---

[1] It may perhaps also be assumed that the sons, when they were driven out and separated from their father, advanced from identification with one another to homosexual object-love, and in this way won freedom to kill their father. [See *Totem and Taboo, Standard Ed.*, 13, 144.]

where all of the sons knew that they were equally *persecuted* by the primal father, and *feared* him equally. This same recasting upon which all social duties are built up is already presupposed by the next form of human society, the totemic clan. The indestructible strength of the family as a natural group formation rests upon the fact that this necessary presupposition of the father's equal love can have a real application in the family.

But we expect even more of this derivation of the group from the primal horde. It ought also to help us to understand what is still incomprehensible and mysterious in group formations—all that lies hidden behind the enigmatic words 'hypnosis' and 'suggestion'. And I think it can succeed in this too. Let us recall that hypnosis has something positively uncanny about it; but the characteristic of uncanniness suggests something old and familiar that has undergone repression.[1] Let us consider how hypnosis is induced. The hypnotist asserts that he is in possession of a mysterious power that robs the subject of his own will; or, which is the same thing, the subject believes it of him. This mysterious power (which is even now often described popularly as 'animal magnetism') must be the same power that is looked upon by primitive people as the source of taboo, the same that emanates from kings and chieftains and makes it dangerous to approach them (*mana*). The hypnotist, then, is supposed to be in possession of this power; and how does he manifest it? By telling the subject to look him in the eyes; his most typical method of hypnotizing is by his look. But it is precisely the *sight* of the chieftain that is dangerous and unbearable for primitive people, just as later that of the Godhead is for mortals. Even Moses had to act as an intermediary between his people and Jehovah, since the people could not support the sight of God; and when he returned from the presence of God his face shone—some of the *mana* had been transferred on to him, just as happens with the intermediary among primitive people.[2]

It is true that hypnosis can also be evoked in other ways, for instance by fixing the eyes upon a bright object or by listening to a monotonous sound. This is misleading and has given occasion to inadequate physiological theories. In point of fact

[1] Cf. 'The "Uncanny" ' (1919*h*).

[2] See *Totem and Taboo* [second essay] and the sources there quoted.

these procedures merely serve to divert conscious attention and to hold it riveted. The situation is the same as if the hypnotist had said to the subject: 'Now concern yourself exclusively with my person; the rest of the world is quite uninteresting.' It would of course be technically inexpedient for a hypnotist to make such a speech; it would tear the subject away from his unconscious attitude and stimulate him to conscious opposition. The hypnotist avoids directing the subject's conscious thoughts towards his own intentions, and makes the person upon whom he is experimenting sink into an activity in which the world is bound to seem uninteresting to him; but at the same time the subject is in reality unconsciously concentrating his whole attention upon the hypnotist, and is getting into an attitude of *rapport*, of transference on to him. Thus the indirect methods of hypnotizing, like many of the technical procedures used in making jokes,[1] have the effect of checking certain distributions of mental energy which would interfere with the course of events in the unconscious, and they lead eventually to the same result as the direct methods of influence by means of staring or stroking.[2]

[1] [The distracting of attention as part of the technique of joking is discussed at some length in the latter half of Chapter V of Freud's book on jokes (1905c). The possibility of this mechanism playing a part in 'thought-transference' is mentioned below, p. 184. But perhaps Freud's earliest allusion to the idea is to be found in his final chapter in *Studies on Hysteria* (Breuer and Freud, 1895). Towards the beginning of the second section of that chapter Freud brings forward this same mechanism as a possible part explanation of the efficacy of his 'pressure' procedure.]

[2] This situation, in which the subject's attitude is unconsciously directed towards the hypnotist, while he is consciously occupied with monotonous and uninteresting perceptions, finds a parallel among the events of psycho-analytic treatment, which deserves to be mentioned here. At least once in the course of every analysis a moment comes when the patient obstinately maintains that just now positively nothing whatever occurs to his mind. His free associations come to a stop and the usual incentives for putting them in motion fail in their effect. If the analyst insists, the patient is at last induced to admit that he is thinking of the view from the consulting-room window, of the wall-paper that he sees before him, or of the gas-lamp hanging from the ceiling. Then one knows at once that he has gone off into the transference and that he is engaged upon what are still unconscious thoughts relating to the physician; and one sees the stoppage in the patient's associations disappear, as soon as he has been given this explanation.

Ferenczi [1909] has made the true discovery that when a hypnotist gives the command to sleep, which is often done at the beginning of hypnosis, he is putting himself in the place of the subject's parents. He thinks that two sorts of hypnotism are to be distinguished: one coaxing and soothing, which he considers is modelled on the mother, and another threatening, which is derived from the father. Now the command to sleep in hypnosis means nothing more nor less than an order to withdraw all interest from the world and to concentrate it on the person of the hypnotist. And it is so understood by the subject; for in this withdrawal of interest from the external world lies the psychological characteristic of sleep, and the kinship between sleep and the state of hypnosis is based on it.

By the measures that he takes, then, the hypnotist awakens in the subject a portion of his archaic heritage which had also made him compliant towards his parents and which had experienced an individual re-animation in his relation to his father; what is thus awakened is the idea of a paramount and dangerous personality, towards whom only a passive-masochistic attitude is possible, to whom one's will has to be surrendered,—while to be alone with him, 'to look him in the face', appears a hazardous enterprise. It is only in some such way as this that we can picture the relation of the individual member of the primal horde to the primal father. As we know from other reactions, individuals have preserved a variable degree of personal aptitude for reviving old situations of this kind. Some knowledge that in spite of everything hypnosis is only a game, a deceptive renewal of these old impressions, may, however, remain behind and take care that there is a resistance against any too serious consequences of the suspension of the will in hypnosis.

The uncanny and coercive characteristics of group formations, which are shown in the phenomena of suggestion that accompany them, may therefore with justice be traced back to the fact of their origin from the primal horde. The leader of the group is still the dreaded primal father; the group still wishes to be governed by unrestricted force; it has an extreme passion for authority; in Le Bon's phrase, it has a thirst for obedience. The primal father is the group ideal, which governs the ego in the place of the ego ideal. Hypnosis has a good claim to being described as a group of two. There remains as a definition for suggestion: a conviction which is not based upon perception and reasoning but upon an erotic tie.[1]

[1] It seems to me worth emphasizing the fact that the discussions in this section have induced us to give up Bernheim's conception of hypnosis and go back to the *naïf* earlier one. According to Bernheim all hypnotic phenomena are to be traced to the factor of suggestion, which is not itself capable of further explanation. We have come to the conclusion that suggestion is a partial manifestation of the state of hypnosis, and that hypnosis is solidly founded upon a predisposition which has survived in the unconscious from the early history of the human family. [Freud had already expressed his scepticism about Bernheim's views on suggestion in the preface to his translation of Bernheim's book on the subject (1888–9).]

[*Addendum to footnote* 2, p. 122 :—Kroeber's original review of *Totem and Taboo*, published in *Amer. Anthropol.*, New Series, 22 (1920), 48, contained no reference to a 'just-so story'. This was pointed out by Kroeber himself in a second review, published nearly twenty years later in *Amer. J. Sociol.* 45, (1939), 446. The comparison with a 'just-so story' was actually made in a review of *Totem and Taboo* by the English anthropologist R. R. Marett in *The Athenaeum*, Feb, 13, 1920, p. 206.]

A DIFFERENTIATING GRADE IN THE EGO

IF we survey the life of an individual man of to-day, bearing in mind the mutually complementary accounts of group psychology given by the authorities, we may lose the courage, in face of the complications that are revealed, to attempt a comprehensive exposition. Each individual is a component part of numerous groups, he is bound by ties of identification in many directions, and he has built up his ego ideal upon the most various models. Each individual therefore has a share in numerous group minds—those of his race, of his class, of his creed, of his nationality, etc.—and he can also raise himself above them to the extent of having a scrap of independence and originality. Such stable and lasting group formations, with their uniform and constant effects, are less striking to an observer than the rapidly formed and transient groups from which Le Bon has made his brilliant psychological character sketch of the group mind. And it is just in these noisy ephemeral groups, which are as it were superimposed upon the others, that we are met by the prodigy of the complete, even though only temporary, disappearance of exactly what we have recognized as individual acquirements.

We have interpreted this prodigy as meaning that the individual gives up his ego ideal and substitutes for it the group ideal as embodied in the leader. And we must add by way of correction that the prodigy is not equally great in every case. In many individuals the separation between the ego and the ego ideal is not very far advanced; the two still coincide readily; the ego has often preserved its earlier narcissistic self-complacency. The selection of the leader is very much facilitated by this circumstance. He need often only possess the typical qualities of the individuals concerned in a particularly clearly marked and pure form, and need only give an impression of greater force and of more freedom of libido; and in that case the need for a strong chief will often meet him half-way and invest him with a predominance to which he would otherwise perhaps have had no claim. The other members of the group, whose ego ideal would not, apart from this, have become embodied in his person without some correction, are then carried away with the rest by 'suggestion', that is to say, by means of identification.

We are aware that what we have been able to contribute towards the explanation of the libidinal structure of groups leads back to the distinction between the ego and the ego ideal and to the double kind of tie which this makes possible—identification, and putting the object in the place of the ego ideal. The assumption of this kind of differentiating grade in the ego as a first step in an analysis of the ego must gradually establish its justification in the most various regions of psychology. In my paper on narcissism [1914c] I have put together all the pathological material that could at the moment be used in support of this differentiation. But it may be expected that when we penetrate deeper into the psychology of the psychoses its significance will be discovered to be far greater. Let us reflect that the ego now enters into the relation of an object to the ego ideal which has been developed out of it, and that all the interplay between an external object and the ego as a whole, with which our study of the neuroses has made us acquainted, may possibly be repeated upon this new scene of action within the ego.

In this place I shall only follow up one of the consequences which seem possible from this point of view, thus resuming the discussion of a problem which I was obliged to leave unsolved elsewhere.[1] Each of the mental differentiations that we have become acquainted with represents a fresh aggravation of the difficulties of mental functioning, increases its instability, and may become the starting-point for its breakdown, that is, for the onset of a disease. Thus, by being born we have made the step from an absolutely self-sufficient narcissism to the perception of a changing external world and the beginnings of the discovery of objects. And with this is associated the fact that we cannot endure the new state of things for long, that we periodically revert from it, in our sleep, to our former condition of absence of stimulation and avoidance of objects. It is true, however, that in this we are following a hint from the external world, which, by means of the periodical change of day and night, temporarily withdraws the greater part of the stimuli that affect us. The second example of such a step, pathologically

[1] 'Mourning and Melancholia' (1917e).

more important, is subject to no such qualification. In the course of our development we have effected a separation of our mental existence into a coherent ego and into an unconscious and repressed portion which is left outside it; and we know that the stability of this new acquisition is exposed to constant shocks. In dreams and in neuroses what is thus excluded knocks for admission at the gates, guarded though they are by resistances; and in our waking health we make use of special artifices for allowing what is repressed to circumvent the resistances and for receiving it temporarily into our ego to the increase of our pleasure. Jokes and humour, and to some extent the comic in general, may be regarded in this light. Everyone acquainted with the psychology of the neuroses will think of similar examples of less importance; but I hasten on to the application I have in view.

It is quite conceivable that the separation of the ego ideal from the ego cannot be borne for long either, and has to be temporarily undone. In all renunciations and limitations imposed upon the ego a periodical infringement of the prohibition is the rule; this indeed is shown by the institution of festivals, which in origin are nothing less nor more than excesses provided by law and which owe their cheerful character to the release which they bring.[1] The Saturnalia of the Romans and our modern carnival agree in this essential feature with the festivals of primitive people, which usually end in debaucheries of every kind and the transgression of what are at other times the most sacred commandments. But the ego ideal comprises the sum of all the limitations in which the ego has to acquiesce, and for that reason the abrogation of the ideal would necessarily be a magnificent festival for the ego, which might then once again feel satisfied with itself.[2]

There is always a feeling of triumph when something in the ego coincides with the ego ideal. And the sense of guilt (as well as the sense of inferiority) can also be understood as an expression of tension between the ego and the ego ideal.

[1] *Totem and Taboo* [*Standard Ed.*, **13**, 140].

[2] Trotter traces repression back to the herd instinct. It is a translation of this into another form of expression rather than a contradiction when I say in my paper on narcissism [1914c, near the beginning of Part III] that 'for the ego the formation of an ideal would be the conditioning factor of repression'.

It is well known that there are people the general colour of whose mood oscillates periodically from an excessive depression through some kind of intermediate state to an exalted sense of well-being. These oscillations appear in very different degrees of amplitude, from what is just noticeable to those extreme instances which, in the shape of melancholia and mania, make the most tormenting or disturbing inroads upon the life of the person concerned. In typical cases of this cyclical depression external precipitating causes do not seem to play any decisive part; as regards internal motives, nothing more, or nothing else is to be found in these patients than in all others. It has consequently become the custom to consider these cases as not being psychogenic. We shall refer presently to those other exactly similar cases of cyclical depression which *can* easily be traced back to mental traumas.

Thus the foundation of these spontaneous oscillations of mood is unknown; we are without insight into the mechanism of the displacement of a melancholia by a mania. So we are free to suppose that these patients are people in whom our conjecture might find an actual application—their ego ideal might be temporarily resolved into their ego after having previously ruled it with especial strictness.

Let us keep to what is clear: On the basis of our analysis of the ego it cannot be doubted that in cases of mania the ego and the ego ideal have fused together, so that the person, in a mood of triumph and self-satisfaction, disturbed by no self-criticism, can enjoy the abolition of his inhibitions, his feelings of consideration for others, and his self-reproaches. It is not so obvious, but nevertheless very probable, that the misery of the melancholic is the expression of a sharp conflict between the two agencies of his ego, a conflict in which the ideal, in an excess of sensitiveness, relentlessly exhibits its condemnation of the ego in delusions of inferiority and in self-depreciation. The only question is whether we are to look for the causes of these altered relations between the ego and the ego ideal in the periodic rebellions, which we have postulated above, against the new institution, or whether we are to make other circumstances responsible for them.

A change into mania is not an indispensable feature of the symptomatology of melancholic depression. There are simple melancholias, some in single and some in recurrent attacks, which never show this development.

On the other hand there are melancholias in which the precipitating cause clearly plays an aetiological part. They are those which occur after the loss of a loved object, whether by death or as the result of circumstances which have necessitated the withdrawal of the libido from the object. A psychogenic melancholia of this sort can end in mania, and this cycle can be repeated several times, just as easily as in a case which appears to be spontaneous. Thus the state of things is somewhat obscure, especially as only a few forms and cases of melancholia have been submitted to psycho-analytic investigation.[1] So far we only understand those cases in which the object is given up because it has shown itself unworthy of love. It is then set up again inside the ego, by means of identification, and severely condemned by the ego ideal. The reproaches and attacks directed towards the object come to light in the shape of melancholic self-reproaches.[2]

A melancholia of this kind, too, may end in a change into mania; so that the possibility of this happening represents a feature which is independent of the other characteristics of the clinical picture.

Nevertheless I see no difficulty in assigning to the factor of the periodic rebellion of the ego against the ego ideal a share in both kinds of melancholia, the psychogenic as well as the spontaneous. In the spontaneous kind it may be supposed that the ego ideal is inclined to display a peculiar strictness, which then results automatically in its temporary suspension. In the psychogenic kind the ego would be incited to rebellion by ill-treatment on the part of its ideal—an ill-treatment which it encounters when there has been identification with a rejected object.[3]

[1] Cf. Abraham (1912).

[2] To speak more accurately, they conceal themselves behind the reproaches directed towards the subject's own ego, and lend them the fixity, tenacity, and imperativeness which characterize the self-reproaches of a melancholic.

[3] [Some further discussion of melancholia will be found in Chapter V of *The Ego and the Id* (1923b).]

POSTSCRIPT

In the course of the enquiry which has just been brought to a provisional end we came across a number of side-paths which we avoided pursuing in the first instance but in which there was much that offered us promises of insight. We propose now to take up a few of the points that have been left on one side in this way.

A. The distinction between identification of the ego with an object and replacement of the ego ideal by an object finds an interesting illustration in the two great artificial groups which we began by studying, the army and the Christian Church.

It is obvious that a soldier takes his superior, that is, in fact, the leader of the army, as his ideal, while he identifies himself with his equals, and derives from this community of their egos the obligations for giving mutual help and for sharing possessions which comradeship implies. But he becomes ridiculous if he tries to identify himself with the general. The soldier in *Wallensteins Lager* laughs at the sergeant for this very reason:

> Wie er räuspert und wie er spuckt,
> Das habt ihr ihm glücklich abgeguckt! [1]

It is otherwise in the Catholic Church. Every Christian loves Christ as his ideal and feels himself united with all other Christians by the tie of identification. But the Church requires more of him. He has also to identify himself with Christ and love all other Christians as Christ loved them. At both points, therefore, the Church requires that the position of the libido which is given by group formation should be supplemented. Identification has to be added where object-choice has taken place, and object-love where there is identification. This addition evidently goes beyond the constitution of the group. One can be a good Christian and yet be far from the idea of putting oneself in

[1] [I grant you, your counterfeit perfectly fits
  The way that he hawks and the way that he spits.
                              (Scene 6 of Schiller's play.)]

Christ's place and of having like him an all-embracing love for mankind. One need not think oneself capable, weak mortal that one is, of the Saviour's largeness of soul and strength of love. But this further development in the distribution of libido in the group is probably the factor upon which Christianity bases its claim to have reached a higher ethical level.

B. We have said that it would be possible to specify the point in the mental development of mankind at which the advance from group psychology to individual psychology was achieved also by the individual members of the group [p. 123].[1]

For this purpose we must return for a moment to the scientific myth of the father of the primal horde. He was later on exalted into the creator of the world, and with justice, for he had produced all the sons who composed the first group. He was the ideal of each one of them, at once feared and honoured, a fact which led later to the idea of taboo. These many individuals eventually banded themselves together, killed him and cut him in pieces. None of the group of victors could take his place, or, if one of them did, the battles began afresh, until they understood that they must all renounce their father's heritage. They then formed the totemic community of brothers, all with equal rights and united by the totem prohibitions which were to preserve and to expiate the memory of the murder. But the dissatisfaction with what had been achieved still remained, and it became the source of new developments. The persons who were united in this group of brothers gradually came towards a revival of the old state of things at a new level. The male became once more the chief of a family, and broke down the prerogatives of the gynaecocracy which had become established during the fatherless period. As a compensation for this he may at that time have acknowledged the mother deities, whose priests were castrated for the mother's protection, after the example that had been given by the father of the primal horde. And yet the new family was only a shadow of the old one; there were numbers of fathers and each one was limited by the rights of the others.

[1] What follows at this point was written under the influence of an exchange of ideas with Otto Rank. [*Added* 1923:] See also Rank (1922). [This passage is to be read in conjunction with Sections 5, 6 and 7 of the fourth essay in *Totem and Taboo, Standard Ed.*, 13, 140 ff.]

It was then, perhaps, that some individual, in the exigency of his longing, may have been moved to free himself from the group and take over the father's part. He who did this was the first epic poet; and the advance was achieved in his imagination. This poet disguised the truth with lies in accordance with his longing. He invented the heroic myth. The hero was a man who by himself had slain the father—the father who still appeared in the myth as a totemic monster. Just as the father had been the boy's first ideal, so in the hero who aspires to the father's place the poet now created the first ego ideal. The transition to the hero was probably afforded by the youngest son, the mother's favourite, whom she had protected from paternal jealousy, and who, in the era of the primal horde, had been the father's successor. In the lying poetic fancies of prehistoric times the woman, who had been the prize of battle and the temptation to murder, was probably turned into the active seducer and instigator to the crime.

The hero claims to have acted alone in accomplishing the deed, which certainly only the horde as a whole would have ventured upon. But, as Rank has observed, fairy tales have preserved clear traces of the facts which were disavowed. For we often find in them that the hero who has to carry out some difficult task (usually the youngest son, and not infrequently one who has represented himself to the father-substitute as being stupid, that is to say, harmless)—we often find, then, that this hero can carry out his task only by the help of a crowd of small animals, such as bees or ants. These would be the brothers in the primal horde, just as in the same way in dream symbolism insects or vermin signify brothers and sisters (contemptuously, considered as babies). Moreover every one of the tasks in myths and fairy tales is easily recognizable as a substitute for the heroic deed.

The myth, then, is the step by which the individual emerges from group psychology. The first myth was certainly the psychological, the hero myth; the explanatory nature myth must have followed much later. The poet who had taken this step and had in this way set himself free from the group in his imagination, is nevertheless able (as Rank has further observed) to find his way back to it in reality. For he goes and relates to the group his hero's deeds which he has invented. At bottom this hero is no one but himself. Thus he lowers himself to the level of reality, and raises his hearers to the level of imagination. But his hearers understand the poet, and, in virtue of their having the same relation of longing towards the primal father, they can identify themselves with the hero.[1]

The lie of the heroic myth culminates in the deification of the hero. Perhaps the deified hero may have been earlier than the Father God and may have been a precursor to the return of the primal father as a deity. The series of gods, then, would run chronologically: Mother Goddess—Hero—Father God. But it is only with the elevation of the never-forgotten primal father that the deity acquires the features that we still recognize in him to-day.[2]

C. A great deal has been said in this paper about directly sexual instincts and those that are inhibited in their aims, and it may be hoped that this distinction will not meet with too much resistance. But a detailed discussion of the question will not be out of place, even if it only repeats what has to a great extent already been said before.

The development of the libido in children has made us acquainted with the first but also the best example of sexual instincts which are inhibited in their aims. All the feelings which a child has towards its parents and those who look after it pass by an easy transition into the wishes which give expression to the child's sexual impulsions. The child claims from these objects of its love all the signs of affection which it knows of; it wants to kiss them, touch them, and look at them; it is curious to see their genitals, and to be with them when they perform their intimate excretory functions; it promises to marry its mother or nurse—whatever it may understand by marriage; it proposes to itself to bear its father a child, etc. Direct observation, as well as the subsequent analytic investigation of the residues of childhood, leave no doubt as to the complete fusion of tender and jealous feelings and of sexual intentions, and show us in what a fundamental way the child makes the person it loves into the object of all its still not properly centred sexual trends.[3]

---

[1] Cf. Hanns Sachs (1920).

[2] In this brief exposition I have made no attempt to bring forward any of the material existing in legends, myths, fairy tales, the history of manners, etc., in support of the construction.

[3] Cf. my *Three Essays* (1905d) [*Standard Ed.*, 7, 199].

This first configuration of the child's love, which in typical cases takes the shape of the Oedipus complex, succumbs, as we know, from the beginning of the period of latency onwards to a wave of repression. Such of it as is left over shows itself as a purely affectionate emotional tie, relating to the same people, but no longer to be described as 'sexual'. Psycho-analysis, which illuminates the depths of mental life, has no difficulty in showing that the sexual ties of the earliest years of childhood also persist, though repressed and unconscious. It gives us courage to assert that wherever we come across an affectionate feeling it is successor to a completely 'sensual' object-tie with the person in question or rather with that person's prototype (or *imago*). It cannot indeed disclose to us without a special investigation whether in a given case this former complete sexual current still exists under repression or whether it has already been exhausted. To speak still more precisely: it is quite certain that this current is still there as a form and possibility, and can always be cathected and put into activity again by means of regression; the only question is (and it cannot always be answered) what degree of cathexis and operative force it still has at the present moment. Equal care must be taken in this connection to avoid two sources of error—the Scylla of under-estimating the importance of the repressed unconscious, and the Charybdis of judging the normal entirely by the standards of the pathological.

A psychology which will not or cannot penetrate the depths of what is repressed regards affectionate emotional ties as being invariably the expression of impulses which have no sexual aim, even though they are derived from impulses which have such an aim.[1]

We are justified in saying that they have been diverted from these sexual aims, even though there is some difficulty in giving a description of such a diversion of aim which will conform to the requirements of metapsychology. Moreover, those instincts which are inhibited in their aims always preserve some few of their original sexual aims; even an affectionate devotee, even a friend or an admirer, desires the physical proximity and

---

[1] Hostile feelings are doubtless a little more complicated in their construction. [In the 1st edition only, this footnote ran: 'Hostile feelings, which are a little more complicated in their construction, offer no exception to this rule.']

the sight of the person who is now loved only in the 'Pauline' sense. If we choose, we may recognize in this diversion of aim a beginning of the *sublimation* of the sexual instincts, or on the other hand we may fix the limits of sublimation at some more distant point. Those sexual instincts which are inhibited in their aims have a great functional advantage over those which are uninhibited. Since they are not capable of really complete satisfaction, they are especially adapted to create permanent ties; while those instincts which are directly sexual incur a loss of energy each time they are satisfied, and must wait to be renewed by a fresh accumulation of sexual libido, so that meanwhile the object may have been changed. The inhibited instincts are capable of any degree of admixture with the uninhibited; they can be transformed back into them, just as they arose out of them. It is well known how easily erotic wishes develop out of emotional relations of a friendly character, based upon appreciation and admiration (compare Molière's 'Kiss me for the love of Greek' [1]), between a master and a pupil, between a performer and a delighted listener, and especially in the case of women. In fact the growth of emotional ties of this kind, with their purposeless beginnings, provides a much frequented pathway to sexual object-choice. Pfister, in his *Frömmigkeit des Grafen von Zinzendorf* (1910), has given an extremely clear and certainly not an isolated example of how easily even an intense religious tie can revert to ardent sexual excitement. On the other hand it is also very usual for directly sexual impulsions, short-lived in themselves, to be transformed into a lasting and purely affectionate tie; and the consolidation of a passionate love marriage rests to a large extent upon this process.

We shall naturally not be surprised to hear that the sexual impulsions that are inhibited in their aims arise out of the directly sexual ones when internal or external obstacles make the sexual aims unattainable. The repression during the period of latency is an internal obstacle of this kind—or rather one which has become internal. We have assumed that the father of the primal horde owing to his sexual intolerance compelled all his sons to be abstinent, and thus forced them into ties that were inhibited in their aims, while he reserved for himself

---

[1] [Quoi! monsieur sait du grec! Ah! permettez, de grâce,
   Que, pour l'amour du grec, monsieur, on vous embrasse.
                              Les femmes savantes. III, 5.]

freedom of sexual enjoyment and in this way remained without ties. All the ties upon which a group depends are of the character of instincts that are inhibited in their aims. But here we have approached the discussion of a new subject, which deals with the relation between directly sexual instincts and the formation of groups.

D. The last two remarks will have prepared us for finding that directly sexual impulsions are unfavourable to the formation of groups. In the history of the development of the family there have also, it is true, been group relations of sexual love (group marriages); but the more important sexual love became for the ego, and the more it developed the characteristics of being in love, the more urgently it required to be limited to two people—*una cum uno*—as is prescribed by the nature of the genital aim. Polygamous inclinations had to be content to find satisfaction in a succession of changing objects.

Two people coming together for the purpose of sexual satisfaction, in so far as they seek for solitude, are making a demonstration against the herd instinct, the group feeling. The more they are in love, the more completely they suffice for each other. Their rejection of the group's influence is expressed in the shape of a sense of shame. Feelings of jealousy of the most extreme violence are summoned up in order to protect the choice of a sexual object from being encroached upon by a group tie. It is only when the affectionate, that is, personal, factor of a love relation gives place entirely to the sensual one, that it is possible for two people to have sexual intercourse in the presence of others or for there to be simultaneous sexual acts in a group, as occurs at an orgy. But at that point a regression has taken place to an early stage in sexual relations, at which being in love as yet played no part, and all sexual objects were judged to be of equal value, somewhat in the sense of Bernard Shaw's malicious aphorism to the effect that being in love means greatly exaggerating the difference between one woman and another.

There are abundant indications that being in love only made its appearance late on in the sexual relations between men and women; so that the opposition between sexual love and group ties is also a late development. Now it may seem as though this assumption were incompatible with our myth of the primal family. For it was after all by their love for their mothers and sisters that the mob of brothers was, as we have supposed, driven to parricide; and it is difficult to imagine this love as being anything but undivided and primitive—that is, as an intimate union of the affectionate and sensual. But further consideration resolves this objection to our theory into a confirmation of it. One of the reactions to the parricide was after all the institution of totemic exogamy, the prohibition of any sexual relation with those women of the family who had been tenderly loved since childhood. In this way a wedge was driven in between a man's affectionate and sensual feelings, one still firmly fixed in his erotic life to-day.[1] As a result of this exogamy the sensual needs of men had to be satisfied with strange and unloved women.

In the great artificial groups, the Church and the army, there is no room for woman as a sexual object. The love relation between men and women remains outside these organizations. Even where groups are formed which are composed of both men and women the distinction between the sexes plays no part. There is scarcely any sense in asking whether the libido which keeps groups together is of a homosexual or of a heterosexual nature, for it is not differentiated according to the sexes, and particularly shows a complete disregard for the aims of the genital organization of the libido.

Even in a person who has in other respects become absorbed in a group, the directly sexual impulsions preserve a little of his individual activity. If they become too strong they disintegrate every group formation. The Catholic Church had the best of motives for recommending its followers to remain unmarried and for imposing celibacy upon its priests; but falling in love has often driven even priests to leave the Church. In the same way love for women breaks through the group ties of race, of national divisions, and of the social class system, and it thus produces important effects as a factor in civilization. It seems certain that homosexual love is far more compatible with group ties, even when it takes the shape of uninhibited sexual impulsions—a remarkable fact, the explanation of which might carry us far.

The psycho-analytic investigation of the psychoneuroses has taught us that their symptoms are to be traced back to directly sexual impulsions which are repressed but still remain active.

[1] See Freud, (1912d).

We can complete this formula by adding—'or, to aim-in-hibited impulsions, whose inhibition has not been entirely successful or has made room for a return to the repressed sexual aim'. It is in accordance with this that a neurosis should make its victim asocial and should remove him from the usual group formations. It may be said that a neurosis has the same disintegrating effect upon a group as being in love. On the other hand it appears that where a powerful impetus has been given to group formation neuroses may diminish and, at all events temporarily, disappear. Justifiable attempts have also been made to turn this antagonism between neuroses and group formation to therapeutic account. Even those who do not regret the disappearance of religious illusions from the civilized world of to-day will admit that so long as they were in force they offered those who were bound by them the most powerful protection against the danger of neurosis.[1] Nor is it hard to discern that all the ties that bind people to mystico-religious or philosophico-religious sects and communities are expressions of crooked cures of all kinds of neuroses. All of this is correlated with the contrast between directly sexual impulsions and those which are inhibited in their aims.

If he is left to himself, a neurotic is obliged to replace by his own symptom formations the great group formations from which he is excluded. He creates his own world of imagination for himself, his own religion, his own system of delusions, and thus recapitulates the institutions of humanity in a distorted way which is clear evidence of the dominating part played by the directly sexual impulsions.[2]

E. In conclusion, we will add a comparative estimate, from the standpoint of the libido theory, of the states with which we have been concerned, of being in love, of hypnosis, of group formation, and of neurosis.

Being in love is based on the simultaneous presence of directly sexual impulsions and of sexual impulsions that are inhibited in their aims, while the object draws a part of the subject's narcissistic ego-libido to itself. It is a condition in which there is only room for the ego and the object.

[1] [Cf. the beginning of Section 2 of Freud, 1910d.]
[2] See *Totem and Taboo*, towards the end of the second essay [*Standard Ed.*, 13. 73–4].

Hypnosis resembles being in love in being limited to these two persons, but it is based entirely on sexual impulsions that are inhibited in their aims and puts the object in the place of the ego ideal.

The group multiplies this process; it agrees with hypnosis in the nature of the instincts which hold it together, and in the replacement of the ego ideal by the object; but to this it adds identification with other individuals, which was perhaps originally made possible by their having the same relation to the object.

Both states, hypnosis and group formation, are an inherited deposit from the phylogenesis of the human libido—hypnosis in the form of a predisposition, and the group, besides this, as a direct survival. The replacement of the directly sexual impulsions by those that are inhibited in their aims promotes in both states a separation between the ego and the ego ideal, a separation with which a beginning has already been made in the state of being in love.

Neurosis stands outside this series. It also is based upon a peculiarity in the development of the human libido—the twice repeated start made by the directly sexual function, with an intervening period of latency.[1] To this extent it resembles hypnosis and group formation in having the character of a regression, which is absent from being in love. It makes its appearance wherever the advance from directly sexual instincts to those that are inhibited in their aims has not been wholly successful; and it represents a *conflict* between those portions of the instincts which have been received into the ego after having passed through this development and those portions of them which, springing from the repressed unconscious, strive—as do other, completely repressed, instinctual impulses—to attain direct satisfaction. Neuroses are extraordinarily rich in content, for they embrace all possible relations between the ego and the object—both those in which the object is retained and others in which it is abandoned or erected inside the ego itself—and also the conflicting relations between the ego and its ego ideal.

[1] See my *Three Essays* (1905d), *Standard Ed.*, 7, 234.

THE PSYCHOGENESIS OF A CASE
OF HOMOSEXUALITY IN A WOMAN
(1920)

ÜBER DIE PSYCHOGENESE EINES FALLES VON WEIBLICHER HOMOSEXUALITÄT

(a) German Editions:

1920   Int. Z. Psychoanal., 6 (1), 1–24.

1922   S.K.S.N., 5, 159–94.

1924   G.S., 5, 312–43.

1926   Psychoanalyse der Neurosen, 87–124.

1931   Sexualtheorie und Traumlehre, 155–88.

1947   G.W., 12, 271–302.

(b) English Translation:

'The Psychogenesis of a Case of Homosexuality in a Woman'

1920   Int. J. Psycho-Anal., 1, 125–49. (Tr. Barbara Low and R. Gabler.)

1924   C.P., 2, 202–31. (Same translators.)

The present translation is a considerably modified version of that published in 1924.

After an interval of nearly twenty years Freud published in the present paper a fairly detailed, if incomplete, case history of a woman patient. But whereas the case of 'Dora' (1905*e* [1901]), as well as his contributions to *Studies on Hysteria* (1895*d*), dealt exclusively with hysteria, he now began to consider more deeply the whole question of sexuality in women. His investigations were to lead subsequently to his papers on the effects of the anatomical distinction between the sexes (1925*j*) and on female sexuality (1931*b*) and to Lecture XXIII of his *New Introductory Lectures* (1933*a*). Apart from this, the paper contains an exposition of some of Freud's later views on homosexuality in general, as well as some interesting remarks on technical points.

THE PSYCHOGENESIS OF A CASE
OF HOMOSEXUALITY IN A
WOMAN

I

HOMOSEXUALITY in women, which is certainly not less common than in men, although much less glaring, has not only been ignored by the law, but has also been neglected by psycho-analytic research. The narration of a single case, not too pronounced in type, in which it was possible to trace its origin and development in the mind with complete certainty and almost without a gap may, therefore, have a certain claim to attention. If this presentation of it furnishes only the most general outlines of the various events concerned and of the conclusions reached from a study of the case, while suppressing all the characteristic details on which the interpretation is founded, this limitation is easily to be explained by the medical discretion necessary in discussing a recent case.

A beautiful and clever girl of eighteen, belonging to a family of good standing, had aroused displeasure and concern in her parents by the devoted adoration with which she pursued a certain 'society lady' who was about ten years older than herself. The parents asserted that, in spite of her distinguished name, this lady was nothing but a *cocotte*. It was well known, they said, that she lived with a friend, a married woman, and had intimate relations with her, while at the same time she carried on promiscuous affairs with a number of men. The girl did not contradict these evil reports, but neither did she allow them to interfere with her worship of the lady, although she herself was by no means lacking in a sense of decency and propriety. No prohibitions and no supervision hindered the girl from seizing every one of her rare opportunities of being together with her beloved, of ascertaining all her habits, of waiting for her for hours outside her door or at a tram-halt, of sending her gifts of flowers, and so on. It was evident that this one interest had swallowed up all others in the girl's mind. She did not trouble herself any further with educational studies, thought nothing of social functions or girlish pleasures, and kept up relations only with a few girl friends who could help her in the matter or serve as confidantes. The parents could not say to what lengths their daughter had gone in her relations with the questionable lady, whether the limits of devoted admiration had already been exceeded or not. They had never remarked in their daughter any interest in young men, nor pleasure in their attentions, while, on the other hand, they were sure that her present attachment to a woman was only a continuation, in a more marked degree, of a feeling she had displayed of recent years for other members of her own sex which had already aroused her father's suspicion and anger.

There were two details of her behaviour, in apparent contrast with each other, that most especially vexed her parents. On the one hand, she did not scruple to appear in the most frequented streets in the company of her undesirable friend, being thus quite neglectful of her own reputation; while, on the other hand, she disdained no means of deception, no excuses and no lies that would make meetings with her possible and cover them. She thus showed herself too open in one respect and full of deceitfulness in the other. One day it happened, indeed, as was sooner or later inevitable in the circumstances, that the father met his daughter in the company of the lady, about whom he had come to know. He passed them by with an angry glance which boded no good. Immediately afterwards the girl rushed off and flung herself over a wall down the side of a cutting on to the suburban railway line which ran close by. She paid for this undoubtedly serious attempt at suicide with a considerable time on her back in bed, though fortunately little permanent damage was done. After her recovery she found it easier to get her own way than before. The parents did not dare to oppose her with so much determination, and the lady, who up till then had received her advances coldly, was moved by such an unmistakable proof of serious passion and began to treat her in a more friendly manner.

About six months after this episode the parents sought medical advice and entrusted the physician with the task of bringing their daughter back to a normal state of mind. The girl's attempted suicide had evidently shown them that strong disciplinary measures at home were powerless to overcome her disorder. Before going further, however, it will be desirable to deal separately with the attitudes of her father and of her mother to the matter. The father was an earnest, worthy man, at bottom very tender-hearted, but he had to some extent estranged his children by the sternness he had adopted towards them. His treatment of his only daughter was too much influenced by consideration for his wife. When he first came to know of his daughter's homosexual tendencies he flew into a rage and tried to suppress them by threats. At that time perhaps he hesitated between different, though equally distressing, views —regarding her either as vicious, as degenerate, or as mentally afflicted. Even after the attempted suicide he did not achieve the lofty resignation shown by one of our medical colleagues who remarked of a similar irregularity in his own family: 'Well, it's just a misfortune like any other.' There was something about his daughter's homosexuality that aroused the deepest bitterness in him, and he was determined to combat it with all the means in his power. The low estimation in which psychoanalysis is so generally held in Vienna did not prevent him from turning to it for help. If this way failed he still had in reserve his strongest counter-measure: a speedy marriage was to awaken the natural instincts of the girl and stifle her unnatural tendencies.

The mother's attitude towards the girl was not so easy to grasp. She was still a youngish woman, who was evidently unwilling to give up her own claims to attractiveness. All that was clear was that she did not take her daughter's infatuation so tragically as did the father, nor was she so incensed at it. She had even for some time enjoyed her daughter's confidence concerning her passion. Her opposition to it seemed to have been aroused mainly by the harmful publicity with which the girl displayed her feelings. She had herself suffered for some years from neurotic troubles and enjoyed a great deal of consideration from her husband; she treated her children in quite different ways, being decidedly harsh towards her daughter and overindulgent to her three sons, the youngest of whom had been born after a long interval and was then not yet three years old. It was not easy to ascertain anything more definite about her character, for, owing to motives that will only later become intelligible, the patient was always reserved in what she said about her mother, whereas in regard to her father there was no question of this.

To a physician who was to undertake psycho-analytic

treatment of the girl there were many grounds for misgiving. The situation he had to deal with was not the one that analysis demands, in which alone it can demonstrate its effectiveness. As is well known, the ideal situation for analysis is when some-one who is otherwise his own master is suffering from an inner conflict which he is unable to resolve alone, so that he brings his trouble to the analyst and begs for his help. The physician then works hand in hand with one portion of the pathologically divided personality, against the other party in the conflict. Any situation which differs from this is to a greater or lesser degree unfavourable for psycho-analysis and adds fresh difficulties to the internal ones already present. Situations like that of a pro-spective house-owner who orders an architect to build him a villa according to his own tastes and requirements, or of a pious donor who commissions an artist to paint a sacred picture in the corner of which is to be a portrait of himself in adoration, are at bottom incompatible with the conditions necessary for psycho-analysis. Thus, it constantly happens that a husband instructs the physician as follows: 'My wife suffers from nerves, and for that reason gets on badly with me; please cure her, so that we may lead a happy married life again.' But often enough it turns out that such a request is impossible to fulfil—that is to say, the physician cannot bring about the result for which the husband sought the treatment. As soon as the wife is freed from her neurotic inhibitions she sets about getting a separation, for her neurosis was the sole condition under which the marriage could be maintained. Or else parents expect one to cure their nervous and unruly child. By a healthy child they mean one who never causes his parents trouble, and gives them nothing but pleasure. The physician may succeed in curing the child, but after that it goes its own way all the more decidedly, and the parents are now far more dissatisfied than before. In short, it is not a matter of indifference whether someone comes to analysis of his own accord or because he is brought to it—whether it is he himself who desires to be changed, or only his relatives, who love him (or who might be expected to love him).

Further unfavourable features in the present case were the facts that the girl was not in any way ill (she did not suffer from anything in herself, nor did she complain of her condition) and that the task to be carried out did not consist in resolving a neurotic conflict but in converting one variety of the genital organization of sexuality into the other. Such an achievement —the removal of genital inversion or homosexuality—is in my experience never an easy matter. On the contrary, I have found success possible only in specially favourable circumstances, and even then the success essentially consisted in making access to the opposite sex (which had hitherto been barred) possible to a person restricted to homosexuality, thus restoring his full bi-sexual functions. After that it lay with him to choose whether he wished to abandon the path that is banned by society, and in some cases he has done so. One must remember that normal sexuality too depends upon a restriction in the choice of object. In general, to undertake to convert a fully developed homo-sexual into a heterosexual does not offer much more prospect of success than the reverse, except that for good practical reasons the latter is never attempted.

The number of successes achieved by psycho-analytic treat-ment of the various forms of homosexuality, which incidentally are manifold, is indeed not very striking. As a rule the homo-sexual is not able to give up the object which provides him with pleasure, and one cannot convince him that if he made the change he would rediscover in the other object the pleasure that he has renounced. If he comes to be treated at all, it is mostly through the pressure of external motives, such as the social disadvantages and dangers attaching to his choice of object, and such components of the instinct of self-preservation prove themselves too weak in the struggle against the sexual impulsions. One then soon discovers his secret plan, namely, to obtain from the striking failure of his attempt a feeling of satis-faction that he has done everything possible against his abnor-mality, to which he can now resign himself with an easy con-science. The case is somewhat different when consideration for beloved parents and relatives has been the motive for his attempt to be cured. Here there really are libidinal impulsions present which may put forth energies opposed to the homo-sexual choice of object; but their strength is rarely sufficient. It is only where the homosexual fixation has not yet become strong enough, or where there are considerable rudiments and vestiges of a heterosexual choice of object, i.e. in a still oscillating or in a definitely bisexual organization, that one may make a more favourable prognosis for psycho-analytic therapy.

For these reasons I refrained altogether from holding out to the parents any prospect of their wish being fulfilled. I merely said I was prepared to study the girl carefully for a few weeks or months, so as then to be able to pronounce how far a continuation of the analysis would be likely to influence her. In quite a number of cases, indeed, an analysis falls into two clearly distinguishable phases. In the first, the physician procures from the patient the necessary information, makes him familiar with the premises and postulates of psycho-analysis, and unfolds to him the reconstruction of the genesis of his disorder as deduced from the material brought up in the analysis. In the second phase the patient himself gets hold of the material put before him; he works on it, recollects what he can of the apparently repressed memories, and tries to repeat the rest as if he were in some way living it over again. In this way he can confirm, supplement, and correct the inferences made by the physician. It is only during this work that he experiences, through overcoming resistances, the inner change aimed at, and acquires for himself the convictions that make him independent of the physician's authority.[1] These two phases in the course of the analytic treatment are not always sharply divided from each other; this can only happen when the resistance obeys certain conditions. But when this is so, one may bring up as an analogy the two stages of a journey. The first comprises all the necessary preparations, to-day so complicated and hard to effect, before, ticket in hand, one can at last go on to the platform and secure a seat in the train. One then has the right, and the possibility, of travelling into a distant country; but after all these preliminary exertions one is not yet there—indeed, one is not a single mile nearer to one's goal. For this to happen one has to make the journey itself from one station to the other, and this part of the performance may well be compared with the second phase of the analysis.

The course of the present patient's analysis followed this two-phased pattern, but it was not continued beyond the beginning of the second phase. A special constellation of the resistance made it possible, nevertheless, to gain full confirmation of my constructions, and to obtain an adequate insight on broad lines into the way in which her inversion had developed. But before relating the findings of the analysis I must deal with a few

[1] [See for a fuller discussion of this 'Recollecting, Repeating and Working Through' (1914g).]

points which have either been touched upon already by myself or which will have roused special interest in the reader.

I had made the prognosis partly dependent on how far the girl had succeeded in satisfying her passion. The information I obtained during the analysis seemed favourable in this respect. With none of the objects of her adoration had the patient enjoyed anything beyond a few kisses and embraces; her genital chastity, if one may use such a phrase, had remained intact. As for the *demi-mondaine* who had roused her most recent and by far her strongest emotions, she had always been treated coldly by her and never been allowed any greater favour than to kiss her hand. She was probably making a virtue of necessity when she kept insisting on the purity of her love and her physical repulsion against the idea of any sexual intercourse. But perhaps she was not altogether wrong when she boasted of her wonderful beloved that, being of good birth as she was, and forced into her present position only by adverse family circumstances, she had preserved, in spite of her situation, much nobility of character. For the lady used to recommend the girl every time they met to withdraw her affection from herself and from women in general, and she had persistently rejected the girl's advances up to the time of the attempted suicide.

A second point, which I at once tried to investigate, concerned any possible motives in the girl herself which might serve as a support for psycho-analytic treatment. She did not try to deceive me by saying that she felt any urgent need to be freed from her homosexuality. On the contrary, she said she could not conceive of any other way of being in love, but she added that for her parents' sake she would honestly help in the therapeutic attempt, for it pained her very much to be the cause of so much grief to them. To begin with, I could not but take this, too, as a propitious sign; for I could not guess the unconscious affective attitude that lay concealed behind it. What came to light later in this connection decisively influenced the course taken by the analysis and determined its premature conclusion.

Readers unversed in psycho-analysis will long have been awaiting an answer to two other questions. Did this homosexual girl show physical characteristics plainly belonging to the opposite sex, and did the case prove to be one of congenital or acquired (later-developed) homosexuality?

I am aware of the importance attaching to the first of these questions. But one should not exaggerate it and allow it to over-shadow the fact that sporadic secondary characteristics of the opposite sex are very often present in normal individuals, and that well-marked physical characteristics of the opposite sex may be found in persons whose choice of object has undergone no change in the direction of inversion; in other words, that in both sexes *the degree of physical hermaphroditism is to a great extent independent of psychical hermaphroditism.* In modification of these statements it must be added that this independence is more evident in men than women, where bodily and mental traits belonging to the opposite sex are apt to coincide.[1] Still I am not in a position to give a satisfactory answer to the first of our questions about my patient. The psycho-analyst customarily forgoes a thorough physical examination of his patients in certain cases. Certainly there was no obvious deviation from the feminine physical type, nor any menstrual disturbance. The beautiful and well-made girl had, it is true, her father's tall figure, and her facial features were sharp rather than soft and girlish, traits which might be regarded as indicating a physical masculinity. Some of her intellectual attributes also could be connected with masculinity: for instance, her acuteness of comprehension and her lucid objectivity, in so far as she was not dominated by her passion. But these distinctions are conventional rather than scientific. What is certainly of greater importance is that in her behaviour towards her love-object she had throughout assumed the masculine part: that is to say, she displayed the humility and the sublime overvaluation of the sexual object so characteristic of the male lover, the renunciation of all narcissistic satisfaction, and the preference for being the lover rather than the beloved. She had thus not only chosen a feminine love-object, but had also developed a masculine attitude towards that object.

The second question, whether this was a case of congenital or acquired homosexuality, will be answered by the whole history of the patient's abnormality and its development. The study of this will show how far this question is a fruitless and inapposite one.

[1] [Cf. the discussion of this point in *Three Essays* (1905d), *Standard Ed.*, 7, 141 ff.]

II

After this highly discursive introduction I am only able to present a very concise summary of the sexual history of the case under consideration. In childhood the girl had passed through the normal attitude characteristic of the feminine Oedipus complex [1] in a way that was not at all remarkable, and had later also begun to substitute for her father a brother slightly older than herself. She did not remember any sexual traumas in early life, nor were any discovered by the analysis. Comparison of her brother's genital organs and her own, which took place about the beginning of the latency period (at five years old or perhaps a little earlier), left a strong impression on her and had far-reaching after-effects. There were very few signs pointing to infantile masturbation, or else the analysis did not go far enough to throw light on this point. The birth of a second brother when she was between five and six years old exercised no special influence upon her development. During the pre-pubertal years at school she gradually became acquainted with the facts of sex, and she received this knowledge with mixed feelings of lasciviousness and frightened aversion, in a way which may be called normal and was not exaggerated in degree. This amount of information about her seems meagre enough, nor can I guarantee that it is complete. It may be that the history of her youth was much richer in experiences; I do not know. As I have already said, the analysis was broken off after a short time, and therefore yielded an anamnesis not much more reliable than the other anamneses of homosexuals, which there is good cause to question. Further, the girl had never been neurotic, and came to the analysis without even one hysterical symptom, so that opportunities for investigating the history of her childhood did not present themselves so readily as usual.

At the age of thirteen to fourteen she displayed a tender and, according to general opinion, exaggeratedly strong affection for a small boy, not quite three years old, whom she used to see regularly in a children's playground. She took to the child so warmly that in consequence a lasting friendship grew up between herself and his parents. One may infer from this episode

---

[1] I do not see any advance or gain in the introduction of the term 'Electra complex', and do not advocate its use.

that at that time she was possessed of a strong desire to be a mother herself and to have a child. However, after a short time she grew indifferent to the boy, and began to take an interest in mature, but still youthful, women. The manifestations of this interest soon brought upon her a severe chastisement at the hands of her father.

It was established beyond all doubt that this change occurred simultaneously with a certain event in the family, and one may therefore look to this for some explanation of the change. Before it happened, her libido was concentrated on a maternal attitude, while afterwards she became a homosexual attracted to mature women, and remained so ever since. The event which is so significant for our understanding of the case was a new pregnancy of her mother's, and the birth of a third brother when she was about sixteen.

The position of affairs which I shall now proceed to lay bare is not a product of my inventive powers; it is based on such trustworthy analytic evidence that I can claim objective validity for it. It was in particular a series of dreams, interrelated and easy to interpret, that decided me in favour of its reality.

The analysis revealed beyond all shadow of doubt that the lady-love was a substitute for—her mother. It is true that the lady herself was not a mother, but then she was not the girl's first love. The first objects of her affection after the birth of her youngest brother were really mothers, women between thirty and thirty-five whom she had met with their children during summer holidays or in the family circle of acquaintances in town. Motherhood as a *sine qua non* in her love-object was later on given up, because that precondition was difficult to combine in real life with another one, which grew more and more important. The specially intense bond with her latest love had still another basis which the girl discovered quite easily one day. Her lady's slender figure, severe beauty, and downright manner reminded her of the brother who was a little older than herself. Her latest choice corresponded, therefore, not only to her feminine but also to her masculine ideal; it combined satisfaction of the homosexual tendency with that of the heterosexual one. It is well known that analysis of male homosexuals has in numerous cases revealed the same combination, which should warn us not to form too simple a conception of the nature and genesis of inversion, and to keep in mind the universal bisexuality of human beings.[1]

But how are we to understand the fact that it was precisely the birth of a child who came late in the family (at a time when the girl herself was already mature and had strong wishes of her own) that moved her to bestow her passionate tenderness upon the woman who gave birth to this child, i.e. her own mother, and to express that feeling towards a substitute for her mother? From all that we know we should have expected just the opposite. In such circumstances mothers with daughters of nearly a marriageable age usually feel embarrassed in regard to them, while the daughters are apt to feel for their mothers a mixture of compassion, contempt and envy which does nothing to increase their tenderness for them. The girl we are considering had in any case altogether little cause to feel affection for her mother. The latter, still youthful herself, saw in her rapidly developing daughter an inconvenient competitor; she favoured the sons at her expense, limited her independence as much as possible, and kept an especially strict watch against any close relation between the girl and her father. A yearning from the beginning for a kinder mother would, therefore, have been quite intelligible, but why it should have flared up just then, and in the form of a consuming passion, is hard to understand.

The explanation is as follows. It was just when the girl was experiencing the revival of her infantile Oedipus complex at puberty that she suffered her great disappointment. She became keenly conscious of the wish to have a child, and a male one; that what she desired was her *father's* child and an image of *him*, her consciousness was not allowed to know. And what happened next? It was not *she* who bore the child, but her unconsciously hated rival, her mother. Furiously resentful and embittered, she turned away from her father and from men altogether. After this first great reverse she forswore her womanhood and sought another goal for her libido.

In doing so she behaved just as many men do who after a first distressing experience turn their backs for ever upon the faithless female sex and become woman-haters. It is related of one of the most attractive and unfortunate princely figures of our time that he became a homosexual because the lady he was engaged to marry betrayed him with another man. I do not

[1] Cf. Sadger (1914).

know whether this is true historically, but an element of psychological truth lies behind the rumour. In all of us, throughout life, the libido normally oscillates between male and female objects; the bachelor gives up his men friends when he marries, and returns to club-life when married life has lost its savour. Naturally, when the swing-over is fundamental and final, we suspect the presence of some special factor which definitely favours one side or the other, and which perhaps has only waited for the appropriate moment in order to turn the choice of object in its direction.

After her disappointment, therefore, this girl had entirely repudiated her wish for a child, her love of men, and the feminine role in general. It is evident that at this point a number of very different things might have happened. What actually happened was the most extreme case. She changed into a man and took her mother in place of her father as the object of her love.[1] Her relation to her mother had certainly been ambivalent from the beginning, and it proved easy to revive her earlier love for her mother and with its help to bring about an overcompensation for her current hostility towards her. Since there was little to be done with the real mother, there arose from this transformation of feeling the search for a substitute mother to whom she could become passionately attached.[2]

There was, in addition, a practical motive for this change, derived from her real relations with her mother, which served as a [secondary] gain from her illness. The mother herself still attached great value to the attentions and the admiration of men. If, then, the girl became homosexual and left men to her mother (in other words, 'retired in favour of' her mother), she

[1] It is by no means rare for a love-relation to be broken off through a process of identification on the part of the lover with the loved object, a process equivalent to a kind of regression to narcissism. After this has been accomplished, it is easy in making a fresh choice of object to direct the libido to a member of the sex opposite to that of the earlier choice.

[2] The displacements of the libido here described are doubtless familiar to every analyst from investigation of the anamneses of neurotics. With the latter, however, they occur in early childhood, at the time of the early efflorescence of erotic life; with our patient, who was in no way neurotic, they took place in the first years following puberty, though, incidentally, they were just as completely unconscious. Perhaps one day this temporal factor may turn out to be of great importance.

would remove something which had hitherto been partly responsible for her mother's dislike.[1]

This libidinal position of the girl's, thus arrived at, was greatly reinforced as soon as she perceived how much it displeased her father. After she had been punished for her over-affectionate attitude to a woman she realized how she could wound her father and take revenge on him. Henceforth she remained homosexual out of defiance against her father. Nor did she scruple to lie to him and to deceive him in every way. Towards her mother, indeed, she was only so far deceitful as was necessary to prevent her father from knowing things. I had the impression that her behaviour followed the principle of the talion: 'Since you have betrayed me, you must put up with my betraying you.' Nor can I come to any other conclusion about the striking lack of caution displayed by this otherwise exceedingly

[1] As 'retiring in favour of someone else' has not previously been mentioned among the causes of homosexuality, or in the mechanism of libidinal fixation in general, I will adduce here another analytic observation of the same kind which has a special feature of interest.   I once knew two twin brothers, both of whom were endowed with strong libidinal impulses. One of them was very successful with women, and had innumerable affairs with women and girls. The other went the same way at first, but it became unpleasant for him to be trespassing on his brother's preserves, and, owing to the likeness between them, to be mistaken for him on intimate occasions; so he got out of the difficulty by becoming homosexual. He left the women to his brother, and thus retired in his favour. Another time I treated a youngish man, an artist, unmistakably bisexual in disposition, in whom the homosexual trend had come to the fore simultaneously with a disturbance in his work. He fled from both women and work together. The analysis, which was able to bring him back to both, showed that fear of his father was the most powerful psychical motive for both the disturbances, which were really renunciations. In his imagination all women belonged to his father, and he sought refuge in men out of submission, so as to retire from the conflict with his father. Such a motivation of the homosexual object-choice must be by no means uncommon; in the primaeval ages of the human race all women presumably belonged to the father and head of the primal horde.

Among brothers and sisters who are not twins this 'retiring' plays a great part in other spheres as well as in that of erotic choice. For example, an elder brother studies music and is admired for it; the younger, far more gifted musically, soon gives up his own musical studies, in spite of his fondness for it, and cannot be persuaded to touch an instrument again. This is only one example of a very frequent occurrence, and investigation of the motives leading to this 'retirement' rather than to open rivalry discloses very complicated conditions in the mind.

shrewd girl. She *wanted* her father to know occasionally of her relations with the lady, otherwise she would be deprived of the satisfaction of her keenest desire—namely, revenge. So she saw to this by showing herself openly in the company of her adored one, by walking with her in the streets near her father's place of business, and the like. This maladroitness, moreover, was by no means unintentional. It was remarkable, too, that both parents behaved as if they understood their daughter's secret psychology. The mother was tolerant, as though she appreciated her daughter's 'retirement' as a favour to her; the father was furious, as though he realized the deliberate revenge directed against himself.

The girl's inversion, however, received its final reinforcement when she found in her 'lady' an object which promised to satisfy not only her homosexual trends, but also that part of her heterosexual libido which was still attached to her brother.

III

Linear presentation is not a very adequate means of describing complicated mental processes going on in different layers of the mind. I am therefore obliged to pause in the discussion of the case and treat more fully and deeply some of the points brought forward above.

I mentioned the fact that in her behaviour to her adored lady the girl had adopted the characteristic masculine type of love. Her humility and her tender lack of pretensions, *'che poco spera e nulla chiede'*,[1] her bliss when she was allowed to accompany the lady a little way and to kiss her hand on parting, her joy when she heard her praised as beautiful (while any recognition of her own beauty by another person meant nothing at all to her), her pilgrimages to places once visited by the loved one, the silence of all more sensual wishes—all these little traits in her resembled the first passionate adoration of a youth for a celebrated actress whom he regards as far above him, to whom he scarcely dares lift his bashful eyes. The correspondence with 'a special type of choice of object made by men' that I have described elsewhere (1910*h*), whose special features I traced to attachment to the mother, held good even to the smallest details. It may seem remarkable that she was not in the least

[1] ['Hoping little and asking for nothing.']

repelled by the bad reputation of her beloved, although her own observations sufficiently confirmed the truth of such rumours. She was after all a well-brought-up and modest girl, who had avoided sexual adventures for herself, and who regarded coarsely sensual satisfactions as unaesthetic. But already her first passions had been for women who were not celebrated for specially strict propriety. The first protest her father made against her love-choice had been evoked by the pertinacity with which she sought the company of a film actress at a summer resort. Moreover, in all these affairs it had never been a question of women who had any reputation for homosexuality, and who might, therefore, have offered her some prospect of homosexual satisfaction; on the contrary, she illogically courted women who were coquettes in the ordinary sense of the word, and she rejected without hesitation the willing advances made by a homosexual friend of her own age. For her, the bad reputation of her 'lady', however, was positively a 'necessary condition for love'. All that is enigmatic in this attitude vanishes when we remember that in the case too of the *masculine* type of object-choice derived from the mother it is a necessary condition that the loved object should be in some way or other 'of bad repute' sexually—someone who really may be called a *cocotte*. When the girl learnt later how far her adored lady deserved this description and that she lived simply by giving her bodily favours, her reaction took the form of great compassion and of phantasies and plans for 'rescuing' her beloved from these ignoble circumstances. We were struck by the same urge to 'rescue' in the men of the type referred to above, and in my description of it I have tried to give the analytic derivation of this urge.

We are led into quite another realm of explanation by the analysis of the attempt at suicide, which I must regard as seriously intended, and which, incidentally, considerably improved her position both with her parents and with the lady she loved. She went for a walk with her one day in a part of the town and at an hour at which she was not unlikely to meet her father on his way from his office. So it turned out. Her father passed them in the street and cast a furious look at her and her companion, about whom he had by that time come to know. A few moments later she flung herself into the railway cutting. The explanation she gave of the immediate reasons determining

her decision sounded quite plausible. She had confessed to the
lady that the man who had given them such an irate glance
was her father, and that he had absolutely forbidden their
friendship. The lady became incensed at this and ordered the
girl to leave her then and there, and never again to wait for her
or to address her—the affair must now come to an end. In her
despair at having thus lost her loved one for ever, she wanted to
put an end to herself. The analysis, however, was able to disclose another and deeper interpretation behind the one she
gave, which was confirmed by the evidence of her own dreams.
The attempted suicide was, as might have been expected, determined by two other motives besides the one she gave: it was
the fulfilment of a punishment (self-punishment), and the fulfilment of a wish. As the latter it meant the attainment of the very
wish which, when frustrated, had driven her into homosexuality—namely, the wish to have a child by her father, for
now she 'fell' through her father's fault.[1] The fact that at that
moment the lady had spoken in just the same terms as her father,
and had uttered the same prohibition, forms the connecting
link between this deep interpretation and the superficial one of
which the girl herself was conscious. From the point of view of
self-punishment the girl's action shows us that she had developed
in her unconscious strong death-wishes against one or other of
her parents—perhaps against her father, out of revenge for im-
peding her love, but more probably against her mother too,
when she was pregnant with the little brother. For analysis has
explained the enigma of suicide in the following way: probably
no one finds the mental energy required to kill himself unless, in
the first place, in doing so he is at the same time killing an
object with whom he has identified himself, and, in the second
place, is turning against himself a death-wish which had been
directed against someone else. Nor need the regular discovery
of these unconscious death-wishes in those who have attempted
suicide surprise us (any more than it ought to make us think
that it confirms our deductions), since the unconscious of all

[1] [In the text there is a play on the word *niederkommen*, which means
both 'to fall' and 'to be delivered of a child'. There is in English, too, a
colloquial use of the verb 'to fall', meaning pregnancy or childbirth.]—
That the various methods of suicide can represent sexual wish-fulfilments
has long been known to all analysts. (To poison oneself = to become
pregnant; to drown = to bear a child; to throw oneself from a height =
to be delivered of a child.)

human beings is full enough of such death-wishes, even against those they love.[1] Since the girl identified herself with her mother, who should have died at the birth of the child denied to herself, this punishment-fulfilment itself was once again a wish-fulfilment. Finally, the discovery that several quite different motives, all of great strength, must have co-operated to make such a deed possible is only in accordance with what we should expect.

In the girl's account of her conscious motives the father did not figure at all; there was not even any mention of fear of his anger. In the motives laid bare by the analysis, on the other hand, he played the principal part. Her relation to her father had the same decisive importance for the course and outcome of the analytic treatment, or rather, analytic exploration. Behind her pretended consideration for her parents, for whose sake she had been willing to make the attempt to be transformed, lay concealed her attitude of defiance and revenge against her father which held her fast to her homosexuality. Secure under this cover, the resistance set a considerable region free to analytic investigation. The analysis went forward almost without any signs of resistance, the patient participating actively with her intellect, though absolutely tranquil emotionally. Once when I expounded to her a specially important part of the theory, one touching her nearly, she replied in an inimitable tone, 'How very interesting', as though she were a *grande dame* being taken over a museum and glancing through her lorgnon at objects to which she was completely indifferent. The impression one had of her analysis was not unlike that of a hypnotic treatment, where the resistance has in the same way withdrawn to a certain boundary line, beyond which it proves to be unconquerable. The resistance very often pursues similar tactics—Russian tactics, as they might be called—in cases of obsessional neurosis. For a time, consequently, these cases yield the clearest results and permit a deep insight into the causation of the symptoms. But presently one begins to wonder how it is that such marked progress in analytic understanding can be unaccompanied by even the slightest change in the patient's compulsions and inhibitions, until at last one perceives that everything that has been accomplished is subject to a mental reservation of doubt, and that behind this protective barrier the

[1] Cf. 'Thoughts for the Times on War and Death' (1915*b*).

neurosis can feel secure. 'It would be all very fine', thinks the patient, often quite consciously, 'if I were obliged to believe what the man says, but there is no question of that, and so long as this is so I need change nothing.' Then, when one comes to close quarters with the motives for this doubt, the fight with the resistances breaks out in earnest.

In the case of our patient, it was not doubt but the affective factor of revenge against her father that made her cool reserve possible, that divided the analysis into two distinct phases, and rendered the results of the first phase so complete and perspicuous. It seemed, further, as though nothing resembling a transference to the physician had been effected. That, however, is of course absurd, or, at least, is a loose way of expressing things. For some kind of relation to the analyst must come into being, and this relation is almost always transferred from an infantile one. In reality she transferred to me the sweeping repudiation of men which had dominated her ever since the disappointment she had suffered from her father. Bitterness against men is as a rule easy to gratify upon the physician; it need not evoke any violent emotional manifestations, it simply expresses itself by rendering futile all his endeavours and by clinging to the illness. I know from experience how difficult it is to make a patient understand just precisely this mute kind of symptomatic behaviour and to make him aware of this latent, and often exceedingly strong, hostility without endangering the treatment. As soon, therefore, as I recognized the girl's attitude to her father, I broke off the treatment and advised her parents that if they set store by the therapeutic procedure it should be continued by a woman doctor. The girl had in the meanwhile promised her father that at any rate she would give up seeing the 'lady', and I do not know whether my advice, the reasons for which are obvious, will be followed.

There was a single piece of material in the course of this analysis which I could regard as a positive transference, as a greatly weakened revival of the girl's original passionate love for her father. Even this manifestation was not quite free from other motives, but I mention it because it brings up, in another direction, an interesting problem of analytic technique. At a certain period, not long after the treatment had begun, the girl brought a series of dreams which, distorted according to rule and couched in the usual dream-language, could nevertheless be easily translated with certainty. Their content, when interpreted, was, however, remarkable. They anticipated the cure of the inversion through the treatment, expressed her joy over the prospects in life that would then be opened before her, confessed her longing for a man's love and for children, and so might have been welcomed as a gratifying preparation for the desired change. The contradiction between them and the girl's utterances in waking life at the time was very great. She did not conceal from me that she meant to marry, but only in order to escape from her father's tyranny and to follow her true inclinations undisturbed. As for the husband, she remarked rather contemptuously, she would easily deal with him, and besides, one could have sexual relations with a man and a woman at one and the same time, as the example of the adored lady showed. Warned through some slight impression or other, I told her one day that I did not believe these dreams, that I regarded them as false or hypocritical, and that she intended to deceive me just as she habitually deceived her father.[1] I was right; after I had made this clear, this kind of dream ceased. But I still believe that, beside the intention to mislead me, the dreams partly expressed the wish to win my favour; they were also an attempt to gain my interest and my good opinion—perhaps in order to disappoint me all the more thoroughly later on.

I can imagine that to point out the existence of lying dreams of this kind, 'obliging' dreams, will arouse a positive storm of helpless indignation in some readers who call themselves analysts. 'What!' they will exclaim, 'the unconscious, the real centre of our mental life, the part of us that is so much nearer the divine than our poor consciousness—it too can lie! Then how can we still build on the interpretations of analysis and the accuracy of our findings?' To which one must reply that the recognition of these lying dreams does not constitute any shattering novelty. I know, indeed, that the craving of mankind for mysticism is ineradicable, and that it makes ceaseless efforts to win back for mysticism the territory it has been deprived of by *The Interpretation of Dreams*, but surely in the case under consideration everything is simple enough. A dream is not the 'unconscious'; it is the form into which a thought left over from preconscious, or even from conscious, waking life, can, thanks

[1] [For other references to 'hypocritical dreams' see *The Interpretation of Dreams, Standard Ed.*, 4, 134 n. and 5, 471 ff.]

to the favouring state of sleep, be recast.[1] In the state of sleep
this thought has been reinforced by unconscious wishful impulses and has thus experienced distortion through the dream-
work, which is determined by the mechanisms prevailing in the
unconscious. With our dreamer, the intention to mislead me,
just as she did her father, certainly emanated from the preconscious, and may indeed have been conscious; it could come
to expression by entering into connection with the unconscious
wishful impulse to please her father (or father-substitute), and
in this way it created a lying dream. The two intentions, to
betray and to please her father, originated in the same complex; the former resulted from the repression of the latter, and
the later one was brought back by the dream-work to the earlier
one. There can therefore be no question of any devaluation of
the unconscious, nor of a shattering of our confidence in the
results of analysis.

I cannot neglect this opportunity of expressing for once my
astonishment that human beings can go through such great and
important moments of their erotic life without noticing them
much, sometimes even, indeed, without having the faintest
suspicion of their existence, or else, having become aware of
those moments, deceive themselves so thoroughly in their judgement of them. This happens not only under neurotic conditions,
where we are familiar with the phenomenon, but seems also to
be common enough in ordinary life. In the present case, for
example, a girl develops a sentimental adoration for women,
which her parents at first find merely vexatious and hardly take
seriously; she herself knows quite well that she is very much
occupied with these relationships, but still she experiences few
of the sensations of intense love until a particular frustration is
followed by a quite excessive reaction, which shows everyone
concerned that they have to do with a consuming passion of
elemental strength. Nor had the girl ever perceived anything of
the state of affairs which was a necessary preliminary to the outbreak of this mental storm. In other cases, too, we come across
girls or women in a state of severe depression, who on being
asked for a possible cause of their condition tell us that they
have, it is true, had a slight feeling for a certain person, but that
it was nothing deep and that they soon got over it when they
had to give it up. And yet it was this renunciation, apparently

[1] [Cf. below, p. 229, and Section V of Freud, 1923c.]

so easily borne, that became the cause of serious mental disturbance. Again, we come across men who have passed through casual love-affairs and realize only from the subsequent effects that they had been passionately in love with the person whom they had apparently regarded lightly. One is also amazed at the unexpected results that may follow an artificial abortion, the killing of an unborn child, which had been decided upon without remorse and without hesitation. It must be admitted that poets are right in liking to portray people who are in love without knowing it, or uncertain whether they do love, or who think that they hate when in reality they love. It would seem that the information received by our consciousness about our erotic life is especially liable to be incomplete, full of gaps, or falsified. Needless to say, in this discussion I have not omitted to allow for the part played by subsequent forgetting.

IV

I now come back, after this digression, to the consideration of my patient's case. We have made a survey of the forces which led the girl's libido from the normal Oedipus attitude into that of homosexuality, and of the psychical paths traversed by it in the process. Most important in this respect was the impression made by the birth of her little brother, and we might from this be inclined to classify the case as one of late-acquired inversion.

But at this point we become aware of a state of things which also confronts us in many other instances in which light has been thrown by psycho-analysis on a mental process. So long as we trace the development from its final outcome backwards, the chain of events appears continuous, and we feel we have gained an insight which is completely satisfactory or even exhaustive. But if we proceed the reverse way, if we start from the premises inferred from the analysis and try to follow these up to the final result, then we no longer get the impression of an inevitable sequence of events which could not have been otherwise determined. We notice at once that there might have been another result, and that we might have been just as well able to understand and explain the latter. The synthesis is thus not so satisfactory as the analysis; in other words, from a knowledge of the premises we could not have foretold the nature of the result.

It is very easy to account for this disturbing state of affairs.

Even supposing that we have a complete knowledge of the aetiological factors that decide a given result, nevertheless what we know about them is only their quality, and not their relative strength. Some of them are suppressed by others because they are too weak, and they therefore do not affect the final result. But we never know beforehand which of the determining factors will prove the weaker or the stronger. We only say at the end that those which succeeded must have been the stronger. Hence the chain of causation can always be recognized with certainty if we follow the line of analysis, whereas to predict it along the line of synthesis is impossible.

We do not, therefore, mean to maintain that every girl who experiences a disappointment such as this of the longing for love that springs from the Oedipus attitude at puberty will necessarily on that account fall a victim to homosexuality. On the contrary, other kinds of reaction to this trauma are undoubtedly commoner. If so, however, there must have been present in this girl special factors that turned the scale, factors outside the trauma, probably of an internal nature. Nor is there any difficulty in pointing them out.

It is well known that even in a normal person it takes a certain time before the decision in regard to the sex of the love-object is finally made. Homosexual enthusiasms, exaggeratedly strong friendships tinged with sensuality, are common enough in both sexes during the first years after puberty. This was also so with our patient, but in her these tendencies undoubtedly showed themselves to be stronger, and lasted longer, than with others. In addition, these presages of later homosexuality had always occupied her *conscious* life, while the attitude arising from the Oedipus complex had remained *unconscious* and had appeared only in such signs as her tender behaviour to the little boy. As a school-girl she had been for a long time in love with a strict and unapproachable mistress, obviously a substitute mother. She had taken a specially lively interest in a number of young mothers long before her brother's birth and therefore all the more certainly long before the first reprimand from her father. From very early years, therefore, her libido had flowed in two currents, the one on the surface being one that we may unhesitatingly designate as homosexual. This latter was probably a direct and unchanged continuation of an infantile fixation on her mother. Possibly the analysis described here actually revealed nothing more than the process by which, on an appropriate occasion, the deeper heterosexual current of libido, too, was deflected into the manifest homosexual one.

The analysis showed, further, that the girl had brought along with her from her childhood a strongly marked 'masculinity complex'. A spirited girl, always ready for romping and fighting, she was not at all prepared to be second to her slightly older brother; after inspecting his genital organs [p. 155] she had developed a pronounced envy for the penis, and the thoughts derived from this envy still continued to fill her mind. She was in fact a feminist; she felt it to be unjust that girls should not enjoy the same freedom as boys, and rebelled against the lot of woman in general. At the time of the analysis the idea of pregnancy and child-birth was disagreeable to her, partly, I surmise, on account of the bodily disfigurement connected with them. Her girlish narcissism had fallen back on this defence,[1] and ceased to express itself as pride in her good looks. Various clues indicated that she must formerly have had strong exhibitionist and scopophilic tendencies. Anyone who is anxious that the claims of acquired as opposed to hereditary factors should not be under-estimated in aetiology will call attention to the fact that the girl's behaviour, as described above, was exactly what would follow from the combined effect in a person with a strong mother-fixation of the two influences of her mother's neglect and her comparison of her genital organs with her brother's. It is possible here to attribute to the impress of the operation of external influence in early life something which one would have liked to regard as a constitutional peculiarity. On the other hand, a part even of this acquired disposition (if it *was* really acquired) has to be ascribed to inborn constitution. So we see in practice a continual mingling and blending of what in theory we should try to separate into a pair of opposites—namely, inherited and acquired characters.

If the analysis had come to an earlier, still more premature end, it might have led to the view that this was a case of late-acquired homosexuality, but as it is, a consideration of the material impels us to conclude that it is rather a case of congenital homosexuality which, as usual, became fixed and

---

[1] Cf. Kriemhilde's admission in the *Nibelungenlied* [I. 15. She declared to her mother that she would never allow a man to love her since that would mean the loss of her beauty.]

unmistakably manifest only in the period following puberty. Each of these classifications does justice only to one part of the state of affairs ascertainable by observation, but neglects the other. It would be best not to attach too much value to this way of stating the problem.

The literature of homosexuality usually fails to distinguish clearly enough between the questions of the choice of object on the one hand, and of the sexual characteristics and sexual attitude of the subject on the other, as though the answer to the former necessarily involved the answers to the latter. Experience, however, proves the contrary: a man with predominantly male characteristics and also masculine in his erotic life may still be inverted in respect to his object, loving only men instead of women. A man in whose character feminine attributes obviously predominate, who may, indeed, behave in love like a woman, might be expected, from this feminine attitude, to choose a man for his love-object; but he may nevertheless be heterosexual, and show no more inversion in respect to his object than an average normal man. The same is true of women; here also mental sexual character and object-choice do not necessarily coincide. The mystery of homosexuality is therefore by no means so simple as it is commonly depicted in popular expositions—'a feminine mind, bound therefore to love a man, but unhappily attached to a masculine body; a masculine mind, irresistibly attracted by women, but, alas! imprisoned in a feminine body'. It is instead a question of three sets of characteristics, namely—

Physical sexual characters
(physical hermaphroditism)

Mental sexual characters
(masculine or feminine attitude)

Kind of object-choice

which, up to a certain point, vary independently of one another, and are met with in different individuals in manifold permutations. Tendentious literature has obscured our view of this interrelationship by putting into the foreground, for practical reasons, the third feature (the kind of object-choice), which is the only one that strikes the layman, and in addition by exaggerating the closeness of the association between this and the first feature. Moreover, it blocks the way to a deeper insight into all that is uniformly designated as homosexuality, by rejecting two fundamental facts which have been revealed by psycho-analytic investigation. The first of these is that homosexual men have experienced a specially strong fixation on their mother; the second, that, in addition to their manifest heterosexuality, a very considerable measure of latent or unconscious homosexuality can be detected in all normal people. If these findings are taken into account, then, clearly, the supposition that nature in a freakish mood created a 'third sex' falls to the ground.

It is not for psycho-analysis to solve the problem of homo-sexuality. It must rest content with disclosing the psychical mechanisms that resulted in determining the object-choice, and with tracing back the paths from them to the instinctual dis-positions. There its work ends, and it leaves the rest to bio-logical research, which has recently brought to light, through Steinach's [1] experiments, such very important results concerning the influence exerted by the first set of characteristics mentioned above upon the second and third. Psycho-analysis has a com-mon basis with biology, in that it presupposes an original bisexuality in human beings (as in animals). But psycho-analysis cannot elucidate the intrinsic nature of what in conventional or in biological phraseology is termed 'masculine' and 'feminine': it simply takes over the two concepts and makes them the foun-dation of its work. When we attempt to reduce them further, we find masculinity vanishing into activity and femininity into passivity,[2] and that does not tell us enough. I have already [p. 150 f.] tried to explain how far we may reasonably expect, or how far experience has already proved, that the work of elucidation which is part of the task of analysis furnishes us with the means of effecting a modification of inversion. When one compares the extent to which we can influence it with the remarkable transformations that Steinach has effected in some cases by his operations, it does not make a very imposing impression. But it would be premature, or a harmful exaggera-tion, if at this stage we were to indulge in hopes of a 'therapy' of inversion that could be generally applied. The cases of male homosexuality in which Steinach has been successful fulfilled

[1] Cf. Lipschütz (1919).

[2] [See also the discussion of these two concepts in Freud's *Three Essays* (1905d), *Standard Ed.*, 7, 219 n.]

the condition, which is not always present, of a very patent physical 'hermaphroditism'. Any analogous treatment of female homosexuality is at present quite obscure. If it were to consist in removing what are probably hermaphroditic ovaries, and in grafting others, which are hoped to be of a single sex, there would be little prospect of its being applied in practice. A woman who has felt herself to be a man, and has loved in masculine fashion, will hardly let herself be forced into playing the part of a woman, when she must pay for this transformation, which is not in every way advantageous, by renouncing all hope of motherhood.[1]

[1] [Cf. the discussion of homosexuality in *Three Essays, Standard Ed.*, 7, 136–48. Freud takes up the subject again in Section C of his paper on jealousy, paranoia and homosexuality (1922b), p. 230 below.]

PSYCHO-ANALYSIS AND TELEPATHY
(1941 [1921])

EDITOR'S NOTE

PSYCHOANALYSE UND TELEPATHIE

(a) GERMAN EDITION:
(1921   August. Date of MS.)
1941   *G.W.*, **17,** 27–44.

(b) ENGLISH TRANSLATION:
'Psychoanalysis and Telepathy'
1953   In *Psychoanalysis and the Occult*, New York, International
Universities Press, 56–68. (Tr. George Devereux.)

The present translation is a new one by James Strachey.

The MS. bears at its beginning the date '2 Aug. 21' and
at its end 'Gastein, 6 Aug. 21'. The original bears no title, and
the one here adopted is that selected by the editors of the
Gesammelte Werke.

A prefatory note to the German edition states that the paper
'was written for the meeting of the Central Executive of the
International Psycho-Analytical Association held in the Harz
mountains at the beginning of September, 1921'. Dr. Ernest
Jones, who was at that time President of the Central Executive,
tells us, however, that no meeting of that body took place in the
Harz mountains at the date in question, though there was a
gathering of Freud's closest followers: Abraham, Eitingon,
Ferenczi, Rank and Sachs, besides Dr. Jones himself. It was to
this unofficial group that the paper seems to have been read.

Freud had intended the paper to give reports of three cases,
but when he came to prepare the MS. at Gastein he found that
he had left the material for the third case behind in Vienna,
and he was obliged to replace it by some material of a rather
different character. The original 'third case' has, however,
survived as a separate MS. This is headed: '*Postscript.* Here is
the report, omitted owing to resistance, on a case of thought-
transference during analytic practice.' The case is in fact that
relating to Dr. Forsyth and the Forsyte Saga, which is the last
of those recorded in Lecture XXX of the *New Introductory*

Lectures. The two versions of the case agree very closely, with scarcely more than verbal differences; and it has therefore not seemed necessary to include it here. Any substantial points of difference will be found recorded in *Standard Ed.*, **22**.

This was the first of Freud's papers on telepathy, and it was never published in his lifetime, though the greater part of the material in it was included in various forms in his later published papers on the subject. His next paper to be written, and the first to be published, is the one immediately following this in the present volume, on the somewhat different topic of 'Dreams and Telepathy' (1922*a*). Soon after this he wrote a short note on 'The Occult Significance of Dreams' (1925*i*). This was apparently designed for inclusion in *The Interpretation of Dreams* and it was actually first printed as part of an appendix in Volume III of the *Gesammelte Schriften* edition of that work, but was not included in any of its later editions. Finally, there was the lecture already referred to on 'Dreams and Occultism' in the *New Introductory Lectures* (1933*a*). It is worth remarking that in this last of his writings on the subject he no longer felt the doubts about the propriety of discussing it which are so evident in the present paper; and, indeed, towards the end of the lecture, he specifically withdraws the fears here expressed that the scientific outlook of psycho-analysts might possibly be endangered if the truth of thought-transference were to be established.

PSYCHO-ANALYSIS AND
TELEPATHY

INTRODUCTORY

WE are not destined, so it seems, to devote ourselves quietly to the extension of our science. Scarcely have we triumphantly repulsed two attacks—one of which sought to deny once more what we had brought to light and only offered us in exchange the theme of disavowal, while the other tried to persuade us that we had mistaken the nature of what we had found and might with advantage take something else in its place[1]— scarcely, then, do we feel ourselves safe from these enemies, when another peril has arisen. And this time it is something tremendous, something elemental, which threatens not us alone but our enemies, perhaps, still more.

It no longer seems possible to keep away from the study of what are known as 'occult' phenomena—of facts, that is, that profess to speak in favour of the real existence of psychical forces other than the human and animal minds with which we are familiar, or that seem to reveal the possession by those minds of faculties hitherto unrecognized. The impetus towards such an investigation seems irresistibly strong. During this last brief vacation I have three times had occasion to refuse to associate myself with newly founded periodicals concerned with these studies. Nor is there much doubt as to the origin of this trend. It is a part expression of the loss of value by which everything has been affected since the world catastrophe of the Great War, a part of the tentative approach to the great revolution towards which we are heading and of whose extent we can form no estimate; but no doubt it is also an attempt at compensation, at making up in another, a supermundane, sphere for the attractions which have been lost by life on this earth. Some, indeed, of the proceedings of the exact sciences themselves may have contributed to this development. The discovery of radium has confused no less than it has advanced the possibilities of explaining the physical world; and the knowledge

[1] [The references are to Adler and Jung.]

177

that has been so very recently acquired of what is called the theory of relativity has had the effect upon many of those who admire without comprehending it of diminishing their belief in the objective trustworthiness of science. You will remember that not long ago Einstein himself took occasion to protest against such misunderstanding.

It does not follow as a matter of course that an intensified interest in occultism must involve a danger to psycho-analysis. We should, on the contrary, be prepared to find reciprocal sympathy between them. They have both experienced the same contemptuous and arrogant treatment by official science. To this day psycho-analysis is regarded as savouring of mysticism, and its unconscious is looked upon as one of the things between heaven and earth which philosophy refuses to dream of. The numerous suggestions made to us by occultists that we should co-operate with them show that they would like to treat us as half belonging to them and that they count on our support against the pressure of exact authority. Nor, on the other hand, has psycho-analysis any interest in going out of its way to defend that authority, for it itself stands in opposition to everything that is conventionally restricted, well-established and generally accepted. Not for the first time would it be offering its help to the obscure but indestructible surmises of the common people against the obscurantism of educated opinion. Alliance and co-operation between analysts and occultists might thus appear both plausible and promising.

But if we look closer, difficulties begin to emerge. The immense majority of occultists are not driven by a desire for knowledge or by a sense of shame that science has so long refused to take cognizance of what are indisputable problems or by a desire to conquer this new sphere of phenomena. They are, on the contrary, convinced believers who are looking for confirmation and for something that will justify them in openly confessing their faith. But the faith which they first adopt themselves and then seek to impose on other people is either the old religious faith which has been pushed into the background by science in the course of human development, or another one even closer to the superseded convictions of primitive peoples. Analysts, on the other hand, cannot repudiate their descent from exact science and their community with its representatives. Moved by an extreme distrust of the power of human wishes and of the temptations of the pleasure principle, they are ready, for the sake of attaining some fragment of objective certainty, to sacrifice everything—the dazzling brilliance of a flawless theory, the exalted consciousness of having achieved a comprehensive view of the universe, and the mental calm brought about by the possession of extensive grounds for expedient and ethical action. In place of all these, they are content with fragmentary pieces of knowledge and with basic hypotheses lacking preciseness and ever open to revision. Instead of waiting for the moment when they will be able to escape from the constraint of the familiar laws of physics and chemistry, they hope for the emergence of more extensive and deeper-reaching natural laws, to which they are ready to submit. Analysts are at bottom incorrigible mechanists and materialists, even though they seek to avoid robbing the mind and spirit of their still unrecognized characteristics. So, too, they embark on the investigation of occult phenomena only because they expect in that way finally to exclude the wishes of mankind from material reality.

In view of this difference between their mental attitudes co-operation between analysts and occultists offers small prospect of gain. The analyst has his own province of work, which he must not abandon: the unconscious element of mental life. If in the course of his work he were to be on the watch for occult phenomena, he would be in danger of overlooking everything that more nearly concerned him. He would be surrendering the impartiality, the lack of prejudices and prepossessions, which have formed an essential part of his analytic armour and equipment. If occult phenomena force themselves on him in the same way in which others do, he will evade them no more than he evades the others. This would appear to be the only plan of behaviour consistent with the activity of an analyst.

By self-discipline the analyst can defend himself against one danger—the subjective one of allowing his interest to be drawn away on to occult phenomena. As regards the *objective* danger, the situation is different. There is little doubt that if attention is directed to occult phenomena the outcome will very soon be that the occurrence of a number of them will be confirmed; and it will probably be a very long time before an acceptable theory covering these new facts can be arrived at. But the eagerly attentive onlookers will not wait so long. At the very first confirmation the occultists will proclaim the triumph of their views. They will carry over an acceptance of one phenomenon on to all the rest and will extend belief in the phenomena to belief in whatever explanations are easiest and most to their taste. They will be ready to employ the methods of scientific enquiry only as a ladder to raise them over the head of science. Heaven help us if they climb to such a height! There will be no scepticism from the surrounding spectators to make them hesitate, there will be no popular outcry to bring them to a halt. They will be hailed as liberators from the burden of intellectual bondage, they will be joyfully acclaimed by all the credulity lying ready to hand since the infancy of the human race and the childhood of the individual. There may follow a fearful collapse of critical thought, of determinist standards and of mechanistic science. Will it be possible for scientific method, by a ruthless insistence on the magnitude of the forces, the masses and qualities of the material concerned, to prevent this collapse?

It is a vain hope to suppose that analytic work, precisely because it relates to the mysterious unconscious, will be able to escape such a collapse in values as this. If spiritual beings who are the intimate friends of human enquirers can supply ultimate explanations of everything, no interest can be left over for the laborious approaches to unknown mental forces made by analytic research. So, too, the methods of analytic technique will be abandoned if there is a hope of getting into direct touch with the operative spirits by means of occult procedures, just as habits of patient humdrum work are abandoned if there is a hope of growing rich at a single blow by means of a successful speculation. We have heard during the war of people who stood half-way between two hostile nations, belonging to one by birth and to the other by choice and domicile; it was their fate to be treated as enemies first by one side and then, if they were lucky enough to escape, by the other. Such might equally be the fate of psycho-analysis. However, one must put up with one's fate whatever it may be; and psycho-analysis will somehow or other come to terms with hers.

Let us return to the present situation, to our immediate task. In the course of the last few years I have made a few observations which I shall not hold back—at all events from the circle that is closest to me. A dislike of falling in with what is to-day a prevailing current, a dread of distracting interest from psycho-analysis and the total absence of any veil of discretion over what I have to say—all these combine as motives for withholding my remarks from a wider public. My material can lay claim to two advantages which are rarely present. In the first place it is exempt from the uncertainties and doubts to which most of the observations of the occultists are prone; and in the second place it only develops its convincing force after it has been worked over analytically. It consists, I should mention, of only two cases of a similar character; a third case, of another kind and open to a different assessment, is only added by way of appendix. The first two cases, which I shall now report at length, are concerned with events of the same sort—namely, with prophecies made by professional fortune-tellers which did *not* come true. In spite of this, these prophecies made an extraordinary impression on the people to whom they were announced, so that their relation to the future cannot be their essential point. Anything that may contribute to their explanation, as well as anything that throws doubt on their evidential force, will be extremely welcome to me. My personal attitude to the material remains unenthusiastic and ambivalent.

I

A few years before the war, a young man from Germany came to me to be analysed.[1] He complained of being unable to work, of having forgotten his past life and of having lost all interest. He was a student of philosophy at Munich and was preparing for his final examination. Incidentally, he was a highly educated, rather sly young man, rascally in a childish way, and the son of a financier, who, as emerged later, had successfully remoulded a colossal amount of anal erotism. When I asked him whether there was really nothing he could remember about his life or his sphere of interest, he recalled the plot of a novel he had sketched out, which was laid in Egypt during the reign of Amenophis IV and in which an important part was played by a particular ring. We took this novel as a starting-point; the ring turned out to be a symbol of marriage, and from there we succeeded in reviving all his

[1] [This case is reported rather more briefly in Lecture XXX of Freud's *New Introductory Lectures* (1933a).]

memories and interests. We found that his break-down had
been the result of a great act of mental self-discipline on his
part. He had an only sister a few years his junior, to whom he
was wholeheartedly and quite undisguisedly devoted. 'Why is
it we can't get married?' they had often asked each other. But
their affection had never gone beyond the point permissible
between brothers and sisters.

A young engineer had fallen in love with the sister. His love
was reciprocated by her but did not meet with the approval of
her strict parents. In their trouble the two young lovers turned
to the brother for help. He gave their cause his support, made
it possible for them to correspond, arranged for them to meet
while he was at home on vacation, and eventually persuaded the
parents to give their consent to an engagement and marriage.
During the time of the engagement there was a highly suspicious
occurrence. The brother took his future brother-in-law to
climb the Zugspitze [1] and himself acted as guide. They lost
their way on the mountain, ran into trouble and only with
difficulty avoided a fall. The patient offered little objection to
my interpretation of this adventure as an attempted murder
and suicide. It was a few months after his sister's marriage that
the young man started analysis.

After some six or nine months he had completely regained his
ability to work, and broke off the analysis in order to take his
examination and write his dissertation. A year or more later he
returned—now a Ph.D.—to resume his analysis, because, as he
said, psycho-analysis had an interest for him as a philosopher
which extended beyond therapeutic success. I know it was in
October that he started again, and it was a few weeks later
that, in some connection or other, he told me the following
story.

There lived in Munich a fortune-teller who enjoyed a great
reputation. The Bavarian princes used to visit her when they
had any undertaking in mind. All that she required was to be
supplied with a date. (I omitted to enquire whether this had
to include the date of the *year*.) It was understood that the date
was that of the birth of some particular person, but she did not
ask whose. Having been given this date, she would consult her
astrological books, make long calculations and finally utter a
prophecy about the person concerned. In the previous March

[1] [The highest peak in the Bavarian Alps.]

my patient resolved to visit the fortune-teller. He presented her with the date of his brother-in-law's birth, without, of course, mentioning his name or betraying the fact that he had him in mind. The oracle pronounced as follows: 'The person in question will die next July or August of crayfish- or oyster-poisoning.' After telling me this, my patient exclaimed: 'It was marvellous!'

I could not understand this and contradicted him vigorously: 'What do you see in it that's marvellous? You've been working with me now for several weeks, and if your brother-in-law had really died you would have told me long ago. So he must be alive. The prophecy was made in March and was to be fulfilled during the height of the summer. It's November now, so it has *not* been fulfilled. What do you find so wonderful in that?'

'No doubt it has not come true,' he replied. 'But the remarkable thing about it is this. My brother-in-law is passionately fond of crayfish and oysters and so on, and *last* August he really did have an attack of crayfish-poisoning [1] and almost died of it.' The matter was not further discussed.

Let us now consider this case.

I believe in the narrator's truthfulness. He is entirely trustworthy and is at present lecturer in philosophy at K——. I can think of no motive which could have induced him to bamboozle me. The story was an incidental one and served no ulterior purpose; nothing further emerged from it and no conclusions were drawn from it. He had no intention of persuading me of the existence of occult mental phenomena; and indeed I had an impression that he was not at all clear about the significance of his experience. I myself was so much struck—to tell the truth, so disagreeably affected—that I omitted to make any analytic use of his tale.

And the observation seems to me equally unobjectionable from another point of view. It is certain that the fortune-teller was not acquainted with the man who put the question. But consider what a degree of intimacy with an acquaintance would be necessary before one could recognize the date of his brother-in-law's birthday. On the other hand, you will no doubt all agree with me in offering the most obstinate resistance to the possibility that so detailed an event as falling ill of crayfish-poisoning could be inferred from the date of the subject's birth by the help of any tables or formulae whatever. Do not

[1] ['Oyster-poisoning' in Freud, 1933a.]

forget how many people are born on the same day. Is it credible that the similarity of the futures of people born on the same day can be carried down to such details as this? I therefore venture to exclude the astrological calculations entirely from the discussion; I believe the fortune-teller might have adopted some other procedure without affecting the outcome of the interrogation. Accordingly, we can also, so it seems to me, leave the fortune-teller (or, as we may say straight out, the 'medium') quite out of account as a possible source of deception.

If you grant the genuineness and truth of this observation, its explanation will be near. And we at once find—and this is the case with the majority of these phenomena—that its explanation on an occult basis is remarkably adequate and covers what has to be explained completely, except that it is so unsatisfying in itself. It is impossible that the knowledge that this man—born on the day in question—had had an attack of crayfish-poisoning could have been present in the fortune-teller's mind; nor can she have arrived at that knowledge from her tables and calculations. It was, however, present in the mind of her questioner. The event becomes completely explicable if we are ready to assume that the knowledge was transferred from him to the supposed prophetess—by some unknown method which excluded the means of communication familiar to us. That is to say, we must draw the inference that there is such a thing as thought-transference. The fortune-teller's astrological activities would in that case have performed the function of diverting her own psychical forces and occupying them in a harmless way, so that she could become receptive and accessible to the effects upon her of her client's thoughts—so that she could become a true 'medium'. We have found similar distracting contrivances employed (for instance, in the case of jokes) where there is a question of securing a more automatic discharge for some mental process.[1]

The application of analysis to this case does more than this, however; it further increases its significance. It teaches us that what has been communicated by this means of induction from one person to another is not merely a chance piece of indifferent knowledge. It shows that an extraordinarily powerful wish harboured by one person and standing in a special relation to his consciousness has succeeded, with the help of a second per-

[1] [See the first footnote on p. 126 above.]

son, in finding conscious expression in a slightly disguised form
—just as the invisible end of the spectrum reveals itself to the
senses on a light-sensitive plate as a coloured extension. It
seems possible to reconstruct the young man's train of thought
after the illness and recovery of the brother-in-law who was
his hated rival: 'Well, he's got over it this time; but he won't
give up his dangerous taste on that account, and let's hope
that next time it will be the end of him.' It was this 'let's hope'
that was changed into the prophecy. I could quote a parallel to
this from a dream (dreamt by another person), in which a
prophecy was part of the subject-matter. The analysis of the
dream showed that the content of the prophecy coincided with
the fulfilment of a wish.[1]

I cannot simplify my statement by describing my patient's
death-wish against his brother-in-law as an unconscious,
repressed one. For it had been made conscious during the
treatment the year before and the consequences which had
followed from its repression had yielded to the treatment. But
it still persisted, and, though it was no longer pathogenic, it
was sufficiently intense. It might be described as a 'suppressed'
wish.

II

In the city of F—— a child grew up who was the eldest of a
family of five, all girls.[2] The youngest was ten years younger than
herself; she once dropped this child out of her arms when it was
a baby; later she called it 'her child'. Her mother was older
than her father and not an agreeable person. Her father—and
it was not in years only that he was the younger—saw a lot of
the little girls and impressed them by his many dexterities. Unfortunately he was not impressive in any other way: he was
incompetent at business and was unable to support the family
without help from relatives. The eldest girl became at an early
age the repository of all the worries that arose from his lack
of earning power.

[1] [This may possibly refer to the 'premonitory dream' noted by
Freud in 1899 but only published after his death (1941c). This dream
did not, however, contain a specific prophecy.]

[2] [This case is reported in less detail in Lecture XXX of Freud's *New
Introductory Lectures* (1933a), and more briefly still in the third section
of Freud, 1925i.]

Once she had left behind the rigid and passionate character
of her childhood, she grew up into a regular mirror of all the
virtues. Her high moral feelings were accompanied by a
narrowly limited intelligence. She became a teacher in an
elementary school and was much respected. The timid homage
paid to her by a young relation who was a music teacher left
her unmoved. No other man had hitherto attracted her notice.

One day a relative of her mother's appeared on the scene,
considerably older than she was, but still (for she was only
nineteen) a youngish man. He was a foreigner who lived in
Russia as the head of a large commercial undertaking and had
grown very rich. It took nothing less than a world war and the
overthrow of a great despotism to impoverish him. He fell in
love with his young and severe cousin and asked her to be his
wife. Her parents put no pressure on her, but she understood
their wishes. Behind all her moral ideals she felt the attraction of
the fulfilment of a wishful phantasy of helping her father and
rescuing him from his necessitous state. She calculated that her
cousin would give her father financial support so long as he
carried on his business and pension him when he finally gave it
up, and that he would provide her sisters with dowries and
trousseaux so that they could get married. And she fell in love
with him, married him soon afterwards and followed him to
Russia.

Except for a few occurrences which were not entirely under-
standable at first sight and whose significance only became
evident in retrospect, everything went very well in the marriage.
She grew into an affectionate wife, sexually satisfied, and a
providential support to her family. Only one thing was wanting:
she was childless. She was now 27 years old and in the eighth
year of her marriage. She lived in Germany, and after overcoming every kind of hesitation she went for a consultation to
a German gynaecologist. With the usual thoughtlessness of a
specialist, he assured her of recovery if she underwent a small
operation. She agreed, and on the eve of the operation discussed
the matter with her husband. It was the hour of twilight and
she was about to turn on the lights when her husband asked
her not to: he had something to say to her and he would prefer
to be in darkness. He told her to countermand the operation,
as the blame for their childlessness was his. During a medical
congress two years earlier he had learnt that certain illnesses

can deprive a man of the capacity to procreate children. An examination had shown that such was the case with him. After this revelation the operation was abandoned. She herself suffered from a temporary collapse, which she vainly sought to disguise. She had only been able to love him as a substitute father, and she had now learnt that he never could be a father. Three paths were open to her, all equally impassable: unfaithfulness, renunciation of her wish for a child, or separation from her husband. The last of them was excluded for the best practical reasons and the middle one for the strongest unconscious ones, which you can easily guess: her whole childhood had been dominated by the thrice disappointed wish to get a child from her father. There remained one other way out, which is what interests us in her case. She fell seriously ill of a neurosis. For a time she put up a defence against various temptations with the help of an anxiety neurosis, but later her symptoms changed into severe obsessional acts. She spent some time in institutions and eventually, after her illness had lasted for ten years, came to me. Her most striking symptom was that when she was in bed she used to fasten [*anstecken* = bring into contact] her sheets to the blankets with safety-pins. In this way she was revealing the secret of her husband's contagion [*Ansteckung*], to which her childlessness was due.

On one occasion, when she was perhaps 40 years old,[1] the patient told me an episode dating back to the time when her depression was beginning, before the outbreak of her obsessional neurosis. To divert her mind, her husband had taken her with him on a business trip to Paris. The couple were sitting with a business friend of her husband's in the hall of their hotel when they became aware of some kind of stir and movement. She asked one of the hotel servants what was happening and was told that Monsieur le Professeur had arrived for consultations in his little room near the hotel entrance. Monsieur le Professeur, it appeared, was a famous fortune-teller; he asked no questions, but got his clients to press down a hand into a dish full of sand and foretold the future by studying the imprint. My patient declared that she would go in and have her fortune told. Her husband dissuaded her, saying it was nonsense. But after he had gone off with his business friend she took off her wedding-ring and slipped into the fortune-teller's cabinet. He

[1] [Forty-three, according to the other two accounts.]

made a long study of the imprint of her hand and then spoke as
follows: 'In the near future you will have to go through some
severe struggles, but all will turn out well. You will get married
and have two children by the time you are 32.' In telling this
story she gave every sign of being greatly impressed by it without understanding it. My comment that it was nevertheless
unfortunate that the date laid down by the prophecy had
already gone by some eight years made no impression on her.
I reflected that perhaps she was admiring the confident boldness
of the prophecy—like the faithful disciple of the long-sighted
Rabbi.[1]

Unluckily my memory, which is usually so trustworthy, is not
certain whether the first part of the prophecy ran: 'All will turn
out well. You will get married.' Or whether it was: 'You will
become happy.' My attention was focused too completely on
my sharp impression of the final phrase with its striking details.
But actually the first remarks, about struggles that will have a
happy ending, are among the vague expressions that figure in
all prophecies—even in those that can be purchased ready-
made. The contrast afforded by the two numbers specified in
the final phrase is all the more remarkable. Nevertheless, it
would certainly have been of interest to know whether the
Professor really spoke of her *marriage*. It is true that she had
taken off her wedding-ring and, at the age of 27, had looked
very youthful and might easily have been taken for an unmarried girl. But, on the other hand, it would not have needed any
great refinement of observation to discover the trace of the ring
on her finger.

Let us restrict ourselves to the problem contained in the last
phrase, which promised her two children at the age of 32.
These details seem quite arbitrary and inexplicable. Even the
most credulous person would scarcely undertake to deduce
them from an interpretation of the lines on a hand. They would
have received an indisputable justification if the future had
confirmed them. But this was not the case. She was now forty
years old and had no children. What, then, were the source and
meaning of these numbers? The patient herself had no notion.
The obvious thing would be to dismiss the question entirely
and to consign it to the rubbish heap among so many other

[1] [The story of the long-sighted Rabbi is told by Freud in the eighth
section of Chapter II of his book on jokes (1905c).]

meaningless and ostensibly occult messages. That would be delightful: the simplest solution and a greatly desirable relief. But unluckily I must add that it was possible—and precisely by the help of analysis—to find an explanation of the two numbers and one which, once again, was completely satisfactory and arose, almost as a matter of course, out of the actual situation.

For the two numbers fitted in perfectly with the life-story of —our patient's *mother*. She had not married till she was thirty and it was in her thirty-second year that (unlike most women and to make up, as it were, for her dilatoriness) she gave birth to two children. So it is easy to translate the prophecy: 'There's no need to worry about your present childlessness. There's nothing in that. You can still follow the example of your mother, who was not even married at your age and nevertheless had two children by the time she was thirty-two.' The prophecy promised her the fulfilment of the identification with her mother which had been the secret of her childhood, and it was spoken through the mouth of a fortune-teller who was in ignorance of all her personal affairs and was busy examining an imprint in the sand. And we may add, as the precondition of this wish-fulfilment (unconscious as it was in every sense): 'You will be set free from your useless husband by his death, or you will find strength to separate from him.' The first alternative would fit in better with the nature of an obsessional neurosis, while the second is suggested by the struggles which, according to the prophecy, she was successfully to overcome.

As you will observe, the part played by analytic interpretation is even more important in this example than in the last one. Analysis may actually be said to have created the occult fact. Accordingly, this example, too, would seem to offer positively conclusive evidence of its being possible to transfer an unconscious wish and the thoughts and knowledge relating to it. I can see only one way of evading the conclusiveness of this last case and you may be sure that I shall not conceal it. It is possible that in the course of the twelve or thirteen years [1] that elapsed between the prophecy and the account of it given during the treatment the patient may have formed a paramnesia: the Professor may have uttered some general and colourless consolation—which would be nothing to wonder at—and the patient may have gradually inserted the significant numbers

[1] [This number is given as 'sixteen' in the other accounts.]

out of her unconscious. If so, we should have avoided the
fact which threatened us with such momentous consequences.
We will gladly identify ourselves with the sceptics who will
only attach value to a report of this kind if it is made immediately after the event—and even then, perhaps, not without
hesitation. I remember that after I was appointed to a pro-
fessorship I had an audience with the Minister [of Education]
to express my thanks. As I was on my way home from this
audience I caught myself in the act of trying to falsify the words
that had passed between us and I was never able to recapture
correctly the actual conversation. I must leave it to you to
decide whether the explanation I have suggested is tenable. I
can neither prove nor disprove it. Thus, this second observation,
though in itself more impressive than the first, is not equally
free from doubt.

The two cases that I have reported to you are both concerned
with unfulfilled prophecies. Observations of this kind, in my
opinion, can provide the best material on the question of
thought-transference, and I should like to encourage you to
collect similar ones. I had also intended to bring you an
example based on material of another kind—a case in which a
patient of a special sort talked during one session of things
which touched in the most remarkable way on an experience
which I had had myself immediately before.[1] But I can now
give you visible proof of the fact that I discuss the subject of
occultism under the pressure of the greatest resistance. When,
while I was at Gastein, I looked out the notes which I had put
together and brought with me [from Vienna] for the purpose
of this paper, the sheet on which I had noted down this last
observation was not there, but in its place I found another sheet
of indifferent memoranda on quite another topic, which I had
brought with me by mistake. Nothing can be done against such
a clear resistance. I must ask you to excuse me for omitting
this case, for I cannot make the loss good from memory.

I will instead add a few remarks about someone who is very
well known in Vienna, a graphologist, Rafael Schermann, who
has a reputation for the most astonishing performances. He is
said to be able not merely to read a person's character from a

[1] [See Editor's Note, p. 176.]

specimen of his handwriting, but also to describe his appearance and to add predictions about him which later come true. Incidentally, many of these remarkable achievements are based on his own stories. A friend of mine once, without my previous knowledge, made the experiment of getting him to allow his imagination to play over a specimen of my writing. All that he produced was that the writing was that of an old gentleman (which it was easy to guess), with whom it was hard to live since he was an intolerable tyrant in his home. Those who share my house would hardly confirm this. But, as we know, the field of the occult is subject to the convenient principle that negative cases prove nothing. I have made no direct observations on Schermann, but through a patient of mine I have been in contact with him without his knowing it. I will tell you about it.[1]

A few years ago a young man came to me who made a particularly sympathetic impression on me, so that I gave him preference over a number of others. It appeared that he was involved with one of the best known *demi-mondaines* and that he wanted to get free from her, because the relationship deprived him of all independence of action, but was unable to do so. I succeeded in setting him free and at the same time I obtained full insight into his compulsion. Not many months ago he contracted a normal and respectable marriage. The analysis soon showed that the compulsion against which he was struggling was not a tie with the *demi-mondaine* but with a married lady in his own circle with whom he had had a *liaison* from his earliest youth. The *demi-mondaine* served merely as a whipping-boy on whom he could satisfy all the feelings of revenge and jealousy which really applied to the other lady. On a model that is familiar to us, he had made use of displacement on to a fresh object in order to escape the inhibition brought about by his ambivalence.

It was his habit to inflict the most refined torment on the *demi-mondaine*, who had fallen in love with him in an almost unselfish fashion. But when she could no longer conceal her sufferings, he in turn passed over on to her the affection he had felt for the woman he had loved since his youth; he made her

[1] [The case which follows is reported also in Lecture XXX of Freud's *New Introductory Lectures* (1933a). One part of the story is given there in greater detail, but others more briefly.]

presents and propitiated her, and the cycle started on its course once more. When finally, under the influence of the treatment, he broke with her, it became clear what it was that he was trying to achieve by his behaviour to this substitute for his early love: revenge for an attempt at suicide of his own when his love had rejected his advances. After the attempted suicide he had at last succeeded in overcoming her reluctance. During this period of the treatment he used to visit the celebrated Schermann. And the latter, on the basis of specimens of the *demi-mondaine's* handwriting, repeatedly told him by way of interpretation that she was at her last gasp, was at the point of suicide and would quite certainly kill herself. This, however, she did not do, but shook off her human weakness, and recalled the principles of her profession and her duties to her official friend. I saw clearly that the miracle-man had merely revealed to my patient his own intimate wish.

After disposing of this spurious figure, my patient set about seriously the task of freeing himself from his real bond. I detected from his dreams a plan that he was forming by means of which he would be able to escape from his relation with his early love without causing her too much mortification or material damage. She had a daughter, who was very fond of the young friend of the family and ostensibly knew nothing of the secret part he played. He now proposed to marry this girl. Soon afterwards the scheme became conscious, and the man took the first steps towards putting it into effect. I supported his intentions, since it offered what was a possible way out of his difficult situation even though an irregular one. But presently there came a dream which showed hostility to the girl; and now once more he consulted Schermann, who reported that the girl was childish and neurotic and should not be married. This time the great observer of human nature was right. The girl, who was by now regarded as the man's *fiancée*, behaved in a more and more contradictory manner, and it was decided that she should be analysed. As a result of the analysis the scheme for the marriage was abandoned. The girl had a complete unconscious knowledge of the relations between her mother and her *fiancé*, and was only attached to him on account of her Oedipus complex.

At about this time our analysis broke off. The patient was free and capable of going his own way in the future. He chose as his wife a respectable girl outside his family circle—a girl on whom Schermann has passed a favourable judgement. Let us hope that this time he will be right once more.

You will have grasped the sense in which I am inclined to interpret these experiences of mine with Schermann. You will see that all my material touches only on the single point of thought-transference. I have nothing to say about all the other miracles that are claimed by occultism. My own life, as I have already openly admitted, has been particularly poor in an occult sense.[1] Perhaps the problem of thought-transference may seem very trivial to you in comparison with the great magical world of the occult. But consider what a momentous step beyond what we have hitherto believed would be involved in this hypothesis alone. What the custodian of [the basilica of] Saint-Denis used to add to his account of the saint's martyrdom remains true. Saint-Denis is said, after his head was cut off, to have picked it up and to have walked quite a distance with it under his arm. But the custodian used to remark: '*Dans des cas pareils, ce n'est que le premier pas qui coûte.*' The rest is easy.[2]

---

[1] [See a passage introduced in 1907 into *The Psychopathology of Everyday Life* (1901*b*), Chapter XII (D).]

[2] [The *mot* was Madame du Deffand's. See her letter to Walpole of June 6, 1767.]

DREAMS AND TELEPATHY
(1922)

TRAUM UND TELEPATHIE

(a) GERMAN EDITIONS:

1922   *Imago*, **8** (1), 1–22.
1925   *G.S.*, **3**, 278–304.
1925   *Traumlehre*, 22–48.
1931   *Sexualtheorie und Traumlehre*, 326–354.
1940   *G.W.*, **13**, 165–91.

(b) ENGLISH TRANSLATION:

'Dreams and Telepathy'

1922   *Int. J. Psycho-Anal.*, **3**, 283–305. (Tr. C. J. M. Hubback.)
1925   *C.P.*, **4**, 408–35. (Same translator.)

The present translation is a considerably modified version of that published in 1925.

This was the first of Freud's writings on telepathy to be published, though it was written after the one above (p. 177). It cannot have been written much before the end of November 1921, since a date eight weeks after September 27 of that year actually occurs in the material under discussion (p. 211). Internal evidence shows that it was designed as a lecture, and in the original MS. (as well as in the editions of 1922 and 1925) the words 'Lecture given before the Vienna Psycho-Analytical Society' appear below the title. On the other hand, the published minutes of the Vienna Society give no evidence of the paper having ever been read before it. It seems likely that Freud's intention to read it was for some reason abandoned after the first number of *Imago* for 1922 was already in type.

DREAMS AND TELEPATHY

AT the present time, when such great interest is felt in what are called 'occult' phenomena, very definite anticipations will doubtless be aroused by the announcement of a paper with this title. I will therefore hasten to explain that there is no ground for any such anticipations. You will learn nothing from this paper of mine about the enigma of telepathy; indeed, you will not even gather whether I believe in the existence of 'telepathy' or not. On this occasion I have set myself the very modest task of examining the relation of the telepathic occurrences in question, whatever their origin may be, to dreams, or more exactly, to our theory of dreams. You will know that the connection between dreams and telepathy is commonly held to be a very intimate one; I shall put forward the view that the two have little to do with each other, and that if the existence of telepathic dreams were to be established there would be no need to alter our conception of dreams in any way.

The material on which the present communication is based is very slight. In the first place, I must express my regret that I could make no use of my own dreams, as I did when I wrote my *Interpretation of Dreams* (1900a). But I have never had a 'telepathic' dream. Not that I have been without dreams of the kind that convey an impression that a certain definite event is happening at some distant place, leaving it to the dreamer to decide whether the event is happening at that moment or will do so at some later time. In waking life, too, I have often become aware of presentiments of distant events. But these hints, foretellings and premonitions have none of them 'come true', as we say; there proved to be no external reality corresponding to them, and they had therefore to be regarded as purely subjective anticipations.

For example, I once dreamt during the war that one of my sons then serving at the front had been killed. This was not directly stated in the dream, but was expressed in an unmistakable manner, by means of the well-known death-symbolism of which an account was first given by Stekel [1911a]. (We must not omit to fulfil the duty, often felt to be inconvenient, of making literary acknowledgements.) I saw the young soldier

197

standing on a landing-stage, between land and water, as it were; he looked to me very pale. I spoke to him but he did not answer. There were other unmistakable indications. He was not wearing military uniform, but a ski-ing costume that he had worn when a serious ski-ing accident had happened to him several years before the war. He stood on something like a footstool with a cupboard in front of him; a situation always closely associated in my mind with the idea of 'falling', through a memory of my own childhood. As a child of little more than two years old I had myself climbed on a footstool like this to get something off the top of a cupboard—probably something good to eat—and I fell down and gave myself an injury, of which I can even now show the scar. My son, however, whom the dream pronounced to be dead, came home from the war unscathed.[1]

Only a short time ago, I had another dream bearing ill-tidings; it was, I think, just before I decided to put together these few remarks. This time there was not much attempt at disguise. I saw my two nieces who live in England. They were dressed in black and said to me, 'We buried her on Thursday.' I knew the reference was to the death of their mother, now eighty-seven years of age, the widow of my eldest brother.

A time of disagreeable anticipation followed; there would of course be nothing surprising in such an old lady suddenly passing away, yet it would be very unpleasant for the dream to coincide exactly with the occurrence. The next letter from England, however, dissipated this fear. For the benefit of those who are concerned for the wish-fulfilment theory of dreams I may interpolate a reassurance by saying that there was no difficulty in detecting by analysis the unconscious motives that might be presumed to exist in these death-dreams just as in others.

I hope you will not object that what I have just related is valueless because negative experiences prove as little here as they do in less occult matters. I am well aware of that and have not adduced these instances with any intention whatever of proving anything or of surreptitiously influencing you in any

[1] [This dream is fully discussed in a passage added in 1919 to *The Interpretation of Dreams* (1900a, Standard Ed., 5, 558 ff.). It may be remarked that the object described above as 'something like a footstool' is referred to in *The Interpretation of Dreams* as a 'basket'.]

particular direction. My sole purpose was to explain the paucity of my material.

Another fact certainly seems to me of more significance, namely, that during some twenty-seven years of work as an analyst I have never been in a position to observe a truly telepathic dream in any of my patients. And yet those patients made up a fair collection of severely neuropathic and 'highly sensitive' natures. Many of them have related to me most remarkable incidents in their earlier life on which they based a belief in mysterious occult influences. Events such as accidents or illnesses of near relatives, in particular the death of a parent, have often enough happened during the treatment and interrupted it; but not on one single occasion did these occurrences, eminently suitable as they were in character, afford me the opportunity of registering a single telepathic dream, although treatment extended over several months or even years. Anyone who cares to may look for an explanation of this fact, which still further restricts the material at my disposal. In any case it will be seen that such an explanation would not affect the subject of this paper.

Nor does it embarrass me to be asked why I have made no use of the abundant store of telepathic dreams that have appeared in the literature of the subject. I should not have had far to seek, since the publications of the English as well as of the American Society for Psychical Research are accessible to me as a member of both societies. In none of these communications is any attempt ever made to subject such dreams to analytic investigation, which would be our first interest in such cases.[1] Moreover, you will soon perceive that for the purposes of this paper one single dream will serve well enough.

My material thus consists simply and solely of two communications which have reached me from correspondents in Germany. The writers are not personally known to me, but they give their names and addresses: I have not the least ground for presuming any intention to mislead on their part.

[1] In two publications by W. Stekel, the author mentioned above (*Der telepathische Traum*, no date, and *Die Sprache des Traumes*, Second Edition, 1922), there are at least attempts to apply the analytic technique to alleged telepathic dreams. The author expresses his belief in the reality of telepathy.

I

With the first of the two [1] I had already been in correspondence; he had been good enough to send me, as many of my readers do, observations of everyday occurrences and the like. He is obviously an educated and highly intelligent man; this time he expressly places his material at my disposal if I care to turn it 'to literary account'.

His letter runs as follows:

'I consider the following dream of sufficient interest for me to hand it on to you as material for your researches.

'I must first state the following facts. My daughter, who is married and lives in Berlin, was expecting her first confinement in the middle of December of this year. I intended to go to Berlin about that time with my (second) wife, my daughter's stepmother. During the night of November 16–17 I dreamt, with a vividness and clearness I have never before experienced, that *my wife had given birth to twins. I saw the two healthy infants quite plainly with their chubby faces lying in their cot side by side. I did not observe their sex; one with fair hair had distinctly my features and something of my wife's, the other with chestnut-brown hair clearly resembled her with a look of me. I said to my wife, who has red-gold hair, "Probably 'your' child's chestnut hair will also go red later on." My wife gave them the breast. In the dream she had also made some jam in a wash-basin and the two children crawled about on all fours in the basin and licked up the contents.*

'So much for the dream. Four or five times I had half woken from it, asked myself if it were true that we had twins, but did not come to the conclusion with any certainty that it was only a dream. The dream lasted till I woke, and after that it was some little time before I felt quite clear about the true state of affairs. At breakfast I told my wife the dream, which much amused her. She said, "Surely Ilse (my daughter) won't have twins?" I answered, "I should hardly think so, as twins are not the usual thing either in my family or in G.'s" (her husband). On November 18, at ten o'clock in the morning, I received a telegram from my son-in-law, handed in the afternoon before, telling me of the birth of twins, a boy and a girl. The birth thus took place at the time when I was dreaming that my wife

[1] [This example will be found described more briefly in Lecture XXX of Freud's *New Introductory Lectures* (1933a).]

had twins. The confinement occurred four weeks earlier than any of us had expected on the basis of my daughter and son-in-law's calculations.

'But there is a further circumstance: the next night [i.e. also before the receipt of the telegram] I dreamt *that my deceased wife, my daughter's own mother, had undertaken the care of forty-eight new-born infants. When the first dozen were being brought in, I protested.* At that point the dream ended.

'My late wife was very fond of children. She often talked about it, saying she would like a whole troop round her, the more the better, and that she would do very well if she had charge of a Kindergarten and would be quite happy so. The noise children make was music to her. From time to time she would invite in a whole troop of children from the streets and regale them with chocolate and cakes in the courtyard of our villa. My daughter must have thought at once of her mother after her confinement, especially because of the surprise of its coming on prematurely, the arrival of twins, and their difference in sex. She knew her mother would have greeted the event with the liveliest joy and sympathy. "Only think what mother would say, if she were with me now!" This thought must undoubtedly have gone through her mind. And then I dream of my dead wife, of whom I very seldom dream, and had neither spoken of nor thought of after the first dream.

'Do you think that the coincidence between dream and event was accidental in both cases? My daughter is much attached to me and was most certainly thinking of me during her labour, particularly because we had often exchanged letters about her mode of living during her pregnancy and I had constantly given her advice.'

It is easy to guess what my answer to this letter was. I was sorry to find that my correspondent's interest in analysis had been so completely killed by his interest in telepathy. I therefore avoided his direct question, and, remarking that the dream contained a good deal besides its connection with the birth of the twins, I asked him to give me any information or ideas that occurred to him which could give me a clue to the meaning of the dream.

Thereupon I received the following second letter which, it must be admitted, did not give me quite all I wanted:

'I have not been able to answer your kind letter of the 24th until to-day. I shall be only too pleased to tell you "without omission or reserve" all the associations that occur to me. Unfortunately there is not much; more would come out in talking.

'Well then—my wife and I do not wish for any more children. We almost never have sexual intercourse; at any rate at the time of the dream there was certainly no "danger". My daughter's confinement, which was expected about the middle of December, was naturally a frequent subject of conversation between us. My daughter had been examined and X-rayed in the summer, and the doctor making the examination was certain that the child would be a boy. My wife said at the time, "I should laugh if it was a girl after all." At the time she also remarked that it would be better if it were an H. rather than a G. (my son-in-law's family name); my daughter is handsomer and has a better figure than my son-in-law, although he has been a naval officer. I have made some study of the question of heredity and am in the habit of looking at babies to see whom they resemble. One more thing. We have a small dog which sits with us at table in the evening to have his food and licks the plates and dishes. All this material appears in the dream.

'I am fond of small children and have often said that I should like to have the bringing up of a child once more, now that I should have so much more understanding, interest and time to devote to it; but with my wife I should not wish it, as she does not possess the necessary qualities for rearing a child judiciously. The dream makes me a present of two children—I did not observe their sex. I see them even at this moment lying in the bed and I recognize the features, the one more "me", the other more my wife, but each with minor traits from the other side. My wife has red-gold hair, but the one child had chestnut (reddish) brown hair. I said, "Oh well, it will go red, too, later on." Both the children crawl round a large wash-basin in which my wife has been stirring jam and lick its bottom and sides (dream). The origin of this detail is easily explicable, just as is the dream as a whole. The dream would not be difficult to understand or interpret if it had not coincided with the unexpectedly early arrival of my grandchildren (three weeks too soon), a coincidence of time almost to the hour. (I cannot exactly say when the dream began; my grandchildren were born at nine p.m. and a quarter past; I went to bed at about eleven and had my dream during the course of the night.) Our knowledge too that the child would be a boy adds to the difficulty, though possibly the doubt whether this had been fully established might account for the appearance of twins in the dream. All the same, there remains the coincidence of the dream with the unexpected and premature appearance of my daughter's twins.

'It is not the first time that distant events have become known to me before I received the actual news. To give one instance among many. In October I had a visit from my three brothers. We had not all been together for thirty years, except for quite a short time, once at my father's funeral and once at my mother's. Both deaths were expected, and I had had no 'presentiments' in either case. But about twenty-five years ago my youngest brother died quite suddenly and unexpectedly when he was ten. As the postman handed me the postcard with the news of his death, before I had glanced at it, the thought came to me at once, "It is to say that your brother is dead." He was the only one left at home, a strong healthy lad, while we four elder brothers were already fully fledged and had left our parents' house. At the time of my brothers' visit the talk by chance came round to this experience of mine, and, as if at the word of command, all three brothers came out with the declaration that exactly the same thing had happened to them. Whether it happened in exactly the same manner I cannot say; at all events each one said that he had felt perfectly certain of the death just before the quite unexpected news had arrived. We are all from the mother's side of a sensitive disposition, though tall, strong men, but not one of us is in the least inclined towards spiritualism or occultism; on the contrary, we disclaim adherence to either. My brothers are all three University men, two are schoolmasters, one a surveyor, all rather pedants than visionaries.—That is all I can tell you in regard to the dream. If you can turn it to literary account, I am delighted to place it at your disposal.'

I am afraid that you may behave like the writer of these two letters. You, too, will be primarily interested in the question whether this dream can really be regarded as a telepathic notification of the unexpected birth of the twin children, and you will not be disposed to submit this dream to analysis like any other. I foresee that it will always be so when psycho-analysis and occultism encounter each other. The former has, so to speak, all our mental instincts against it; the latter is met half-way by powerful and mysterious sympathies. I am not, however, going to take up the position that I am nothing but a psycho-analyst, that the problems of occultism do not concern me: you would rightly judge that to be only an evasion of a problem. On the contrary, I may say that it would be a great satisfaction to me if I could convince myself and others on unimpeachable evidence of the existence of telepathic processes, but I also consider that the information provided about this dream is altogether inadequate to justify any such pronounce-ment. You will observe that it does not once occur to this intelligent man, deeply interested as he is in the problem of his dream, to tell us when he had last seen his daughter or what news he had lately had from her. He writes in the first letter that the birth was a month too soon; in the second, however, the month has become three weeks only, and in neither are we told whether the birth was really premature, or whether, as so often happens, those concerned were out in their reckoning. But we should have to consider these and other details of the occurrence if we are to weigh the probability of the dreamer having made unconscious estimates and guesses. I felt too that it would be of no use even if I succeeded in getting answers to such questions. In the course of arriving at the information new doubts would constantly arise, which could only be set at rest if one had the man in front of one and could revive all the relevant memories which he had perhaps dismissed as unes-sential. He is certainly right in what he says at the beginning of his second letter that more would have come out in talking.

Consider another and similar case, in which the disturbing interest of occultism has no part. You must often have been in a position to compare the anamnesis and the information about the illness given during the first session by any neurotic with what you have gained from him after some months of psycho-analysis. Apart from inevitable abbreviations, how many essentials were left out or suppressed, how many connections were displaced—in fact, how much that was incorrect or untrue was told you on that first occasion! You will not call me hyper-critical if I refuse in the circumstances to make any pronouncement whether the dream in question is a telepathic event or a particularly subtle achievement on the part of the dreamer's unconscious or whether it is simply to be taken as a striking coincidence. Our curiosity must be satisfied with the hope of some later occasion on which it may be possible to make a detailed oral examination of the dreamer. But you cannot say that this outcome of our investigation has disappointed you, for I prepared you for it; I said you would hear nothing which would throw any light on the problem of telepathy.

If we now pass on to the analytic treatment of this dream, we are obliged once more to express dissatisfaction. The thoughts that the dreamer associates with the manifest content of the dream are again insufficient; they do not enable us to make any analysis of the dream. For instance, the dream goes into great detail over the likeness of the children to the parents, discusses the colour of their hair and the probable change of colour at a later age, and as an explanation of these elaborate details we only have the dry piece of information from the dreamer that he has always been interested in questions of likeness and heredity. We are accustomed to expect rather more material than this! But at *one* point the dream does admit of an analytic interpretation, and precisely at this point analysis, which has otherwise no connection with occultism, comes to the aid of telepathy in a remarkable way. It is only on account of this single point that I am asking for your attention to this dream at all.

Correctly speaking, this dream has no right whatever to be called 'telepathic'. It did not inform the dreamer of anything which (outside his normal knowledge) was taking place elsewhere. What the dream did relate was something quite different from the event reported in the telegram received on the second day after the night of the dream. The dream and the actual occurrence diverge at a particularly important point; but they agree, apart from the coincidence of time, in another very interesting element. In the dream the dreamer's *wife* had twins. The occurrence, however, was that his *daughter* had given birth to twins in her distant home. The dreamer did not overlook this difference; he did not seem to know any way of getting over it and, as according to his own account he had no leaning towards the occult, he only asked quite tentatively whether the coincidence between dream and occurrence on the point of the twin-birth could be more than an accident. The psycho-analytic interpretation of dreams, however, does away with this difference between the dream and the event, and gives both the same content. If we consult the associative material to this dream, it shows, in spite of its sparseness, that an intimate bond of feeling existed between the father and daughter, a bond of feeling which is so usual and so natural that we ought to cease to be ashamed of it, one that in daily life merely finds expression as a tender interest and is only pushed to its logical conclusion in dreams. The father knew that his daughter clung to him, he was convinced that she often thought of him during her labour. In his heart I think he grudged her to his son-in-law, to whom in one letter he makes a few disparaging references. On the occasion of her confinement (whether expected or communicated by telepathy) the unconscious wish became active in the repressed part of his mind: 'she ought to be my (second) wife instead'; it was this wish that had distorted the dream-thoughts and was the cause of the difference between the manifest content of the dream and the event. We are entitled to replace the second wife in the dream by the daughter. If we possessed more associations to the dream, we could undoubtedly verify and deepen this interpretation.

And now I have reached the point I wish to put before you. We have endeavoured to maintain the strictest impartiality and have allowed two conceptions of the dream to rank as equally probable and equally unproved. According to the first the dream is a reaction to a telepathic message: 'your daughter has just brought twins into the world.' According to the second an unconscious process of thought underlies the dream, which may be reproduced somewhat as follows: 'To-day is the day the confinement should take place if the young people in Berlin are really out in their reckoning by a month, as I suspect. And if my (first) wife were still alive, she certainly would not be content with one grandchild. To please her there would have to be at least twins!' If this second view is right, no new problems arise. It is simply a dream like any other. The (preconscious) dream-thoughts as outlined above are reinforced by the (unconscious) wish that no other than the daughter should be the dreamer's second wife, and thus the manifest dream as described to us arises.

If you prefer to assume that a telepathic message about the

daughter's confinement reached the sleeper, further questions arise of the relation of a message such as this to a dream and of its influence on the formation of dreams. The answer is not far to seek and is quite unambiguous. A telepathic message will be treated as a portion of the material that goes to the formation of a dream, like any other external or internal stimulus, like a disturbing noise in the street or an insistent organic sensation in the sleeper's own body. In our example it is evident how the message, with the help of a lurking repressed wish, became remodelled into a wish-fulfilment; it is unfortunately less easy to show that it combined with other material that had become active at the same time and was blended into a dream. Telepathic messages—if we are justified in recognizing their existence —can thus make no alteration in the process of forming a dream; telepathy has nothing to do with the nature of dreams. And in order to avoid the impression that I am trying to conceal a vague notion behind abstract and fine-sounding words, I am willing to repeat: the essential nature of dreams consists in the peculiar process of 'dream-work' which, with the help of an unconscious wish, carries the preconscious thoughts (day's residues) over into the manifest content of the dream. The problem of telepathy concerns dreams as little as does the problem of anxiety.[1]

I am hoping that you will grant this, but that you will raise the objection that there are, nevertheless, other telepathic dreams in which there is no difference between the event and the dream, and in which there is nothing else to be found but an undistorted reproduction of the event. I have no knowledge of such dreams from my own experience, but I know they have often been reported. If we assume that we have such an undisguised and unadulterated telepathic dream to deal with, another question arises. Ought we to call such a telepathic experience a 'dream' at all? You will certainly do so as long as you keep to popular usage, in which everything that takes place in mental life during sleep is called a dream. You, too, perhaps say, 'I tossed about in my dream', and still less are you conscious of anything incorrect when you say, 'I shed tears in my dream' or 'I felt apprehensive in my dream'. But you will no doubt notice that in all these cases you are using 'dream'

[1] [See *The Interpretation of Dreams*, Chapter VII (D), *Standard Ed.*, 5, 582.]

and 'sleep' and 'state of being asleep' interchangeably, as if there were no distinction between them. I think it would be in the interests of scientific accuracy to keep 'dream' and 'state of sleep' more distinctly separate. Why should we provide a counterpart to the confusion evoked by Maeder who, by refusing to distinguish between the dream-work and the latent dream-thoughts, has discovered a new function for dreams? [1] Supposing, then, that we are brought face to face with a pure telepathic 'dream', let us rather call it instead a telepathic experience in a state of sleep. A dream without condensation, distortion, dramatization, above all, without wish-fulfilment, surely does not deserve the name. You will remind me that, if so, there are *other* mental products in sleep to which the right to be called 'dreams' would have to be refused. Actual experiences of the day are sometimes simply repeated in sleep; reproductions of traumatic scenes in 'dreams' [p. 13] have led us only lately to revise the theory of dreams. There are dreams which are to be distinguished from the usual type by certain special qualities, which are, properly speaking, nothing but night-phantasies, not having undergone additions or alterations of any kind and being in all other ways similar to the familiar day-dreams. It would be awkward, no doubt, to exclude these structures from the domain of 'dreams'.[2] But still they all come from within, are products of our mental life, whereas the very conception of the purely 'telepathic dream' lies in its being a perception of something external, in relation to which the mind remains passive and receptive.[3]

II

The second case which I shall bring before your notice in fact follows along other lines. This is not a telepathic dream, but a dream that has recurred from childhood onwards, in a person who has had many telepathic experiences. Her letter, which I reproduce here, contains some remarkable things, about which we cannot form any judgement. A part of it is of interest in

[1] [The supposed 'prospective' function of dreams is fully discussed in two footnotes added in 1914 and 1925 to *The Interpretation of Dreams* (*Standard Ed.*, 5, 506–7 and 579–80).]

[2] [Cf. *The Interpretation of Dreams*, *Standard Ed.*, 4, 331.]

[3] [A general discussion of the definition of dreams will be found in the fifth of Freud's *Introductory Lectures* (1916–17).]

connection with the problem of the relation of telepathy to dreams.

(1) '. . . My doctor, Herr Dr. N., advises me to give you an account of a dream that has pursued me for some thirty or thirty-two years. I am following his advice, and perhaps the dream may possess interest for you in some scientific respect. Since, in your opinion, such dreams are to be traced to an experience of a sexual nature in the first years of my childhood, I relate some reminiscences of childhood. They are experiences whose impression on me still persists and which were of so marked a character as to have determined my religion for me.

'May I beg of you to send me word in what way you explain this dream and whether it is not possible to banish it from my life, for it haunts me like a ghost, and the circumstances that always accompany it—I always fall out of bed, and have inflicted on myself not inconsiderable injuries—make it particularly disagreeable and distressing.'

(2) 'I am thirty-seven years old, very strong and in good physical health, but in childhood I had, besides measles and scarlet fever, an attack of nephritis. Furthermore, in my fifth year I had a very severe inflammation of the eyes, which left double vision. The images are at an angle to each other and their outline is blurred, as the scars from the ulcers affect clearness of vision. In the specialist's opinion there is nothing more to be done to the eyes and no chance of improvement. The left side of my face is drawn up from having screwed up my left eye to see better. By dint of practice and determination I can do the finest needlework; and, similarly, when a six-year-old child, I broke myself of squinting by practising in front of a looking-glass, so that now there is no external sign of the defect in vision.

'From my very earliest years I was always solitary. I kept apart from other children, and had visions (clairvoyance and clairaudience). I was not able to distinguish these from reality, and in consequence often found myself in conflict with other people in embarrassing positions, with the result that I have become a very reserved and shy person. Since as a quite small child I already knew far more than I could have learnt, I simply did not understand children of my own age. I am myself the eldest of a family of twelve.

'From six to ten years old I attended the parish school and up to sixteen the high-school of the Ursuline Nuns in B——. At ten I had taken in as much French in four weeks, in eight lessons, as other children learn in two years. I had only to say it over. It was just as if I had already learnt it and only forgotten it. I have never had any need to learn French, in contradistinction to English, which gave me no trouble, certainly, but which was not known to me beforehand. The same thing happened to me with Latin as with French and I have never properly learnt it, only knowing it from Church Latin, which is, however, quite familiar to me. If I read a French book to-day, then I immediately begin thinking in French, whereas this never happens to me with English, although I have more command of English. My parents are peasant people who for generations have never spoken any languages except German and Polish.

'*Visions.*—Sometimes reality vanishes for some moments and I see something quite different. In my house, for example, I often see an old married couple and a child; and the house is then differently furnished. In the sanatorium a friend once came into my room at about four in the morning; I was awake, had the lamp burning, and was sitting at my table reading, as I suffer much from sleeplessness. This apparition of her always means a trying time for me—as it did on this occasion.

'In 1914 my brother was on active service; I was not with my parents in B——, but in Ch——. It was ten a.m. on August 22 when I heard my brother's voice calling, "Mother! Mother!" It came again ten minutes later, but I saw nothing. On August 24 I came home, found my mother greatly depressed, and in answer to my questions she said that she had had a message from the boy on August 22. She had been in the garden in the morning, when she had heard him call, "Mother! Mother!" I comforted her and said nothing about myself. Three weeks after there came a card from my brother, written on August 22 between nine and ten in the morning; shortly after that he died.

'On September 27, 1921, while in the sanatorium, I received a message of some kind. There were violent knockings two or three times repeated on the bed of the patient who shared my room. We were both awake; I asked if she had knocked; she had not even heard anything. Eight weeks later I heard that one of my friends had died in the night of September 26–7.

'Now something which is regarded as a hallucination—a matter of opinion! I have a friend who married a widower with five children; I got to know the husband only through my friend. Nearly every time that I have been to see her, I have seen a lady going in and out of the house. It was natural to suppose that this was the husband's first wife. I asked at some convenient opportunity for a portrait of her, but could not identify the apparition with the photograph. Seven years later I saw a picture with the features of the lady, belonging to one of the children. It was the first wife after all. In the picture she looked in much better health: she had just been through a feeding-up treatment and that alters the appearance of a consumptive patient.—These are only a few examples out of many.

'*The [recurrent] dream.—I saw a tongue of land surrounded by water. The waves were being driven forward and then back by the breakers. On this piece of land stood a palm-tree, bent somewhat towards the water. A woman had her arm wound round the stem of the palm and was bending low towards the water, where a man was trying to reach the shore. At last she lay down on the ground, held tightly to the palm-tree with her left hand and stretched out her right hand as far as she could towards the man in the water, but without reaching him.* At that point I would fall out of bed and wake. I was about fifteen or sixteen years old when I realized that this woman was myself, and from that time I not only experienced all the woman's apprehensions on behalf of the man but sometimes stood there as a third person looking on at the scene without taking part in it. I dreamed this dream too in separate scenes. As an interest in men awoke in me (at eighteen to twenty years old), I tried to see the man's face; but this was never possible. The foam hid everything but his neck and the back of his head. I have twice been engaged to be married, but judging by his head and build he was neither of the two men I was engaged to.—Once, when I was lying in the sanatorium under the influence of paraldehyde, I saw the man's face, which I now always see in this dream. It was that of the doctor under whose care I was. I liked him as a doctor, but I was not drawn to him in any other way.

'*Memories. Six to nine months old.*—I was in a perambulator. On my right were two horses; one, a brown, was looking at me very intently and expressively. This was my most vivid experience; I had the feeling that it was a human being.

'*One year old.*—Father and I in the town-park, where a park-keeper was putting a little bird into my hand. Its eyes looked back into mine. I felt "That is a creature like yourself".

'*Animals being slaughtered.*—When I heard the pigs squealing I always called for help and cried out "You are killing a person" (four years old). I always refused to eat meat. Pork always makes me vomit. It was not till the war that I came to eat meat, and only unwillingly; now I am learning to do without it again.

'*Five years old.*—My mother was confined and I heard her cry out. I had the feeling, "There is a human being or an animal in the greatest distress", just as I had over the pig-killing.

'I was quite indifferent as a child to sexual matters; at ten years old I had as yet no conception of offences against chastity. Menstruation came on at the age of twelve. The woman first awakened in me at six-and-twenty, after I had given life to a child; up to that time (six months) I constantly had violent vomiting after intercourse. This also came on whenever I was at all oppressed in mood.

'I have extraordinarily keen powers of observation, and quite exceptionally sharp hearing, also a very keen sense of smell. With my eyes bandaged I can pick out by smell people I know from among a number of others.

'I do not regard my abnormal powers of sight and hearing as pathological, but ascribe them to finer perceptions and greater quickness of thought; but I have only spoken of it to my pastor and to Dr.—— (very unwillingly to the latter, as I was afraid he would tell me that what I regarded as *plus*-qualities were *minus*-qualities, and also because from being misunderstood in childhood I am very reserved and shy).'

The dream which the writer of the letter asks us to interpret is not hard to understand. It is a dream of rescuing from water, a typical birth-dream.[1] The language of symbolism, as you are aware, knows no grammar; it is an extreme case of a language of infinitives, and even the active and passive are represented by one and the same image. If in a dream a woman pulls (or tries to pull) a man out of the water, that may mean that she

[1] [See *The Interpretation of Dreams* (1900a), *Standard Ed.*, 5, 403.]

wants to be his mother (takes him for her son as Pharaoh's daughter did with Moses). Or it may mean that she wants him to make her into a mother: she wants to have a son by him, who, as a likeness of him, can be his equivalent. The tree-trunk to which the woman was clinging is easily recognized as a phallic symbol, even though it is not standing straight up, but inclined towards the surface of the water—in the dream the word is 'bent'. The onrush and recoil of the breakers brought to the mind of another dreamer who was relating a similar dream a comparison with the intermittent pains of labour; and when, knowing that she had not yet borne a child, I asked her how she knew of this characteristic of labour, she said that she imagined labour as a kind of colic—a quite unimpeachable description physiologically. She gave the association '*The Waves of the Sea and of Love*'.[1] How our present dreamer at so early an age can have arrived at the finer details of symbolism—tongue of land, palm-tree—I am naturally unable to say. We must not, moreover, overlook the fact that, when people assert that they have for years been pursued by the same dream, it often turns out that the manifest content is not quite the same. Only the kernel of the dream has recurred each time; the details of the content are changed or additions are made to them.[2]

At the end of this dream, which is clearly charged with anxiety, the dreamer falls out of bed. This is a fresh representation of childbirth. Analytic investigation of the fear of heights, of the dread of an impulse to throw oneself out of the window, has doubtless led you all to the same conclusion.

Who then is the man, by whom the dreamer wishes to have a child, or of whose likeness she would like to be the mother? She often tried to see his face, but the dream never allowed her to; the man had to remain *incognito*. We know from countless analyses what this concealment means, and the conclusion we should base on analogy is verified by another statement of the dreamer's. Under the influence of paraldehyde she once recognized the face of the man in the dream as that of the hospital physician who was treating her, and who meant nothing more to her conscious emotional life. The original thus never divulged

---

[1] [*Des Meeres und der Liebe Wellen*, the title of a play about Hero and Leander by Grillparzer.]

[2] [This point is discussed at some length in Freud's analysis of the case of 'Dora' (1905e), *Standard Ed.*, 7, 92–3.]

its identity, but this impression of it in 'transference' establishes the conclusion that earlier it must always have been her father. Ferenczi [1917] is perfectly right in pointing out that these 'dreams of the unsuspecting' are valuable sources of information, as confirming the conjectures of analysis. Our dreamer was the eldest of twelve children; how often must she have suffered the pangs of jealousy and disappointment when it was not she but her mother who obtained from her father the child she longed for!

Our dreamer quite correctly supposed that her first memories of childhood would be of value in the interpretation of her early and recurrent dream. In the first scene, before she was one year old, as she was sitting in her perambulator she saw two horses beside her, one looking at her. This she described as her most vivid experience; she had the feeling that it was a human being. This was a feeling which we can understand only if we assume that the two horses represented, in this case as so often, a married couple, father and mother. It was, as it were, a flash of infantile totemism. If we could, we should ask the writer whether the *brown* horse who looked at her so humanly could not be recognized by its colouring as her father. The second recollection was associatively connected with the first through the same 'understanding' gaze. Taking the little bird in her hand, however, reminds the analyst, who has prejudices of his own, of a feature in the dream in which the woman's hand was in contact with another phallic symbol.

The next two memories belong together; they make still slighter demands on the interpreter. The mother crying out during her confinement reminded the daughter directly of the pigs squealing when they were being killed and put her into the same frenzy of pity. But we may also conjecture that this was a violent reaction against an angry death-wish directed at the mother.

With these indications of tenderness for her father, of contact with his genitals, and of death-wishes against her mother, the outline of the female Oedipus complex is sketched in. Her long retention of her ignorance of sexual matters, and her frigidity at a later period bear out these suppositions. The writer of the letter became potentially—and at times no doubt actually —a hysterical neurotic. The forces of life have, for her own happiness, carried her along with them. They have awakened in her the sexual feelings of a woman and brought her the joys of motherhood, and the capacity to work. But a portion of her libido still clings to its points of fixation in childhood; she still dreams the dream that throws her out of bed and punishes her for her incestuous object-choice by 'not inconsiderable injuries'.

And now an explanation, given in writing by a doctor who was a stranger to her, was expected to effect what all the most important experiences of her later life had failed to do! Probably a regular analysis continued for a considerable time would have succeeded in this. As things were, I was obliged to content myself with writing to her that I was convinced she was suffering from the after-effects of a strong emotional tie binding her to her father and from a corresponding identification with her mother, but that I did not myself expect that this explanation would help her. Spontaneous cures of neurosis usually leave scars behind, and these become painful again from time to time. We are very proud of our art if we achieve a cure through psycho-analysis, yet here too we cannot always prevent the formation of a painful scar as an outcome.

The little series of reminiscences must engage our attention for a while longer. I have stated elsewhere that such scenes of childhood are 'screen memories' [1] selected at a later period, put together, and not infrequently falsified in the process. This subsequent remodelling serves a purpose that is sometimes easy to guess. In our case one can almost hear the writer's ego glorifying or soothing itself by means of this series of recollections. 'I was from infancy a particularly noble and compassionate creature. I learnt quite early that animals have souls as we have, and could not endure cruelty to animals. The sins of the flesh were far from me and I preserved my chastity till late in life.' With declarations such as these she was loudly contradicting the inferences that we have to make about her early childhood on the basis of our analytical experience, namely, that she had an abundance of premature sexual impulses and violent feelings of hatred for her mother and her younger brothers and sisters. (Besides the genital significance I have just assigned to it, the little bird may also be a symbol of a child, like all small animals; her recollection thus accentuated very insistently the fact that this small creature had the

---

[1] [See Freud's paper on 'Screen Memories' (1899a), and Chapter IV of his *Psychopathology of Everyday Life* (1901b).]

same right to exist as she herself.) Hence the short series of recollections furnishes a very nice example of a mental structure with a twofold aspect. Viewed superficially, we may find in it the expression of an abstract idea, here, as usually, with an ethical reference. In Silberer's nomenclature the structure has an *anagogic* content. On deeper investigation it reveals itself as a chain of phenomena belonging to the region of the repressed life of the instincts—it displays its *psycho-analytic* content. As you know, Silberer, who was among the first to issue a warning to us not to lose sight of the nobler side of the human soul, has put forward the view that all or nearly all dreams permit such a twofold interpretation, a purer, anagogic one beside the ignoble, psycho-analytic one. This is, however, unfortunately not so. On the contrary, an over-interpretation of this kind is rarely possible. To my knowledge no valid example of such a dream-analysis with a double meaning has been published up to the present time. But observations of this kind can often be made upon the series of associations that our patients produce during analytic treatment. On the one hand the successive ideas are linked by a line of association which is plain to the eye, while on the other hand you become aware of an underlying theme which is kept secret but which at the same time plays a part in all these ideas. The contrast between the two themes that dominate the same series of ideas is not always one between the lofty anagogic and the low psycho-analytic, but one rather between offensive and respectable or indifferent ideas—a fact that easily explains why such a chain of associations with a twofold determination arises. In our present example it is of course not accidental that the anagogic and the psycho-analytic interpretations stood in such a sharp contrast to each other; both related to the same material, and the later trend was no other than that of the reaction-formations which had been erected against the disowned instinctual impulses.[1]

But why do we look for a psycho-analytic interpretation at all instead of contenting ourselves with the more accessible anagogic one? The answer to this is linked up with many other problems—with the existence in general of neurosis and the explanations it inevitably demands—with the fact that virtue does not reward a man with as much joy and strength in life

[1] [Cf. the passage added in 1919 to *The Interpretation of Dreams*, Standard Ed., 5, 523 f.]

as one would expect, as though it brought with it too much of its origin (our dreamer, too, had not been well rewarded for her virtue), and with other things which I need not discuss before this audience.

So far, however, we have completely neglected the question of telepathy, the other point of interest for us in this case; it is time to return to it. In a sense we have here an easier task than in the case of Herr H.[1] With a person who so easily and so early in life lost touch with reality and replaced it by the world of phantasy, the temptation is irresistible to connect her telepathic experiences and 'visions' with her neurosis and to derive them from it, although here too we should not allow ourselves to be deceived as to the cogency of our own arguments. We shall merely be replacing what is unknown and unintelligible by possibilities that are at least comprehensible.

On August 22, 1914, at ten o'clock in the morning, our correspondent experienced a telepathic impression that her brother, who was at the time on active service, was calling, 'Mother! Mother!'; the phenomenon was purely acoustic, it was repeated shortly after, but nothing was seen. Two days later she saw her mother and found her much depressed because the boy had announced himself to her with a repeated call of 'Mother! Mother!' She immediately remembered the same telepathic message, which she had experienced at the same time, and as a matter of fact some weeks later it was established that the young soldier had died on that day at the hour in question.

It cannot be proved, but also cannot be disproved, that instead of this, what happened was the following. Her mother told her one day that her son had sent a telepathic message; whereupon the conviction at once arose in her mind that she had had the same experience at the same time. Such illusions of memory arise in the mind with a compelling force which they draw from real sources; but they turn psychical reality into material reality. The strength of the illusion lies in its being an excellent way of expressing the sister's proneness to identify herself with her mother. 'You are anxious about the boy, but I am really his mother, and his cry was meant for me; *I* had this telepathic message.' The sister would naturally firmly reject our attempt at explanation and would hold to her belief in the

[1] [All the German editions read 'Herr G.', which is an evident slip. (See p. 202.) The mistake was pointed out in Devereux (1953).]

authenticity of her experience. But she could not do otherwise. She would be bound to believe in the reality of the pathological effect so long as the reality of its unconscious premises were unknown to her. Every such delusion derives its strength and its unassailable character from having a source in unconscious psychical reality. I note in passing that it is not incumbent on us here to explain the mother's experience or to investigate its authenticity.

The dead brother, however, was not only our correspondent's imaginary child; he also represented a rival whom she had regarded with hatred from the time of his birth. By far the greater number of all telepathic intimations relate to death or the possibility of death; when patients under analysis keep telling us of the frequency and infallibility of their gloomy forebodings, we can with equal regularity show them that they are fostering particularly strong death-wishes in their unconscious against their nearest relations and have long been thus suppressing them. The patient whose history I related in 1909 [1] was an example to the point; he was called a 'carrion crow' by his relations. But when this kindly and highly intelligent man—who has since himself perished in the war—began to make progress towards recovery, he himself gave me considerable assistance in clearing up his own psychological conjuring tricks. In the same way, the account given in our first correspondent's letter, of how he and his three brothers had received the news of their youngest brother's death as a thing they had long been inwardly aware of [p. 203], appears to need no other explanation. The elder brothers would all have been equally convinced of the superfluousness of the youngest arrival.

Here is another of our dreamer's 'visions' which will probably become more intelligible in the light of analytic knowledge. Women friends obviously had a great significance in her emotional life. Only recently the death of one of them was conveyed to her by a knocking at night on the bed of a room-mate in the sanatorium. Another friend had many years before married a widower with several (five) children. On the occasion of her visits to their house she regularly saw the apparition of a lady, who she could not help supposing was the husband's first wife; this did not at first permit of confirmation, and only became a matter of certainty with her seven years later, on the

[1] 'Notes upon a Case of Obsessional Neurosis' [*Standard Ed.*, 10, 235]

discovery of a fresh photograph of the dead woman. This achievement in the way of a vision on the part of our correspondent had the same intimate dependence on the family-complexes familiar to us as had her presentiment of her brother's death. By identifying herself with her friend she could in the person of the latter find the fulfilment of her own wishes; for every eldest daughter of a numerous family builds up in her unconscious the phantasy of becoming her father's second wife by the death of her mother. If the mother is ill or dies, the eldest daughter takes her place as a matter of course in relation to her younger brothers and sisters, and may even take over some part of the functions of the wife in respect to the father. The unconscious wish fills in the other part.

I am now almost at the end of what I wish to say. I might, however, add the observation that the instances of telepathic messages or productions which have been discussed here are clearly connected with emotions belonging to the sphere of the Oedipus complex. This may sound startling; I do not intend to give it out as a great discovery, however. I would rather revert to the result we arrived at through investigating the dream I considered first. Telepathy has no relation to the essential nature of dreams; it cannot deepen in any way what we already understand of them through analysis. On the other hand, psycho-analysis may do something to advance the study of telepathy, in so far as, by the help of its interpretations, many of the puzzling characteristics of telepathic phenomena may be rendered more intelligible to us; or other, still doubtful, phenomena may for the first time definitely be ascertained to be of a telepathic nature.

There remains one element of the apparently intimate connection between telepathy and dreams which is not affected by any of these considerations: namely, the incontestable fact that sleep creates favourable conditions for telepathy. Sleep is not, it is true, indispensable to the occurrence of telepathic processes—whether they originate in messages or in unconscious activity. If you are not already aware of this, you will learn it from the instance given by our second correspondent, of the young man's message which came between nine and ten in the morning. We must add, however, that no one has a right to take exception to telepathic occurrences if the event and the intimation (or message) do not exactly coincide in astronomical time. It is perfectly conceivable that a telepathic message might arrive contemporaneously with the event and yet only penetrate to consciousness the following night during sleep (or even in waking life only after a while, during some pause in the activity of the mind). We are, as you know, of opinion that dream-formation itself does not necessarily wait for the onset of sleep before it begins.[1] Often the latent dream-thoughts may have been being got ready during the whole day, till at night they find the contact with the unconscious wish that shapes them into a dream. But if the phenomenon of telepathy is only an activity of the unconscious mind, then, of course, no fresh problem lies before us. The laws of unconscious mental life may then be taken for granted as applying to telepathy.

Have I given you the impression that I am secretly inclined to support the reality of telepathy in the occult sense? If so, I should very much regret that it is so difficult to avoid giving such an impression. For in reality I have been anxious to be strictly impartial. I have every reason to be so, since I have no opinion on the matter and know nothing about it.

[1] [See *The Interpretation of Dreams, Standard Ed.*, 5, 575–6.]

SOME NEUROTIC MECHANISMS IN JEALOUSY, PARANOIA AND HOMOSEXUALITY
(1922)

ÜBER EINIGE NEUROTISCHE MECHANISMEN BEI EIFERSUCHT, PARANOIA UND HOMOSEXUALITÄT

(a) GERMAN EDITIONS:

1922   *Int. Z. Psychoanal.*, **8** (3), 249–58.

1924   *G.S.*, **5**, 387–99.

1924   *Psychoanalyse der Neurosen*, 125–39.

1931   *Neurosenlehre und Technik*, 173–86.

1940   *G.W.*, **13**, 195–207.

(b) ENGLISH TRANSLATION:

'Certain Neurotic Mechanisms in Jealousy,
Paranoia and Homosexuality'

1923   *Int. J. Psycho-Anal.*, **4**, 1–10. (Tr. Joan Riviere.)

1924   *C.P.*, **2**, 232–43. (Same translator.)

The present translation is based on the one published in 1924; the title has been modified.

We learn from Dr. Ernest Jones that this paper was read by Freud to a small group of friends in the Harz mountains in September, 1921, on the same occasion as the paper on 'Psycho-Analysis and Telepathy'. (See above, p. 175.)

SOME NEUROTIC MECHANISMS
IN JEALOUSY, PARANOIA AND
HOMOSEXUALITY

A

JEALOUSY is one of those affective states, like grief, that may be described as normal. If anyone appears to be without it, the inference is justified that it has undergone severe repression and consequently plays all the greater part in his unconscious mental life. The instances of abnormally intense jealousy met with in analytic work reveal themselves as constructed of three layers. The three layers or grades of jealousy may be described as (1) *competitive* or normal, (2) *projected*, and (3) *delusional* jealousy.

There is not much to be said from the analytic point of view about normal jealousy. It is easy to see that essentially it is compounded of grief, the pain caused by the thought of losing the loved object, and of the narcissistic wound, in so far as this is distinguishable from the other wound; further, of feelings of enmity against the successful rival, and of a greater or lesser amount of self-criticism which tries to hold the subject's own ego accountable for his loss. Although we may call it normal, this jealousy is by no means completely rational, that is, derived from the actual situation, proportionate to the real circumstances and under the complete control of the conscious ego; for it is rooted deep in the unconscious, it is a continuation of the earliest stirrings of the child's affective life, and it originates in the Oedipus or brother-and-sister complex of the first sexual period. Moreover, it is noteworthy that in some people it is experienced bisexually. That is to say, a man will not only feel pain about the woman he loves and hatred of the man who is his rival, but also grief about the man, whom he loves unconsciously, and hatred of the woman as his rival; and this latter set of feelings will add to the intensity of his jealousy. I even know of a man who suffered exceedingly during his attacks of jealousy and who, according to his own account, went through unendurable torments by consciously imagining himself in the position of the faithless woman. The sensation of helplessness which then came over him and the images he used to describe his condition—exposed to the vulture's beak like Prometheus, or thrown bound into a nest of serpents—were referred by him to impressions received during several homosexual acts of aggression to which he had been subjected as a boy.

The jealousy of the second layer, *projected* jealousy, is derived in both men and women either from their own actual unfaithfulness in real life or from impulses towards it which have succumbed to repression. It is a matter of everyday experience that fidelity, especially that degree of it required in marriage, is only maintained in the face of continual temptations. Anyone who denies these temptations in himself will nevertheless feel their pressure so strongly that he will be glad enough to make use of an unconscious mechanism to alleviate his situation. He can obtain this alleviation—and, indeed, acquittal by his conscience—if he projects his own impulses to faithlessness on to the partner to whom he owes faith. This strong motive can then make use of the perceptual material which betrays unconscious impulses of the same kind in the partner, and the subject can justify himself with the reflection that the other is probably not much better than he is himself.[1]

Social conventions have wisely taken this universal state of things into account, by granting a certain amount of latitude to the married woman's craving to attract and the married man's thirst to make conquests, in the expectation that this inevitable tendency to unfaithfulness will thus find a safety-valve and be rendered innocuous. Convention has laid down that neither partner is to hold the other accountable for these little excursions in the direction of unfaithfulness, and they usually result in the desire that has been awakened by the new object finding satisfaction in some kind of return to faithfulness to the original object. A jealous person, however, does not recognize this convention of tolerance; he does not believe in any such thing as a halt or a turning-back once the path has been trodden, nor that a flirtation may be a safeguard against actual infidelity. In the treatment of a jealous person like this, one must refrain from disputing with him the material on

[1] Cf. Desdemona's song [*Othello* IV, 3]:

> I called my love false love; but what said he then?
> If I court moe women, you'll couch with moe men.

which he bases his suspicions; one can only aim at bringing him to regard the matter in a different light.

The jealousy that arises from such a projection has, it is true, an almost delusional character; it is, however, amenable to the analytic work of exposing the unconscious phantasies of the subject's own infidelity. The position is worse as regards jealousy belonging to the third layer, the true *delusional* type. It too has its origin in repressed impulses towards unfaithfulness; but the object in these cases is of the same sex as the subject. Delusional jealousy is what is left of a homosexuality that has run its course, and it rightly takes its position among the classical forms of paranoia. As an attempt at defence against an unduly strong homosexual impulse it may, in a man, be described in the formula: '*I* do not love him, *she* loves him!' [1] In a delusional case one will be prepared to find jealousy belonging to all three layers, never to the third alone.

B

Paranoia.—Cases of paranoia are for well-known reasons not usually amenable to analytic investigation. I have recently been able, nevertheless, by an intensive study of two paranoics, to discover something new to me.

The first case was that of a youngish man with a fully developed paranoia of jealousy, the object of which was his impeccably faithful wife. A stormy period in which the delusion had possessed him uninterruptedly already lay behind him. When I saw him he was only subject to clearly separated attacks, which lasted for several days and which, curiously enough, regularly appeared on the day after he had had sexual intercourse with his wife, which was, incidentally, satisfying to both of them. The inference is justified that after every satiation of the heterosexual libido the homosexual component, likewise stimulated by the act, forced an outlet for itself in the attack of jealousy.

These attacks drew their material from his observation of minute indications, by which his wife's quite unconscious coquetry, unnoticeable to any one else, had betrayed itself to him. She had unintentionally touched the man sitting next her with her hand; she had turned too much towards him, or she had

[1] See the Schreber analysis (1911c) [Part III].

smiled more pleasantly than when alone with her husband. He was extraordinarily observant of all these manifestations of her unconscious, and always knew how to interpret them correctly, so that he really was always in the right about it, and could furthermore call in analysis to justify his jealousy. His abnormality really reduced itself to this, that he watched his wife's unconscious mind much more closely and then regarded it as far more important than anyone else would have thought of doing.

We are reminded that sufferers from persecutory paranoia act in just the same way. They, too, cannot regard anything in other people as indifferent, and they, too, take up minute indications with which these other, unknown, people present them, and use them in their delusions of reference. The meaning of their delusion of reference is that they expect from all strangers something like love. But these people show them nothing of the kind; they laugh to themselves, flourish their sticks, even spit on the ground as they go by—and one really does not do such things while a person in whom one takes a friendly interest is near. One does them only when one feels quite indifferent to the passer-by, when one can treat him like air; and, considering, too, the fundamental kinship of the concepts of 'stranger' and 'enemy', the paranoic is not so far wrong in regarding this indifference as hate, in contrast to his claim for love.

We begin to see that we describe the behaviour of both jealous and persecutory paranoics very inadequately by saying that they project outwards on to others what they do not wish to recognize in themselves. Certainly they do this; but they do not project it into the blue, so to speak, where there is nothing of the sort already. They let themselves be guided by their knowledge of the unconscious, and displace to the unconscious minds of others the attention which they have withdrawn from their own. Our jealous husband perceived his wife's unfaithfulness instead of his own; by becoming conscious of hers and magnifying it enormously he succeeded in keeping his own unconscious. If we accept his example as typical, we may infer that the enmity which the persecuted paranoic sees in others is the reflection of his own hostile impulses against them. Since we know that with the paranoic it is precisely the most loved person of his own sex that becomes his persecutor, the question arises where this reversal of affect takes its origin; the answer is not far to seek—the ever-present ambivalence of feeling provides its source and the non-fulfilment of his claim for love strengthens it. This ambivalence thus serves the same purpose for the persecuted paranoic as jealousy served for my patient—that of a defence against homosexuality.

The dreams of my jealous patient presented me with a great surprise. They were not simultaneous with the outbreaks of the attacks, it is true, but they occurred within the period which was under the dominance of the delusion; yet they were completely free from delusion and they revealed the underlying homosexual impulses with no more than the usual degree of disguise. Since I had had little experience of the dreams of paranoics, it seemed plausible at the time to suppose that it was true in general that paranoia does not penetrate into dreams.

This patient's homosexual position was easily surveyed. He had made no friendships and developed no social interests; one had the impression that only the delusion had carried forward the development of his relations with men, as if it had taken over some of the arrears that had been neglected. The fact that his father was of no great importance in the family, combined with a humiliating homosexual trauma in early boyhood, had forced his homosexuality into repression and barred the way to its sublimation. The whole of his youth was governed by a strong attachment to his mother. Of all her many sons he was her declared favourite, and he developed marked jealousy of the normal type in regard to her. When later he made his choice of a wife—mainly prompted by an impulse to enrich his mother—his longing for a virgin mother expressed itself in obsessive doubts about his fiancée's virginity. The first years of his marriage were free from jealousy. Then he became unfaithful to his wife and entered upon an intimate relationship with another woman that lasted for a considerable time. Frightened by a certain suspicion, he at length made an end of this love affair, and not until then did jealousy of the second, projected type break out, by means of which he was able to assuage his self-reproaches about his own unfaithfulness. It was soon complicated by an accession of homosexual impulses, of which his father-in-law was the object, and became a fully formed jealous paranoia.

My second case would probably not have been classified as persecutory paranoia, apart from analysis; but I had to recognize the young man as a candidate for a terminal illness of that kind. In his attitude to his father there existed an ambivalence which in its range was quite extraordinary. On the one hand, he was the most pronounced rebel imaginable, and had developed manifestly in every direction in opposition to his father's wishes and ideals; on the other hand, at a deeper level he was still the most submissive of sons, who after his father's death denied himself all enjoyment of women out of a tender sense of guilt. His actual relations with men were clearly dominated by suspiciousness; his keen intellect easily rationalized this attitude; and he knew how to bring it about that both friends and acquaintances deceived and exploited him. The new thing I learned from studying him was that classical persecutory ideas may be present without finding belief or acceptance. They flashed up occasionally during the analysis, but he regarded them as unimportant and invariably scoffed at them. This may occur in many cases of paranoia; it may be that the delusions which we regard as new formations when the disease breaks out have already long been in existence.

It seems to me that we have here an important discovery—namely, that the qualitative factor, the presence of certain neurotic formations, has less practical significance than the quantitative factor, the degree of attention or, more correctly, the amount of cathexis that these structures are able to attract to themselves. Our consideration of the first case, the jealous paranoia, led to a similar estimate of the importance of the quantitative factor, by showing that there also the abnormality essentially consisted in the hypercathexis of the interpretations of someone else's unconscious. We have long known of an analogous fact in the analysis of hysteria. The pathogenic phantasies, derivatives of repressed instinctual impulses, are for a long time tolerated alongside the normal life of the mind, and have no pathogenic effect until by a revolution in the libidinal economy they receive a hypercathexis; not till then does the conflict which leads to the formation of symptoms break out. Thus as our knowledge grows we are increasingly impelled to bring the *economic* point of view into the foreground. I should also like to throw out the question whether this quantitative factor that I am now dwelling on does not suffice to cover the phenomena which Bleuler [1916] and others have lately proposed to name 'switching'. One need only assume that an increase in resistance in the course taken by the psychical current in one direction results in a hypercathexis of another path and thus causes the flow to be switched into that path.[1]

My two cases of paranoia showed an instructive contrast in the behaviour of their dreams. Whereas those of the first case were free from delusion, as has already been said, the other patient produced great numbers of persecutory dreams, which may be regarded as forerunners of or substitutes for the delusional ideas. The pursuer, whom he only managed to escape with great fear, was usually a powerful bull or some other male symbol which even in the dream itself he sometimes recognized as representing his father. One day he produced a very characteristic paranoic transference-dream. He saw me shaving in front of him, and from the scent he realized that I was using the same soap as his father had used. I was doing this in order to oblige him to make a father-transference on to me. The choice of this incident for his dream quite unmistakably betrays the patient's depreciatory attitude to his paranoic phantasies and his disbelief in them; for his own eyes could tell him every day that I was never in a position to make use of shaving-soap and that therefore there was in this respect nothing to which a father-transference could attach itself.

A comparison of the dreams of the two patients shows, however, that the question whether or not paranoia (or any other psychoneurosis) can penetrate into dreams is based on a false conception of dreams. Dreams are distinguished from waking thought by the fact that they can include material (belonging to the region of the repressed) which must not emerge in waking thought. Apart from this, dreams are merely a *form of thinking*, a transformation of preconscious material of thought by the dream-work and its conditions.[2] Our terminology of the neuroses is not applicable to repressed material; this cannot be called hysterical, nor obsessional, nor paranoic. As against this, the other part of the material which is subjected to the process of dream-formation—the preconscious thoughts— may be normal or may bear the character of any neurosis; they

[1] [The idea underlying this goes back to the picture of the psychical apparatus which Freud had already drawn in his 'Project' of 1895 (Freud 1950a).]   [2] [Cf. above, pp. 165–6.]

may be the products of any of the pathogenic processes in which the essence of a neurosis lies. There seems to be no reason why any such pathological idea should not be transformed into a dream. A dream may therefore quite simply represent a hysterical phantasy, an obsessional idea, or a delusion—that is, may reveal one or other of these upon interpretation. Observation of the two paranoics shows that the dreams of the one were quite normal while he was subject to his delusion, and that those of the other were paranoic in content while he was treating his delusional ideas with contempt. In both cases, therefore, the dream took up the material that was at the time forced into the background in waking life. This too, however, need not necessarily be an invariable rule.

C

Homosexuality.—Recognition of the organic factor in homosexuality does not relieve us of the obligation of studying the psychical processes connected with its origin. The typical process,[1] already established in innumerable cases, is that a few years after the termination of puberty a young man, who until this time has been strongly fixated to his mother, changes his attitude; he identifies himself with his mother, and looks about for love-objects in whom he can re-discover himself, and whom he might then love as his mother loved him. The characteristic mark of this process is that for several years one of the necessary conditions for his love is usually that the male object shall be of the same age as he himself was when the change took place. We have come to know of various factors contributing to this result, probably in different degrees. First there is the fixation on the mother, which makes it difficult to pass on to another woman. Identification with the mother is an outcome of this attachment, and at the same time in a certain sense it enables the son to keep true to her, his first object. Then there is the inclination towards a narcissistic object-choice, which in general lies readier to hand and is easier to put into effect than a move towards the other sex. Behind this latter factor there lies concealed another of quite exceptional strength, or perhaps it coincides with it: the high value set upon the male organ and the

[1] [Described by Freud in Chapter III of his study on Leonardo (1910c).]

inability to tolerate its absence in a love-object. Depreciation of women, and aversion to them, even horror of them, are generally derived from the early discovery that women have no penis. We subsequently discovered, as another powerful motive urging towards homosexual object-choice, regard for the father or fear of him; for the renunciation of women means that all rivalry with him (or with all men who may take his place) is avoided. The two last motives—the clinging to the condition of a penis in the object, as well as the retiring in favour of the father—may be ascribed to the castration complex. Attachment to the mother, narcissism, fear of castration—these are the factors (which incidentally have nothing specific about them) that we have hitherto found in the psychical aetiology of homosexuality; and with these must be reckoned the effect of seduction, which is responsible for a premature fixation of the libido, as well as the influence of the organic factor which favours the passive role in love.

We have, however, never regarded this analysis of the origin of homosexuality as complete. I can now point to a new mechanism leading to homosexual object-choice, although I cannot say how large a part it plays in the formation of the extreme, manifest and exclusive type of homosexuality. Observation has directed my attention to several cases in which during early childhood impulses of jealousy, derived from the mother-complex and of very great intensity, arose [in a boy] against rivals, usually older brothers. This jealousy led to an exceedingly hostile and aggressive attitude towards these brothers which might sometimes reach the pitch of actual death-wishes, but which could not maintain themselves in the face of the subject's further development. Under the influences of upbringing—and certainly not uninfluenced also by their own continuing powerlessness—these impulses yielded to repression and underwent a transformation, so that the rivals of the earlier period became the first homosexual love-objects. Such an outcome of the attachment to the mother shows various interesting relations with other processes known to us. First of all it is a complete contrast to the development of persecutory paranoia, in which the person who has before been loved becomes the hated persecutor, whereas here the hated rivals are transformed into love-objects. It represents, too, an exaggeration of the process which, according to my view, leads to the birth of social instincts in the individual.[1] In both processes there is first the presence of jealous and hostile impulses which cannot achieve satisfaction; and both the affectionate and the social feelings of identification arise as reactive formations against the repressed aggressive impulses.

This new mechanism of homosexual object-choice—its origin in rivalry which has been overcome and in aggressive impulses which have become repressed—is sometimes combined with the typical conditions already familiar to us. In the history of homosexuals one often hears that the change in them took place after the mother had praised another boy and set him up as a model. The tendency to a narcissistic object-choice was thus stimulated, and after a short phase of keen jealousy the rival became a love-object. As a rule, however, the new mechanism is distinguished by the change taking place at a much earlier period, and the identification with the mother receding into the background. Moreover, in the cases I have observed, it led only to homosexual attitudes which did not exclude heterosexuality and did not involve a *horror feminae*.

It is well known that a good number of homosexuals are characterized by a special development of their social instinctual impulses and by their devotion to the interests of the community. It would be tempting, as a theoretical explanation of this, to say that the behaviour towards men in general of a man who sees in other men potential love-objects must be different from that of a man who looks upon other men in the first instance as rivals in regard to women. The only objection to this is that jealousy and rivalry play their part in homosexual love as well, and that the community of men also includes these potential rivals. Apart from this speculative explanation, however, the fact that homosexual object-choice not infrequently proceeds from an early overcoming of rivalry with men cannot be without a bearing on the connection between homosexuality and social feeling.

In the light of psycho-analysis we are accustomed to regard social feeling as a sublimation of homosexual attitudes towards objects. In the homosexuals with marked social interests, it would seem that the detachment of social feeling from object-choice has not been fully carried through.

[1] Cf. my *Group Psychology and the Analysis of the Ego* (1921c). [See above, p. 119 ff.]

TWO ENCYCLOPAEDIA ARTICLES
(1923 [1922])

'PSYCHOANALYSE' UND 'LIBIDOTHEORIE'

(*a*) GERMAN EDITIONS:

1923   In *Handwörterbuch der Sexualwissenschaft*, ed. M. Marcuse,
       Bonn. Pp. 296–8 and 377–83.
1928   *G.S.*, **11**, 201–23.
1940   *G.W.*, **13**, 211–33.

(*b*) ENGLISH TRANSLATION:
           'Two Encyclopaedia Articles'
1942   *Int. J. Psycho-Anal.*, **23**, 97–107. (Tr. James Strachey.)
1950   *C.P.*, **5**, 107–35. (Same translator.)

The present translation is that of 1950, slightly modified.

According to a note to be found in *Gesammelte Schriften*, **11**,
201, these articles were written during the summer of 1922, that
is to say, before Freud's final re-casting of his views upon the
structure of the mind in *The Ego and the Id* (1923*b*). But the new
views, though unexpressed in these articles, must already have
been clearly present in his thoughts while he was writing them,
for it was in September, 1922, at the Berlin International
Psycho-Analytical Congress, which is actually mentioned in
one of the articles (p. 248), that he first made public his newly-
defined conceptions of ego, super-ego and id. A somewhat
similarly-conceived didactic article, written not long afterwards
for an American publication (1924*f*), takes these new ideas into
account.

TWO ENCYCLOPAEDIA ARTICLES

(A) PSYCHO-ANALYSIS

Psycho-Analysis is the name (1) of a procedure for the investigation of mental processes which are almost inaccessible in any other way, (2) of a method (based upon that investigation) for the treatment of neurotic disorders and (3) of a collection of psychological information obtained along those lines, which is gradually being accumulated into a new scientific discipline.

History.—The best way of understanding psycho-analysis is still by tracing its origin and development. In 1880 and 1881 Dr. Josef Breuer of Vienna, a well-known physician and experimental physiologist, was occupied in the treatment of a girl who had fallen ill of a severe hysteria while she was nursing her sick father. The clinical picture was made up of motor paralyses, inhibitions, and disturbances of consciousness. Following a hint given him by the patient herself, who was a person of great intelligence, he put her into a state of hypnosis and contrived that, by describing to him the moods and thoughts that were uppermost in her mind, she returned on each particular occasion to a normal mental condition. By consistently repeating the same laborious process, he succeeded in freeing her from all her inhibitions and paralyses, so that in the end he found his trouble rewarded by a great therapeutic success as well as by an unexpected insight into the nature of the puzzling neurosis. Nevertheless, Breuer refrained from following up his discovery or from publishing anything about the case until some ten years later, when the personal influence of the present writer (Freud, who had returned to Vienna in 1886 after studying in the school of Charcot) prevailed on him to take up the subject afresh and embark upon a joint study of it. These two, Breuer and Freud, published a preliminary paper 'On the Psychical Mechanism of Hysterical Phenomena' in 1893, and in 1895 a volume entitled *Studies on Hysteria* (which reached its fourth edition in 1922), in which they described their therapeutic procedure as '*cathartic*'.

Catharsis.—The investigations which lay at the root of Breuer and Freud's studies led to two chief results, and these have not been shaken by subsequent experience: first, that hysterical symptoms have sense and meaning, being substitutes for normal mental acts; and secondly, that the uncovering of this unknown meaning is accompanied by the removal of the symptoms—so that in this case scientific research and therapeutic effort coincide. The observations were carried out upon a series of patients who were treated in the same manner as Breuer's first patient, that is to say, put into a state of deep hypnosis; and the results seemed brilliant, until later their weak side became evident. The theoretical ideas put forward at that time by Breuer and Freud were influenced by Charcot's theories on traumatic hysteria and could find support in the findings of his pupil Pierre Janet, which, though they were published earlier than the *Studies*, were in fact subsequent to Breuer's first case. From the very beginning the factor of *affect* was brought into the foreground: hysterical symptoms, the authors maintained, came into existence when a mental process with a heavy charge of affect was in any way prevented from being levelled out along the normal path leading to consciousness and movement (i.e. was prevented from being *'abreacted'*); as a result of this the affect, which was in a sense *'strangulated'*, was diverted along wrong paths and flowed off into the somatic innervation (a process named *'conversion'*). The occasions upon which 'pathogenic ideas' of this kind arose were described by Breuer and Freud as *'psychical traumas'*, and, since these often dated back to the very remote past, it was possible for the authors to say that hysterics suffered mainly from reminiscences (which had not been dealt with). Under the treatment, therefore, *'catharsis'* came about when the path to consciousness was opened and there was a normal discharge of affect. It will be seen that an essential part of this theory was the assumption of the existence of *unconscious* mental processes. Janet too had made use of unconscious acts in mental life; but, as he insisted in his later polemics against psycho-analysis, to him the phrase was no more than a make-shift expression, a *'manière de parler'*, and he intended to suggest no new point of view by it.

In a theoretical section of the *Studies* Breuer brought forward some speculative ideas about the processes of excitation in the mind. These ideas determined the direction of future lines of thought and even to-day have not received sufficient appreciation. But they brought his contributions to this branch of science to an end, and soon afterwards he withdrew from the common work.

The Transition to Psycho-Analysis.—Contrasts between the views of the two authors had been visible even in the *Studies*. Breuer supposed that the pathogenic ideas produced their traumatic effect because they arose during '*hypnoid states*', in which mental functioning was subject to special limitations. The present writer rejected this explanation and inclined to the belief that an idea became pathogenic if its content was in opposition to the predominant trend of the subject's mental life so that it provoked him into '*defence*'. (Janet had attributed to hysterical patients a constitutional incapacity for holding together the contents of their minds; and it was at this point that his path diverged from that of Breuer and Freud.) Moreover, the two innovations which led the present writer to move away from the cathartic method had already been mentioned in the *Studies*. After Breuer's withdrawal they became the starting-point of fresh developments.

Abandonment of Hypnosis.—The first of these innovations was based on practical experience and led to a change in technique. The second consisted in an advance in the clinical understanding of neuroses. It soon appeared that the therapeutic hopes which had been placed upon cathartic treatment in hypnosis were to some extent unfulfilled. It was true that the disappearance of the symptoms went hand-in-hand with the catharsis, but total success turned out to be entirely dependent upon the patient's relation to the physician and thus resembled the effect of 'suggestion'. If that relation was disturbed, all the symptoms reappeared, just as though they had never been cleared up. In addition to this, the small number of people who could be put into a deep state of hypnosis involved a very considerable limitation, from the medical standpoint, of the applicability of the cathartic procedure. For these reasons the present writer decided to give up the use of hypnosis. But at the same time the impressions he had derived from hypnosis afforded him the means of replacing it.

Free Association.—The effect of the hypnotic condition upon the patient had been so greatly to increase his ability to make associations that he was able straight away to find the path—inaccessible to his conscious reflection—which led from the symptom to the thoughts and memories connected with it. The abandonment of hypnosis seemed to make the situation hope-less, until the writer recalled a remark of Bernheim's to the effect that things that had been experienced in a state of som-nambulism were only *apparently* forgotten and that they could be brought into recollection at any time if the physician insisted forcibly enough that the patient knew them. The writer there-fore endeavoured to insist on his *unhypnotized* patients giving him their associations, so that from the material thus provided he might find the path leading to what had been forgotten or fended off. He noticed later that the insistence was unnecessary and that copious ideas almost always arose in the patient's mind, but that they were held back from being communicated and even from becoming conscious by certain objections put by the patient in his own way. It was to be expected—though this was still unproved and not until later confirmed by wide experience —that everything that occurred to a patient setting out from a particular starting-point must also stand in an internal con-nection with that starting-point; hence arose the technique of educating the patient to give up the whole of his critical attitude and of making use of the material which was thus brought to light for the purpose of uncovering the connections that were being sought. A strong belief in the strict determination of mental events certainly played a part in the choice of this technique as a substitute for hypnosis.

The '*Fundamental Technical Rule*' of this procedure of 'free association' has from that time on been maintained in psycho-analytic work. The treatment is begun by the patient being required to put himself in the position of an attentive and dis-passionate self-observer, merely to read off all the time the surface of his consciousness, and on the one hand to make a duty of the most complete honesty while on the other not to hold back any idea from communication, even if (1) he feels that it is too disagreeable or if (2) he judges that it is nonsensical or (3) too unimportant or (4) irrelevant to what is being looked for. It is uniformly found that precisely those ideas which provoke these last-mentioned reactions are of particular value in dis-covering the forgotten material.

Psycho-Analysis as an Interpretative Art.—The new technique altered the picture of the treatment so greatly, brought the physician into such a new relation to the patient and produced so many surprising results that it seemed justifiable to distinguish the procedure from the cathartic method by giving it a new name. The present writer gave this method of treatment, which could now be extended to many other forms of neurotic disorder, the name of *psycho-analysis*. Now, in the first resort, this psycho-analysis was an art of *interpretation* and it set itself the task of carrying deeper the first of Breuer's great discoveries —namely, that neurotic symptoms are significant substitutes for other mental acts which have been omitted. It was now a question of regarding the material produced by the patients' associations as though it hinted at a hidden meaning and of discovering that meaning from it. Experience soon showed that the attitude which the analytic physician could most advantageously adopt was to surrender himself to his own unconscious mental activity, in a state of *evenly suspended attention*, to avoid so far as possible reflection and the construction of conscious expectations, not to try to fix anything that he heard particularly in his memory, and by these means to catch the drift of the patient's unconscious with his own unconscious. It was then found that, except under conditions that were too unfavourable, the patient's associations emerged like allusions, as it were, to one particular theme and that it was only necessary for the physician to go a step further in order to guess the material which was concealed from the patient himself and to be able to communicate it to him. It is true that this work of interpretation was not to be brought under strict rules and left a great deal of play to the physician's tact and skill; but, with impartiality and practice, it was usually possible to obtain trustworthy results—that is to say, results which were confirmed by being repeated in similar cases. At a time when so little was as yet known of the unconscious, the structure of the neuroses and the pathological processes underlying them, it was a matter for satisfaction that a technique of this kind should be available, even if it had no better theoretical basis. Moreover it is still employed in analyses at the present day in the same manner, though with a sense of greater assurance and with a better understanding of its limitations.

The Interpretation of Parapraxes and Haphazard Acts.—It was a triumph for the interpretative art of psycho-analysis when it succeeded in demonstrating that certain common mental acts of normal people, for which no one had hitherto attempted to put forward a psychological explanation, were to be regarded in the same light as the symptoms of neurotics: that is to say, they had a *meaning*, which was unknown to the subject but which could easily be discovered by analytic means. The phenomena in question were such events as the temporary forgetting of familiar words and names, forgetting to carry out prescribed tasks, everyday slips of the tongue and of the pen, misreadings, losses and mislayings of objects, certain errors, instances of apparently accidental self-injury, and finally habitual movements carried out seemingly without intention or in play, tunes hummed 'thoughtlessly', and so on. All of these were shorn of their physiological explanation, if any such had ever been attempted, were shown to be strictly determined and were revealed as an expression of the subject's suppressed intentions or as a result of a clash between two intentions one of which was permanently or temporarily unconscious. The importance of this contribution to psychology was of many kinds. The range of mental determinism was extended by it in an unforeseen manner; the supposed gulf between normal and pathological mental events was narrowed; in many cases a useful insight was afforded into the play of mental forces that must be suspected to lie behind the phenomena. Finally, a class of material was brought to light which is calculated better than any other to stimulate a belief in the existence of unconscious mental acts even in people to whom the hypothesis of something at once mental and unconscious seems strange and even absurd. The study of one's own parapraxes and haphazard acts, for which most people have ample opportunities, is even to-day the best preparation for an approach to psycho-analysis. In analytic treatment, the interpretation of parapraxes retains a place as a means of uncovering the unconscious, alongside the immeasurably more important interpretation of associations.

The Interpretation of Dreams.—A new approach to the depths of mental life was opened when the technique of free association was applied to dreams, whether one's own or those of patients in analysis. In fact, the greater and better part of what we know of the processes in the unconscious levels of the mind is derived from the interpretation of dreams. Psycho-analysis has restored to dreams the importance which was generally ascribed to them in ancient times, but it treats them differently. It does not rely upon the cleverness of the dream-interpreter but for the most part hands the task over to the dreamer himself by asking him for his associations to the separate elements of the dream. By pursuing these associations further we obtain knowledge of thoughts which coincide entirely with the dream but which can be recognized—up to a certain point—as genuine and completely intelligible portions of waking mental activity. Thus the recollected dream emerges as the *manifest dream-content*, in contrast to the *latent dream-thoughts* discovered by interpretation. The process which has transformed the latter into the former, that is to say into 'the dream', and which is undone by the work of interpretation, may be called the '*dream-work*'.

We also describe the latent dream-thoughts, on account of their connection with waking life, as '*residues of the [previous] day*'. By the operation of the dream-work (to which it would be quite incorrect to ascribe any 'creative' character) the latent dream-thoughts are *condensed* in a remarkable way, are *distorted* by the *displacement* of psychical intensities and are arranged with a view to being *represented in visual pictures*; and, besides all this, before the manifest dream is arrived at, they are submitted to a process of *secondary revision* which seeks to give the new product something in the nature of sense and coherence. Strictly speaking, this last process does not form a part of the dream-work.[1]

The Dynamic Theory of Dream-Formation.—An understanding of the dynamics of dream-formation did not involve any very great difficulties. The motive power for the formation of dreams is not provided by the latent dream-thoughts or day's residues, but by an unconscious impulse, repressed during the day, with which the day's residues have been able to establish contact and which contrives to make a *wish-fulfilment* for itself out of the material of the latent thoughts. Thus every dream is on the one hand the fulfilment of a wish on the part of the unconscious and on the other hand (in so far as it succeeds in guarding the state of sleep against being disturbed) the fulfilment of the normal wish to sleep which set the sleep going. If we disregard the unconscious contribution to the formation of the dream and limit the dream to its latent thoughts, it can represent anything with which waking life has been concerned—a reflection, a warning, an intention, a preparation for the immediate future or, once again, the satisfaction of an unfulfilled wish. The unrecognizability, strangeness and absurdity of the manifest dream are

[1] [In *The Interpretation of Dreams, Standard Ed.*, **5**, 490, secondary revision is regarded as part of the dream-work.]

partly the result of the translation of the thoughts into a different, so to say *archaic*, method of expression, but partly the effect of a restrictive, critically disapproving agency in the mind, which does not entirely cease to function during sleep. It is plausible to suppose that the '*dream-censorship*', which we regard as being responsible in the first instance for the distortion of the dream-thoughts into the manifest dream, is an expression of the same mental forces which during the day-time had held back or *repressed* the unconscious wishful impulse.

It has been worth while to enter in some detail into the explanation of dreams, since analytic work has shown that the dynamics of the formation of dreams are the same as those of the formation of symptoms. In both cases we find a struggle between two trends, of which one is unconscious and ordinarily repressed and strives towards satisfaction—that is, wish-fulfilment—while the other, belonging probably to the conscious ego, is disapproving and repressive. The outcome of this conflict is a *compromise-formation* (the dream or the symptom) in which both trends have found an incomplete expression. The theoretical importance of this conformity between dreams and symptoms is illuminating. Since dreams are not pathological phenomena, the fact shows that the mental mechanisms which produce the symptoms of illness are equally present in normal mental life, that the same uniform law embraces both the normal and the abnormal and that the findings of research into neurotics or psychotics cannot be without significance for our understanding of the healthy mind.

Symbolism.—In the course of investigating the form of expression brought about by the dream-work, the surprising fact emerged that certain objects, arrangements and relations are represented, in a sense indirectly, by 'symbols', which are used by the dreamer without his understanding them and to which as a rule he offers no associations. Their translation has to be provided by the analyst, who can himself only discover it empirically by experimentally fitting it into the context. It was later found that linguistic usage, mythology and folklore afford the most ample analogies to dream-symbols. Symbols, which raise the most interesting and hitherto unsolved problems, seem to be a fragment of extremely ancient inherited mental equipment. The use of a common symbolism extends far beyond the use of a common language.

The Aetiological Significance of Sexual Life.—The second novelty which emerged after the hypnotic technique had been replaced by free associations was of a clinical nature. It was discovered in the course of the prolonged search for the traumatic experiences from which hysterical symptoms appeared to be derived. The more carefully the search was pursued the more extensive seemed to be the network of aetiologically significant impressions, but the further back, too, did they reach into the patient's puberty or childhood. At the same time they assumed a uniform character and eventually it became inevitable to bow before the evidence and recognize that at the root of the formation of every symptom there were to be found traumatic experiences from early sexual life. Thus a sexual trauma stepped into the place of an ordinary trauma and the latter was seen to owe its aetiological significance to an associative or symbolic connection with the former, which had preceded it. An investigation of cases of common nervousness (falling into the two classes of *neurasthenia* and *anxiety neurosis*) which was simultaneously undertaken led to the conclusion that these disorders could be traced to *contemporary* abuses in the patients' sexual life and could be removed if these were brought to an end. It was thus easy to infer that neuroses in general are an expression of disturbances in sexual life, the so-called *actual-neuroses* being the consequences (by chemical agency) of *contemporary* injuries and the *psychoneuroses* the consequences (by psychical modification) of *bygone* injuries to a biological function which had hitherto been gravely neglected by science. None of the theses of psycho-analysis has met with such tenacious scepticism or such embittered resistance as this assertion of the preponderating aetiological significance of sexual life in the neuroses. It should, however, be expressly remarked that, in its development up to the present day, psycho-analysis has found no reason to retreat from this opinion.

Infantile Sexuality.—As a result of its aetiological researches, psycho-analysis found itself in the position of dealing with a subject the very existence of which had scarcely been suspected previously. Science had become accustomed to consider sexual life as beginning with puberty and regarded manifestations of sexuality in children as rare signs of abnormal precocity and degeneracy. But now psycho-analysis revealed a wealth of phenomena, remarkable, yet of regular occurrence, which made it necessary to date back the beginning of the sexual function in children almost to the commencement of extra-uterine existence; and it was asked with astonishment how all this could have come to be overlooked. The first glimpses of sexuality in children had indeed been obtained through the analytic examination of adults and were consequently saddled with all the doubts and sources of error that could be attributed to such a belated retrospect; but subsequently (from 1908 onwards) a beginning was made with the analysis of children themselves and with the unembarrassed observation of their behaviour, and in this way direct confirmation was reached for the whole factual basis of the new view.

Sexuality in children showed a different picture in many respects from that in adults, and, surprisingly enough, it exhibited numerous traces of what, in adults, were condemned as *'perversions'*. It became necessary to enlarge the concept of what was sexual, till it covered more than the impulsion towards the union of the two sexes in the sexual act or towards provoking particular pleasurable sensations in the genitals. But this enlargement was rewarded by the new possibility of grasping infantile, normal and perverse sexual life as a single whole.

The analytic researches carried out by the writer fell, to begin with, into the error of greatly overestimating the importance of *seduction* as a source of sexual manifestations in children and as a root for the formation of neurotic symptoms. This misapprehension was corrected when it became possible to appreciate the extraordinarily large part played in the mental life of neurotics by the activities of *phantasy*, which clearly carried more weight in neurosis than did external reality. Behind these phantasies there came to light the material which allows us to draw the picture which follows of the development of the sexual function.

The Development of the Libido.—The sexual instinct, the dynamic manifestation of which in mental life we shall call *'libido'*, is made up of component instincts into which it may once more break up and which are only gradually united into well-defined organizations. The sources of these component instincts are the organs of the body and in particular certain specially marked *erotogenic zones*; but contributions are made to libido from every important functional process in the body. At first the individual component instincts strive for satisfaction independently of one another, but in the course of development they become more and more convergent and concentrated. The first (pregenital) stage of organization to be discerned is the *oral* one, in which—in conformity with the suckling's predominant interest—the oral zone plays the leading part. This is followed by the *sadistic-anal* organization, in which the *anal* zone and the component instinct of *sadism* are particularly prominent; at this stage the difference between the sexes is represented by the contrast between active and passive. The third and final stage of organization is that in which the majority of the component instincts converge under the *primacy of the genital zones*. As a rule this development is passed through swiftly and unobtrusively; but some individual portions of the instincts remain behind at the prodromal stages of the process and thus give rise to *fixations* of libido, which are important as constituting predispositions for subsequent irruptions of repressed impulses and which stand in a definite relation to the later development of neuroses and perversions. (See the article on 'The Libido Theory' [p. 255 below].)

The Process of Finding an Object, and the Oedipus Complex.—In the first instance the oral component instinct finds satisfaction by attaching itself to the sating of the desire for nourishment; and its object is the mother's breast. It then detaches itself, becomes independent and at the same time *auto-erotic*, that is, it finds an object in the child's own body. Others of the component instincts also start by being auto-erotic and are not until later diverted on to an external object. It is a particularly important fact that the component instincts belonging to the genital zone habitually pass through a period of intense auto-erotic satisfaction. The component instincts are not all equally serviceable in the final genital organization of libido; some of them (for instance, the anal components) are consequently left aside and suppressed, or undergo complicated transformations.

In the very earliest years of childhood (approximately between the ages of two and five) a convergence of the sexual impulses occurs of which, in the case of boys, the object is the mother. This choice of an object, in conjunction with a corresponding attitude of rivalry and hostility towards the father, provides the content of what is known as the *Oedipus complex*, which in every human being is of the greatest importance in determining the final shape of his erotic life. It has been found to be characteristic of a normal individual that he learns to master his Oedipus complex, whereas the neurotic subject remains involved in it.

The Diphasic Onset of Sexual Development.—Towards the end of the fifth year this early period of sexual life normally comes to an end. It is succeeded by a period of more or less complete *latency*, during which ethical restraints are built up, to act as defences against the desires of the Oedipus complex. In the subsequent period of *puberty*, the Oedipus complex is revivified in the unconscious and embarks upon further modifications. It is only at puberty that the sexual instincts develop to their full intensity; but the direction of that development, as well as all the predispositions for it, have already been determined by the early efflorescence of sexuality during childhood which preceded it. This diphasic development of the sexual function—in two stages, interrupted by the latency period—appears to be a biological peculiarity of the human species and to contain the determining factor for the origin of neuroses.

The Theory of Repression.—These theoretical considerations, taken together with the immediate impressions derived from analytic work, lead to a view of the neuroses which may be described in the roughest outline as follows. The neuroses are the expression of conflicts between the ego and such of the sexual impulses as seem to the ego incompatible with its integrity or with its ethical standards. Since these impulses are not *ego-syntonic*, the ego has *repressed* them: that is to say, it has withdrawn its interest from them and has shut them off from becoming conscious as well as from obtaining satisfaction by motor discharge. If in the course of analytic work one attempts to make these repressed impulses conscious, one becomes aware of the repressive forces in the form of *resistance*. But the achievement of repression fails particularly readily in the case of the sexual instincts. Their dammed-up libido finds other ways out from the unconscious: for it *regresses* to earlier phases of development and earlier attitudes towards objects, and, at weak points in the libidinal development where there are infantile fixations, it breaks through into consciousness and obtains discharge. What results is a *symptom* and consequently in its essence a substitutive sexual satisfaction. Nevertheless the symptom cannot entirely escape from the repressive forces of the ego and must therefore submit to modifications and displacements— exactly as happens with dreams—by means of which its characteristic of being a sexual satisfaction becomes unrecognizable. Consequently symptoms are in the nature of compromises between the repressed sexual instincts and the repressing ego instincts; they represent a wish-fulfilment for both partners to the conflict simultaneously, but one which is incomplete for each of them. This is quite strictly true of the symptoms of hysteria, while in the symptoms of obsessional neurosis there is often a stronger emphasis upon the side of the repressing function owing to the erection of reaction-formations, which are assurances against sexual satisfaction.

Transference.—If further proof were needed of the truth that the motive forces behind the formation of neurotic symptoms are of a sexual nature, it would be found in the fact that in the course of analytic treatment a special emotional relation is regularly formed between the patient and the physician. This goes far beyond rational limits. It varies between the most affectionate devotion and the most obstinate enmity and derives all of its characteristics from earlier erotic attitudes of the patient's which have become unconscious. This *transference* alike in its positive and in its negative form is used as a weapon by the resistance; but in the hands of the physician it becomes the most powerful therapeutic instrument and it plays a part scarcely to be over-estimated in the dynamics of the process of cure.

The Corner-Stones of Psycho-Analytic Theory.—The assumption that there are unconscious mental processes, the recognition of the theory of resistance and repression, the appreciation of the importance of sexuality and of the Oedipus complex—these constitute the principal subject-matter of psycho-analysis and the foundations of its theory. No one who cannot accept them all should count himself a psycho-analyst.

Later History of Psycho-Analysis.—Psycho-analysis was carried approximately thus far by the work of the writer of this article, who for more than ten years was its sole representative. In 1906 the Swiss psychiatrists Bleuler and C. G. Jung began to play a lively part in analysis; in 1907 a first conference of its supporters took place at Salzburg; and the young science soon found itself the centre of interest both among psychiatrists and laymen. Its reception in Germany, with her morbid craving for authority, was not precisely to the credit of German science and moved even so cool a partisan as Bleuler to an energetic protest. Yet no condemnation or dismissal at official congresses served to hold up the internal growth or external expansion of psycho-analysis. In the course of the next ten years it extended far beyond the frontiers of Europe and became especially popular in the United States of America, and this was due in no small degree to the advocacy and collaboration of Putnam (Boston), Ernest Jones (Toronto; later London), Flournoy (Geneva), Ferenczi (Budapest), Abraham (Berlin), and many others besides. The anathema which was imposed upon psycho-analysis led its supporters to combine in an international organization which in the present year (1922) is holding its eighth private Congress in Berlin and now includes local groups in Vienna, Budapest, Berlin, Holland, Zurich, London, New York, Calcutta and Moscow. This development was not interrupted even by the World War. In 1918–19 Dr. Anton von Freund of Budapest founded the Internationaler Psychoanalytischer Verlag, which publishes journals and books concerned with psycho-analysis, and in 1920 Dr. M. Eitingon opened in Berlin the first psycho-analytic clinic for the treatment of neurotics without private means. Translations of the writer's principal works, which are now in preparation, into French, Italian and Spanish, testify to a growing interest in psycho-analysis in the Latin world as well.

Between 1911 and 1913 two movements of divergence from psycho-analysis took place, evidently with the object of mitigating its repellent features. One of these (sponsored by C. G. Jung), in an endeavour to conform to ethical standards, divested the Oedipus complex of its real significance by giving it only a *symbolic* value, and in practice neglected the uncovering of the forgotten and, as we may call it, 'prehistoric' period of childhood. The other (originated by Alfred Adler in Vienna) reproduced many factors from psycho-analysis under other names—repression, for instance, appeared in a sexualized version as the 'masculine protest'. But in other respects it turned away from the unconscious and the sexual instincts, and endeavoured to trace back the development of character and of the neuroses to the 'will to power', which by means of overcompensation strives to check the dangers arising from 'organ inferiority'. Neither of these movements, with their systematic structures, had any permanent influence on psycho-analysis. In the case of Adler's theories it soon became clear that they had very little in common with psycho-analysis, which they were designed to replace.

More Recent Advances in Psycho-Analysis.—Since psycho-analysis has become the field of work for such a large number of observers it has made advances, both in extent and depth; but unfortunately these can receive only the briefest mention in the present article.

Narcissism.—The most important theoretical advance has certainly been the application of the libido theory to the repressing ego. The ego itself came to be regarded as a reservoir of what was described as narcissistic libido, from which the libidinal cathexes of objects flowed out and into which they could be once more withdrawn. By the help of this conception it became possible to embark upon the analysis of the ego and to make a clinical distinction of the psychoneuroses into *transference neuroses* and *narcissistic* disorders. In the former (hysteria and obsessional neurosis) the subject has at his disposal a quantity of libido striving to be transferred on to extraneous objects, and use is made of this in carrying out analytic treatment; on the other hand, the narcissistic disorders (dementia praecox, paranoia, melancholia) are characterized by a withdrawal of the libido from objects and they are therefore scarcely accessible to analytic therapy. But their therapeutic inaccessibility has not prevented analysis from making the most fruitful beginnings in the deeper study of these illnesses, which are counted among the psychoses.

Development of Technique.—After the analyst's curiosity had, as it were, been gratified by the elaboration of the technique of interpretation, it was inevitable that interest should turn to the problem of discovering the most effective way of influencing the patient. It soon became evident that the physician's immediate task was to assist the patient in getting to know, and afterwards in overcoming, the resistances which emerged in him during treatment and of which, to begin with, he himself was unaware. And it was found at the same time that the essential part of the process of cure lay in the overcoming of these resistances and that unless this was achieved no permanent mental change could be brought about in the patient. Since the analyst's efforts have in this way been directed upon the patient's resistance, analytic technique has attained a certainty and delicacy rivalling that of surgery. Consequently, everyone is strongly advised against undertaking psycho-analytic treatments without a strict training, and a physician who ventures upon them on the strength of his medical qualification is in no respect better than a layman.

Psycho-Analysis as a Therapeutic Procedure.—Psycho-analysis has never set itself up as a panacea and has never claimed to perform miracles. In one of the most difficult spheres of medical activity it is the only possible method of treatment for certain illnesses and for others it is the method which yields the best or the most permanent results—though never without a corresponding expenditure of time and trouble. A physician who is not wholly absorbed in the work of giving help will find his labours amply repaid by obtaining an unhoped-for insight into the complications of mental life and the interrelations between the mental and the physical. Where at present it cannot offer help but only theoretical understanding, it may perhaps be preparing the way for some later, more direct means of influencing neurotic disorders. Its province is above all the two transference neuroses, hysteria and obsessional neurosis, in which it has contributed to the discovery of their internal structure and operative mechanisms; and, beyond them, all kinds of phobias, inhibitions, deformities of character, sexual perversions and difficulties in erotic life. Some analysts (Jelliffe, Groddeck, Felix Deutsch) have reported too that the analytic treatment of gross organic diseases is not unpromising, since a mental factor not infrequently contributes to the origin and continuance of such illnesses. Since psycho-analysis demands a certain amount of psychical plasticity from its patients, some kind of age-limit must be laid down in their selection; and since it necessitates the devotion of long and intense attention to the individual patient, it would be uneconomical to squander such expenditure upon completely worthless persons who happen to be neurotic. Experience upon material in clinics can alone show what modifications may be necessary in order to make psycho-analytic treatment accessible to wider strata of the population or to adapt it to weaker intelligences.

Comparison between Psycho-Analysis and Hypnotic and Suggestive Methods.—Psycho-analytic procedure differs from all methods making use of suggestion, persuasion, etc., in that it does not seek to suppress by means of authority any mental phenomenon that may occur in the patient. It endeavours to trace the causation of the phenomenon and to remove it by bringing about a permanent modification in the conditions that led to it. In psycho-analysis the suggestive influence which is inevitably exercised by the physician is diverted on to the task assigned to the patient of overcoming his resistances, that is, of carrying forward the curative process. Any danger of falsifying the products of a patient's memory by suggestion can be avoided by prudent handling of the technique; but in general the arousing of resistances is a guarantee against the misleading effects of suggestive influence. It may be laid down that the aim of the treatment is to remove the patient's resistances and to pass his repressions in review and thus to bring about the most far-reaching unification and strengthening of his ego, to enable him to save the mental energy which he is expending upon internal conflicts, to make the best of him that his inherited capacities will allow and so to make him as efficient and as capable of enjoyment as is possible. The removal of the symptoms of the illness is not specifically aimed at, but is achieved, as it were, as a by-product if the analysis is properly carried through. The analyst respects the patient's individuality and does not seek to remould him in accordance with his own—that is, according to the physician's—personal ideals; he is glad to avoid giving advice and instead to arouse the patient's power of initiative.

Its Relation to Psychiatry.—Psychiatry is at present essentially a descriptive and classificatory science whose orientation is still towards the somatic rather than the psychological and which is without the possibility of giving explanations of the phenomena which it observes. Psycho-analysis does not, however, stand in opposition to it, as the almost unanimous behaviour of the psychiatrists might lead one to believe. On the contrary, as a *depth-psychology*, a psychology of those processes in mental life which are withdrawn from consciousness, it is called upon to provide psychiatry with an indispensable groundwork and to free it from its present limitations. We can foresee that the future will give birth to a scientific psychiatry, to which psycho-analysis has served as an introduction.

Criticisms and Misunderstandings of Psycho-Analysis.—Most of what is brought up against psycho-analysis, even in scientific works, is based upon insufficient information which in its turn seems to be determined by emotional resistances. Thus it is a mistake to accuse psycho-analysis of 'pan-sexualism' and to allege that it derives all mental occurrences from sexuality and traces them all back to it. On the contrary, psycho-analysis has from the very first distinguished the sexual instincts from others which it has provisionally termed 'ego instincts'. It has never dreamt of trying to explain 'everything', and even the neuroses it has traced back not to sexuality alone but to the conflict between the sexual impulses and the ego. In psycho-analysis (unlike the works of C. G. Jung) the term '*libido*' does not mean psychical energy in general but the motive force of the sexual instincts. Some assertions, such as that every dream is the fulfilment of a sexual wish, have never been maintained by it at all. The charge of one-sidedness made against psycho-analysis, which, as *the science of the unconscious mind*, has its own definite and restricted field of work, is as inapplicable as it would be if it were made against chemistry. To believe that psycho-analysis seeks a cure for neurotic disorders by giving a free rein to sexuality is a serious misunderstanding which can only be excused by ignorance. The making conscious of repressed sexual desires in analysis makes it possible, on the contrary, to obtain a mastery over them which the previous repression had been unable to achieve. It can more truly be said that analysis sets the neurotic free from the chains of his sexuality. Moreover, it is quite unscientific to judge analysis by whether it is calculated to undermine religion, authority and morals; for, like all sciences, it is entirely non-tendentious and has only a single aim —namely to arrive at a consistent view of one portion of reality. Finally, one can only characterize as simple-minded the fear which is sometimes expressed that all the highest goods of humanity, as they are called—research, art, love, ethical and social sense—will lose their value or their dignity because psycho-analysis is in a position to demonstrate their origin in elementary and animal instinctual impulses.

The Non-Medical Applications and Correlations of Psycho-Analysis.—Any estimate of psycho-analysis would be incomplete if it failed to make clear that, alone among the medical disciplines, it has the most extensive relations with the mental sciences, and that it is in a position to play a part of the same importance in the studies of religious and cultural history and in the sciences of mythology and literature as it is in psychiatry. This may seem strange when we reflect that originally its only object was the understanding and improvement of neurotic symptoms. But it is easy to indicate the starting-point of the bridge that leads over to the mental sciences. The analysis of dreams gave us an insight into the unconscious processes of the mind and showed us that the mechanisms which produce pathological symptoms are also operative in the normal mind. Thus psycho-analysis became a *depth-psychology* and capable as such of being applied to the mental sciences, and it was able to answer a good number of questions with which the academic psychology of consciousness was helpless to deal. At quite an early stage problems of human *phylogenesis* arose. It became clear that pathological function was often nothing more than a *regression* to an earlier stage in the development of normal function. C. G. Jung was the first to draw explicit attention to the striking similarity between the disordered phantasies of sufferers from dementia praecox and the myths of primitive peoples; while the present writer pointed out that the two wishes which combine to form the Oedipus complex coincide precisely with the two principal prohibitions imposed by *totemism* (not to kill the tribal ancestor and not to marry any woman belonging to one's own clan) and drew far-reaching conclusions from this fact. The significance of the Oedipus complex began to grow to gigantic proportions and it looked as though social order, morals, justice and religion had arisen together in the primaeval ages of mankind as reaction-formations against the Oedipus complex. Otto Rank threw a brilliant light upon mythology and the history of literature by the application of psycho-analytic views, as did Theodor Reik upon the history of morals and religions, while Dr. Pfister, of Zurich, aroused the interest of religious and secular teachers and demonstrated the importance of the psycho-analytic standpoint for education. Further discussion of these applications of psycho-analysis would be out of place here, and it is enough to say that the limits of their influence are not yet in sight.

Psycho-Analysis an Empirical Science.—Psycho-analysis is not, like philosophies, a system starting out from a few sharply defined basic concepts, seeking to grasp the whole universe with the help of these and, once it is completed, having no room for fresh discoveries or better understanding. On the contrary, it keeps close to the facts in its field of study, seeks to solve the immediate problems of observation, gropes its way forward by the help of experience, is always incomplete and always ready to correct or modify its theories. There is no incongruity (any more than in the case of physics or chemistry) if its most general concepts lack clarity and if its postulates are provisional; it leaves their more precise definition to the results of future work.

(B) THE LIBIDO THEORY

LIBIDO is a term used in the theory of the instincts for describing the dynamic manifestation of sexuality. It was already used in this sense by Moll (1898)[1] and was introduced into psycho-analysis by the present writer. What follows is limited to a description of the developments which the theory of the instincts has passed through in psycho-analysis—developments which are still proceeding.

Contrast between Sexual Instincts and Ego Instincts.—Psychoanalysis early became aware that all mental occurrences must be regarded as built on the basis of an interplay of the forces of the elementary instincts. This, however, led to a difficult predicament, since psychology included no theory of the instincts. No one could say what an instinct really was, the question was left entirely to individual caprice, and every psychologist was in the habit of postulating any instincts in any number that he chose. The first sphere of phenomena to be studied by psycho-analysis comprised what are known as the transference neuroses (hysteria and obsessional neurosis). It was found that their symptoms came about by sexual instinctual impulses being rejected (repressed) by the subject's personality (his ego) and then finding expression by circuitous paths through the unconscious. These facts could be met by drawing a contrast between the sexual instincts and ego instincts (*instincts of self-preservation*), which was in line with the popular saying that hunger and love are what make the world go round: libido was the manifestation of the force of love in the same sense as was hunger of the self-preservative instinct. The nature of the ego instincts remained for the time being undefined and, like all the other characteristics of the ego, inaccessible to analysis. There was no means of deciding whether, and if so what, qualitative differences were to be assumed to exist between the two classes of instincts.

Primal Libido.—C. G. Jung attempted to resolve this obscurity along speculative lines by assuming that there was only a

---

[1] [Freud himself had in fact used the term 'libido' in his first paper on anxiety neurosis (1895*b*) and in his correspondence with Fliess as early as August 18, 1894 (1950*a*).]

single primal libido which could be either sexualized or desexualized and which therefore coincided in its essence with mental energy in general. This innovation was methodologically disputable, caused a great deal of confusion, reduced the term 'libido' to the level of a superfluous synonym and was still in practice confronted with the necessity for distinguishing between sexual and asexual libido. The difference between the sexual instincts and instincts with other aims was not to be got rid of by means of a new definition.

Sublimation.—An attentive examination of the sexual trends, which alone were accessible to psycho-analysis, had meanwhile led to some remarkable detailed findings. What is described as the sexual instinct turns out to be of a highly composite nature and is liable to disintegrate once more into its component instincts. Each component instinct is unalterably characterized by its *source*, that is, by the region or zone of the body from which its excitation is derived. Each has furthermore as distinguishable features an *object* and an *aim*. The aim is always discharge accompanied by satisfaction, but it is capable of being changed from activity to passivity. The object is less closely attached to the instinct than was at first supposed; it is easily exchanged for another one, and, moreover, an instinct which had an external object can be turned round upon the subject's own self. The separate instincts can either remain independent of one another or—in what is still an inexplicable manner—can be combined and merged into one another to perform work in common. They are also able to replace one another and to transfer their libidinal cathexis to one another, so that the satisfaction of one instinct can take the place of the satisfaction of others. The most important vicissitude which an instinct can undergo seems to be *sublimation*; here both object and aim are changed, so that what was originally a sexual instinct finds satisfaction in some achievement which is no longer sexual but has a higher social or ethical valuation. These different features do not as yet combine to form an integral picture.

Narcissism.—A decisive advance was made when the analysis of dementia praecox and other psychotic disorders was ventured upon and thus the examination was begun of the ego itself, which had so far been known only as the agency of repression and opposition. It was found that the pathogenic process in dementia praecox is the withdrawal of the libido from objects and its introduction into the ego, while the clamorous symptoms of the disease arise from the vain struggles of the libido to find a pathway back to objects. It thus turned out to be possible for object-libido to change into cathexis of the ego and *vice versa*. Further reflection showed that this process must be presumed to occur on the largest scale and that the ego is to be regarded as a great reservoir of libido from which libido is sent out *to* objects and which is always ready to absorb libido flowing back *from* objects. Thus the instincts of self-preservation were also of a libidinal nature: they were sexual instincts which, instead of external objects, had taken the subject's own ego as an object. Clinical experience had made us familiar with people who behaved in a striking fashion as though they were in love with themselves and this perversion had been given the name of *narcissism*. The libido of the self-preservative instincts was now described as *narcissistic libido* and it was recognized that a high degree of this self-love constituted the primary and normal state of things. The earlier formula laid down for the transference neuroses consequently required to be modified, though not corrected. It was better, instead of speaking of a conflict between sexual instincts and ego instincts, to speak of a conflict between object-libido and ego-libido, or, since the nature of these instincts was the same, between the object-cathexes and the ego.

Apparent Approach to Jung's Views.—It thus seemed on the face of it as though the slow process of psycho-analytic research was following in the steps of Jung's speculation about a primal libido, especially because the transformation of object-libido into narcissism necessarily carried along with it a certain degree of desexualization, or abandonment of the specifically sexual aims. Nevertheless, it has to be borne in mind that the fact that the self-preservative instincts of the ego are recognized as libidinal does not necessarily prove that there are no other instincts operating in the ego.

The Herd Instinct.—It has been maintained in many quarters that there is a special innate and not further analysable 'herd instinct', which determines the social behaviour of human beings and impels individuals to come together into larger communities. Psycho-analysis finds itself in contradiction to this view. Even if the social instinct is innate, it may without any difficulty be traced back to what were originally libidinal object-cathexes and may have developed in the childhood of the individual as a reaction-formation against hostile attitudes of rivalry. It is based on a peculiar kind of identification with other people.

Aim-inhibited Sexual Impulses.—The social instincts belong to a class of instinctual impulses which need not be described as sublimated, though they are closely related to these. They have not abandoned their directly sexual aims, but they are held back by internal resistances from attaining them; they rest content with certain approximations to satisfaction and for that very reason lead to especially firm and permanent attachments between human beings. To this class belong in particular the affectionate relations between parents and children, which were originally fully sexual, feelings of friendship, and the emotional ties in marriage which had their origin in sexual attraction.

Recognition of Two Classes of Instincts in Mental Life.—Though psycho-analysis endeavours as a rule to develop its theories as independently as possible from those of other sciences, it is nevertheless obliged to seek a basis for the theory of the instincts in biology. On the ground of a far-reaching consideration of the processes which go to make up life and which lead to death, it becomes probable that we should recognize the existence of two classes of instincts, corresponding to the contrary processes of construction and dissolution in the organism. On this view, the one set of instincts, which work essentially in silence, would be those which follow the aim of leading the living creature to death and therefore deserve to be called the *'death instincts'*; these would be directed outwards as the result of the combination of numbers of unicellular elementary organisms, and would manifest themselves as *destructive* or *aggressive* impulses. The other set of instincts would be those which are better known to us in analysis—the libidinal, sexual or life instincts, which are best comprised under the name of *Eros*; their purpose would be to form living substance into ever greater unities, so that life may be prolonged and brought to higher development. The erotic instincts and the death instincts would be present in living beings in regular mixtures or fusions; but 'defusions' [1]

[1] [This seems to be the earliest appearance of this term, which is discussed at greater length near the beginning of Chapter II of *The Ego and the Id* (1923*b*).]

would also be liable to occur. Life would consist in the manifestations of the conflict or interaction between the two classes of instincts; death would mean for the individual the victory of the destructive instincts, but reproduction would mean for him the victory of Eros.

The Nature of the Instincts.—This view would enable us to characterize instincts as tendencies inherent in living substance towards restoring an earlier state of things: that is to say, they would be historically determined and of a conservative nature and, as it were, the expression of an inertia or elasticity present in what is organic. Both classes of instincts, Eros as well as the death instinct, would, on this view, have been in operation and working against each other from the first origin of life.

SHORTER WRITINGS
(1920–1922)

A NOTE ON THE PREHISTORY OF
THE TECHNIQUE OF ANALYSIS[1]

(1920)

A RECENT book by Havelock Ellis (so justly admired for his researches into sexual science, and an eminent critic of psychoanalysis), which bears the title of *The Philosophy of Conflict* (1919), includes an essay on 'Psycho-Analysis in Relation to Sex.' The aim of this essay is to show that the writings of the creator of analysis should be judged not as a piece of scientific work but as an artistic production. We cannot but regard this view as a fresh turn taken by resistance and as a repudiation of analysis, even though it is diguised in a friendly, indeed in too flattering a manner. We are inclined to meet it with a most decided contradiction.

It is not, however, with a view to contradicting him on this point that we are now concerned with Havelock Ellis's essay, but for another reason. His wide reading has enabled him to bring forward an author who practised and recommended free association as a technique, though for purposes other than ours, and thus has a claim to be regarded as a forerunner of psychoanalysis.

'In 1857, Dr. J. J. Garth Wilkinson, more noted as a Swedenborgian mystic and poet than as a physician, published a volume of mystic doggerel verse written by what he considered "a new method", the method of "Impression". "A theme is chosen or written down," he stated; "as soon as this is done the first impression upon the mind which succeeds the act of writing the title is the beginning of the evolution of that theme, no matter how strange or alien the word or phrase may seem." "The first mental movement, the first word that comes" is "the response to the mind's desire for the unfolding of the subject." It is continued by the same method, and Garth

[1] ['Zur Vorgeschichte der analytischen Technik.' First published anonymously, over the signature 'F', *Int. Z. Psychoanal.*, 6 (1920), 79; reprinted *S.K.S.N.*, 5 (1922), 141; *Technik u. Metapsychol.* (1924), 148; *G.S.*, 6 (1925), 148; *Neurosenlehre u. Technik* (1931), 423; *G.W.*, 12 (1947), 309. The present translation, by James Strachey, is reprinted from *C.P.*, 5 (1950), 101.]

Wilkinson adds: "I have always found it lead by an infallible instinct into the subject." The method was, as Garth Wilkinson viewed it, a kind of exalted *laissez-faire*, a command to the deepest unconscious instincts to express themselves. Reason and will, he pointed out, are left aside; you trust to "an influx", and the faculties of the mind are "directed to ends they know not of". Garth Wilkinson, it must be clearly understood, although he was a physician, used this method for religious and literary, and never for scientific or medical ends; but it is easy to see that essentially it is the method of psycho-analysis applied to oneself, and it is further evidence how much Freud's method is an artist's method.'

Those who are familiar with psycho-analytic literature will recall at this point the interesting passage in Schiller's correspondence with Körner [1] in which (1788) the great poet and thinker recommends anyone who desires to be productive to adopt the method of free association. It is to be suspected that what is alleged to be Garth Wilkinson's new technique had already occurred to the minds of many others and that its systematic application in psycho-analysis is not evidence so much of Freud's artistic nature as of his conviction, amounting almost to a prejudice, that all mental events are completely determined. It followed from this view that the first and most likely possibility was that a free association [2] would be related to the subject designated; and this was confirmed by experience in analysis except in so far as too great resistances made the suspected connection unrecognizable.

Meanwhile it is safe to assume that neither Schiller nor Garth Wilkinson had in fact any influence on the choice of psycho-analytic technique. It is from another direction that there are indications of a personal influence at work.

A short time ago in Budapest Dr. Hugo Dubowitz drew Dr. Ferenczi's attention to a short essay covering only four and a half pages, by Ludwig Börne. This was written in 1823 and was reprinted in the first volume of the 1862 edition of his collected

----

[1] Pointed out by Otto Rank and quoted in my *Interpretation of Dreams* (1900a) [*Standard Ed.*, 4, 102–3].

[2] [The German phrase here is '*freier Einfall*', that is, an idea occurring to the mind spontaneously. Thus the German avoids the unfortunate appearance of a circular argument, which is inevitably produced by the use in English of the word 'association' in two senses.]

works. It is entitled 'The Art of Becoming an Original Writer in Three Days', and shows the familiar stylistic features of Jean Paul, of whom Börne was at that time a great admirer. He ends the essay with the following sentences:

'And here follows the practical application that was promised. Take a few sheets of paper and for three days on end write down, without fabrication or hypocrisy, everything that comes into your head. Write down what you think of yourself, of your wife, of the Turkish War, of Goethe, of Fonk's trial, of the Last Judgement, of your superiors—and when three days have passed you will be quite out of your senses with astonishment at the new and unheard-of thoughts you have had. This is the art of becoming an original writer in three days.'

When Professor Freud came to read this essay of Börne's, he brought forward a number of facts that may have an important bearing on the question that is under discussion here as to the prehistory of the psycho-analytic use of free associations. He said that when he was fourteen he had been given Börne's works as a present, that he still possessed the book now, fifty years later, and that it was the only one that had survived from his boyhood. Börne, he said, had been the first author into whose writings he had penetrated deeply. He could not remember the essay in question, but some of the others that were contained in the same volume—such as 'A Tribute to the Memory of Jean Paul,' 'The Artist in Eating', and 'The Fool at the White Swan Inn'—kept on recurring to his mind for no obvious reason over a long period of years. He was particularly astonished to find expressed in the advice to the original writer some opinions which he himself had always cherished and vindicated. For instance: 'A disgraceful cowardliness in regard to thinking holds us all back. The censorship of governments is less oppressive than the censorship exercised by public opinion over our intellectual productions.' (Moreover there is a reference here to a 'censorship', which reappears in psychoanalysis as the dream-censorship.) 'It is not lack of intellect but lack of character that prevents most writers from being better than they are. . . . Sincerity is the source of all genius, and men would be cleverer if they were more moral. . . .'

Thus it seems not impossible that this hint may have brought to light the fragment of cryptomnesia which in so many cases may be suspected to lie behind apparent originality.

ASSOCIATIONS OF A FOUR-YEAR-OLD
CHILD [1]
(1920)

HERE is part of a letter from an American mother: 'I must tell you what my little girl said yesterday. I have not yet recovered from my astonishment. Cousin Emily was talking of how she was going to take an apartment. Whereupon the child said: "If Emily gets married, she'll have a baby." I was very much surprised and asked her: "Why, how do you know that?" And she replied: "Well, when anyone gets married, a baby always comes." I repeated: "But how can you tell that?" And the little girl answered: "Oh, I know a lot besides. I know that trees grow in the ground." What a strange association! That is precisely what I intend to say to her one day by way of enlightening her. Then she went on: "And I know that God makes the world." [2] When she talks like this I can scarcely believe that she is not yet four years old.'

The mother herself seems to have understood the transition from the child's first remark to her second one. What she was trying to say was: 'I know that babies grow inside their mother.' She was not expressing this knowledge directly, but symbolically, by replacing the mother by Mother Earth. We have already learnt from numerous incontestable observations the early age at which children know how to make use of symbols. But the little girl's third remark carries on the same context. We can only suppose that she was trying to convey a further piece of her knowledge about the origin of babies: 'I know that it's all the work of the father.' But this time she was replacing the direct thought by the appropriate sublimation—that God makes the world.

[1] ['Gedankenassoziation eines vierjährigen Kindes', *Int. Z. Psychoanal.*, 6 (1920), 157; *G.S.*, 5 (1924), 244; *Psychoanalyse der Neurosen* (1926), 85; *Neurosenlehre u. Technik* (1931), 172; *G.W.*, 12 (1947), 305. The present translation, the first into English, is by James Strachey.]

[2] ['In the ground' and 'makes the world' are in English in the original.]

DR. ANTON VON FREUND [1]
(1920)

DR. ANTON VON FREUND, who has been General Secretary of the International Psycho-Analytical Association since the Budapest Congress in September 1918, died on January 20, 1920, in a Vienna sanatorium, a few days after completing his fortieth year. He was the most powerful promoter of our science and one of its brightest hopes. Born in Budapest in 1880, he obtained a doctorate in philosophy. He intended to become a teacher, but was persuaded to enter his father's industrial undertaking. But the great successes he attained as a manufacturer and organizer failed to satisfy the two needs which were active in the depths of his nature—for social benefaction and scientific activity. Seeking nothing for himself, and possessing every gift which can charm and captivate, he used his material powers to assist others and to soften the hardness of their destiny as well as to sharpen in all directions the sense of social justice. In this way he acquired a wide circle of friends, who will deeply mourn his loss.

When, during his last years, he came to know psychoanalysis, it seemed to him to promise the fulfilment of his two great wishes. He set himself the task of helping the masses by psycho-analysis and of making use of the therapeutic effects of that medical technique, which had hitherto only been at the service of the rich, in order to mitigate the neurotic suffering of the poor. Since the State took no heed of the neuroses of the common people, since hospital clinics for the most part rejected psycho-analytic therapy without being able to offer any substitute for it, and since the few psycho-analytic physicians, tied by the necessity for maintaining themselves, were unequal to such a gigantic task, Anton von Freund sought, by his private initiative, to open a path for every one towards the fulfilment of this important social duty. During the years of

[1] ['Dr. Anton v. Freund.' First published over the signature 'Redaktion und Herausgeber der Internationalen Zeitschrift für Psychoanalyse', *Int. Z. Psychoanal.*, **6** (1920), 95; reprinted *G.S.*, **11** (1928), 280; *G.W.*, **13** (1940), 435. Possibly in collaboration with Otto Rank. The present translation, the first into English, is by James Strachey.]

the war he had collected what was then the very considerable sum of one and a half million *kronen* [1] for humanitarian purposes in the city of Budapest. With the concurrence of Dr. Stephan von Bárczy, the then Burgomaster, he assigned this sum for the foundation of a psycho-analytic Institute in Budapest, in which analysis was to be practised, taught and made accessible to the people. It was intended to train a considerable number of physicians in this Institute who would then receive an honorarium from it for the treatment of poor neurotics in an out-patient clinic. The Institute, furthermore, was to be a centre for further scientific research in analysis. Dr. Ferenczi was to be the scientific head of the Institute; von Freund himself was to undertake its organization and finances. The founder handed over a relatively smaller sum to Professor Freud for the foundation of an international psycho-analytic publishing house. [2] But,

> Was sind Hoffnungen, was sind Entwürfe,
> die der Mensch, der vergängliche, baut? [3]

Von Freund's premature death has put an end to these philanthropic schemes, with all their scientific hopes. Though the fund which he collected is still in existence, the attitude of those who are now in power in the Hungarian capital gives no promise that his intentions will be fulfilled. Only the psychoanalytical publishing house has come to birth in Vienna.

None the less, the example which von Freund sought to set has already had its effect. A few weeks after his death, thanks to the energy and liberality of Dr. Max Eitingon, the first psycho-analytical out-patients' clinic has been opened in Berlin. Thus von Freund's work is carried on, though he himself can never be replaced or forgotten.

[1] [Before 1914 equivalent to some £62,500 or $312,500.]

[2] [See 'A Note on Psycho-Analytic Publications and Prizes' (Freud, 1919c).]

[3] ['What becomes of the hopes, what becomes of the plans built by Man, that transient creature?' (Schiller, *Die Braut von Messina*, III, 5.)]

PREFACE TO J. J. PUTNAM'S
ADDRESSES ON PSYCHO-ANALYSIS [1]
(1921)

THE Editor of this series[2] must feel a special satisfaction in being able to issue as its opening volume this collection of the psycho-analytical writings of Professor James J. Putnam, the distinguished neurologist of Harvard University. Professor Putnam, who died in 1918 at the age of seventy-two, was not only the first American to interest himself in psycho-analysis, but soon became its most decided supporter and its most influential representative in America. In consequence of the established reputation which he had gained through his activities as a teacher, as well as through his important work in the domain of organic nervous disease, and thanks to the universal respect which his personality enjoyed, he was able to do perhaps more than anyone for the spread of psycho-analysis in his own country, and was able to protect it from aspersions which, on the other side of the Atlantic no less than this, would inevitably have been cast upon it. But all such reproaches were bound to be silenced when a man of Putnam's lofty ethical standards and moral rectitude had ranged himself among the supporters of the new science and of the therapeutics based upon it.

The papers here collected into a single volume, which were written by Putnam between 1909 and the end of his life, give a good picture of his relations to psycho-analysis. They show how he was at first occupied in correcting a provisional judgement which was based on insufficient knowledge; how he then accepted the essence of analysis, recognized its capacity for throwing a clear light upon the origin of human imperfections and failings, and how he was struck by the prospect of contributing towards the improvement of humanity along analytical lines; how he then became convinced by his own activities as

---

[1] [No German text extant. The translation by Ernest Jones, here reprinted, first appeared in J. J. Putnam's *Addresses on Psycho-Analysis*, London, 1921. Also reprinted *G.S.*, 11 (1928), 262 and *G.W.*, 13 (1940), 437.—Cf. also Freud's obituary of Putnam (1919*b*).]

[2] [The International Psycho-Analytical Library, edited by Ernest Jones.]

a physician as to the truth of most of the psycho-analytical conclusions and postulates, and then in his turn bore witness to the fact that the physician who makes use of analysis understands far more about the sufferings of his patients and can do far more for them than was possible with the earlier methods of treatment; and finally how he began to extend beyond the limits of analysis, demanding that as a science it should be linked on to a particular philosophical system, and that its practice should be openly associated with a particular set of ethical doctrines.

So it is not to be wondered at that a mind with such pre-eminently ethical and philosophical tendencies as Putnam's should have desired, after he had plunged deep into psycho-analysis, to establish the closest relation between it and the aims which lay nearest his heart. But his enthusiasm, so admirable in a man of his advanced age, did not succeed in carrying others along with him. Younger people remained cooler. It was especially Ferenczi who expressed the opposite view. The decisive reason for the rejection of Putnam's proposals was the doubt as to which of the countless philosophical systems should be accepted, since they all seemed to rest on an equally insecure basis, and since everything had up till then been sacrificed for the sake of the relative certainty of the results of psycho-analysis. It seemed more prudent to wait, and to discover whether a particular attitude towards life might be forced upon us with all the weight of necessity by analytical investigation itself.

It is our duty to express our thanks to the author's widow, Mrs. Putnam, for her assistance with the manuscripts, with the copyrights, and with financial support, without all of which the publication of this volume would have been impossible. No English manuscripts were forthcoming in the case of the papers numbered VI, VII, and X. They have been translated into English by Dr. Katherine Jones from the German text which originated from Putnam himself.

This volume will keep fresh in analytical circles the memory of the friend whose loss we so profoundly deplore. May it be the first of a series of publications which shall serve the end of furthering the understanding and application of psycho-analysis among those who speak the English tongue—an end to which James J. Putnam dedicated the last ten years of his fruitful life.

January 1921

INTRODUCTION TO J. VARENDONCK'S
THE PSYCHOLOGY OF DAY-DREAMS [1]
(1921)

THIS present volume of Dr. Varendonck's contains a significant novelty, and will justly arouse the interest of all philosophers, psychologists and psycho-analysts. After an effort lasting for some years the author has succeeded in getting hold of the mode of thought-activity to which one abandons oneself during the state of distraction into which we readily pass before sleep or upon incomplete awakening. He has brought to the consciousness the chains of thought originating in these conditions without the interference of the will; he has written them down, studied their peculiarities and differences with directed conscious thinking, and has made thereby a series of important discoveries which lead to still vaster problems and give rise to the formulation of still more far-reaching questions. Many a point in the psychology of the dream and the defective act finds, thanks to the observations of Dr. Varendonck, a trustworthy settlement.

It is not my intention to give a review of the author's results. I will content myself with pointing to the significance of his work and will permit myself only a remark concerning the terminology which he has adopted. He includes the sort of thought-activity which he has observed in Bleuler's autistic thinking, but calls it, as a rule, *fore-conscious thinking*, according to the custom prevailing in psycho-analysis. However, the

---

[1] [First published in English in J. Varendonck's *The Psychology of Day-Dreams*, London, 1921. The original English text was probably written by Freud himself and is here reprinted without any alteration. Some of the terminology therefore differs from that employed elsewhere in this edition—e.g. 'fore-conscious' for 'preconscious'. The book was translated into German by Anna Freud (*Über das vorbewusste phantasierende Denken*, Vienna, 1922), and this translation included a German version, also probably written by Freud himself, of the first paragraph only of his preface. This part of the preface was reprinted (in German) in *G.S.*, **11** (1928), 264, and again in *G.W.*, **13** (1940), 439. The latter contained in addition the English version of the last part of the preface (of which no German text is extant).—A short reference to Varendonck's book will be found above on p. 5.]

autistic thinking of Bleuler does not by any means correspond with the extension and the contents of the fore-conscious, neither can I admit that the name used by Bleuler has been happily chosen. The designation 'fore-conscious' thinking itself as a characteristic appears to me misleading and unsatisfactory. The point in question is that the sort of thought-activity of which the well-known day-dream is an example—complete by itself, developing a situation or an act that is being brought to a close—constitutes the best and until now the only studied example. This day-dreaming does not owe its peculiarities to the circumstances that it proceeds mostly fore-consciously, nor are the forms changed when it is accomplished consciously. From another point of view we know also that even strictly directed reflection may be achieved without the co-operation of consciousness, that is to say, fore-consciously. For that reason I think it is advisable, when establishing a distinction between the different modes of thought-activity, not to utilize the relation to consciousness in the first instance, and to designate the day-dream, as well as the chains of thought studied by Varendonck, as freely wandering or phantastic thinking, in opposition to intentionally directed reflection. At the same time it should be taken into consideration that even phantastic thinking is not invariably in want of an aim and end-representations.[1]

[1] [This introduction is reprinted here by arrangement with Messrs. George Allen and Unwin, the publishers of Varendonck's book.]

MEDUSA'S HEAD [1]
(1940 [1922])

WE have not often attempted to interpret individual mythological themes, but an interpretation suggests itself easily in the case of the horrifying decapitated head of Medusa.

To decapitate = to castrate. The terror of Medusa is thus a terror of castration that is linked to the sight of something. Numerous analyses have made us familiar with the occasion for this: it occurs when a boy, who has hitherto been unwilling to believe the threat of castration, catches sight of the female genitals, probably those of an adult, surrounded by hair, and essentially those of his mother.

The hair upon Medusa's head is frequently represented in works of art in the form of snakes, and these once again are derived from the castration complex. It is a remarkable fact that, however frightening they may be in themselves, they nevertheless serve actually as a mitigation of the horror, for they replace the penis, the absence of which is the cause of the horror. This is a confirmation of the technical rule according to which a multiplication of penis symbols signifies castration. [2]

The sight of Medusa's head makes the spectator stiff with terror, turns him to stone. Observe that we have here once again the same origin from the castration complex and the same transformation of affect! For becoming stiff means an erection. Thus in the original situation it offers consolation to the spectator: he is still in possession of a penis, and the stiffening reassures him of the fact.

This symbol of horror is worn upon her dress by the virgin goddess Athene. And rightly so, for thus she becomes a woman who is unapproachable and repels all sexual desires—since she

---

[1] ['Das Medusenhaupt.' First published posthumously *Int. Z. Psycho-anal. Imago*, 25 (1940), 105; reprinted *G.W.*, 17 (1941), 47. The manuscript is dated May 14, 1922, and appears to be a sketch for a more extensive work. The present translation, by James Strachey, is reprinted from *Int. J. Psycho-Anal.*, 22 (1941), 69 and *C.P.*, 5 (1950), 105.]

[2] [This is referred to in Freud's paper on 'The "Uncanny" ' (1919h), middle of Section II.]

displays the terrifying genitals of the Mother. Since the Greeks were in the main strongly homosexual, it was inevitable that we should find among them a representation of woman as a being who frightens and repels because she is castrated.

If Medusa's head takes the place of a representation of the female genitals, or rather if it isolates their horrifying effects from their pleasure-giving ones, it may be recalled that displaying the genitals is familiar in other connections as an apotropaic act. What arouses horror in oneself will produce the same effect upon the enemy against whom one is seeking to defend oneself. We read in Rabelais of how the Devil took to flight when the woman showed him her vulva.

The erect male organ also has an apotropaic effect, but thanks to another mechanism. To display the penis (or any of its surrogates) is to say: 'I am not afraid of you. I defy you. I have a penis.' Here, then, is another way of intimidating the Evil Spirit.[1]

In order seriously to substantiate this interpretation it would be necessary to investigate the origin of this isolated symbol of horror in Greek mythology as well as parallels to it in other mythologies.[2]

[1] [It may be worth quoting a footnote added by Freud to a paper of Stekel's, 'Zur Psychologie des Exhibitionismus', in *Zentralbl. Psychoanal.*, 1 (1911), 495: 'Dr. Stekel here proposes to derive exhibitionism from unconscious narcissistic motive forces. It seems to me probable that the same explanation can be applied to the apotropaic exhibiting found among the peoples of antiquity.']

[2] [The same topic was dealt with by Ferenczi (1923) in a very short paper which was itself briefly commented upon by Freud in his 'Infantile Genital Organization of the Libido' (1923e).]

BIBLIOGRAPHY
AND AUTHOR INDEX

[Titles of books and periodicals are in italics; titles of papers are in inverted commas. Abbreviations are in accordance with the *World List of Scientific Periodicals* (London, 1952). Further abbreviations used in this volume will be found in the List at the end of this bibliography. Numerals in thick type refer to volumes; ordinary numerals refer to pages. The figures in round brackets at the end of each entry indicate the page or pages of this volume on which the work in question is mentioned. In the case of the Freud entries, the letters attached to the dates of publication are in accordance with the corresponding entries in the complete bibliography of Freud's writings to be included in the last volume of the *Standard Edition*.

For non-technical authors, and for technical authors where no specific work is mentioned, see the General Index.]

ABRAHAM, K. (1912) 'Ansätze zur psychoanalytischen Erforschung und Behandlung des manisch-depressiven Irreseins und verwandter Zustände', *Zbl. Psychoanal.*, **2**, 302. (133)
[*Trans.*: 'Notes on the Psycho-Analytic Investigation and Treatment of Manic-Depressive Insanity and Allied Conditions', *Selected Papers on Psycho-Analysis*, London, 1927, Chap. VI.]
(1916) 'Untersuchungen über die früheste prägenitale Entwicklungsstufe der Libido', *Int. Z. Psychoanal.*, **4**, 71. (105)
[*Trans.*: 'The First Pregenital Stage of the Libido', *Selected Papers on Psycho-Analysis*, London, 1927, Chap. XII.]

ADLER, A. (1908) 'Der Aggressionsbetrieb im Leben und in der Neurose', *Fortschr. Med.*, No. 19. (53)

BLEULER, E. (1912) 'Das autistische Denken', *Jb. psychoanal. psychopath. Forsch.*, **4**, 1. (69, 271-2)
(1916) 'Physisch und Psychisch in der Pathologie', *Z. ges. Neurol. Psychiatr.*, **30**, 426. (229)

BREUER, J., and FREUD, S. (1893) See FREUD, S. (1893a)
(1895) See FREUD, S. (1895d)
(1940) See FREUD, S. (1940d)

BRUGEILLES, R. (1913) 'L'essence du phénomène social: la suggestion', *Rev. phil.*, **75**, 593. (88)

DEVEREUX, G. (1953) *Psychoanalysis and the Occult*, New York. (175, 217)

DOFLEIN, F. (1919) *Das Problem des Todes und der Unsterblichkeit bei den Pflanzen und Tieren*, Jena. (47)

ELLIS, HAVELOCK (1919) *The Philosophy of Conflict and Other Essays in Wartime*, 2nd Series, London. (263)

FECHNER, G. T. (1873) *Einige Ideen zur Schöpfungs- und Entwicklungsgeschichte der Organismen*, Leipzig. (8, 10)

FEDERN, P. (1919) *Die vaterlose Gesellschaft*, Vienna. (98)

FELSZEGHY, BÉLA VON (1920) 'Pan und Pankomplex', *Imago*, **6**, 1. (97)

FERENCZI, S. (1909) 'Introjektion und Übertragung', *Jb. psychoanal. psychopath. Forsch.*, **1**, 422. (113, 127)
[*Trans.*: 'Introjection and Transference', *First Contributions to Psycho-Analysis*, London, 1952, Chap. II.]

(1913) 'Entwicklungsstufen des Wirklichkeitssinnes', *Int. Z. Psychoanal.*, **1**, 124. (41)
[*Trans.*: 'Stages in the Development of the Sense of Reality', *First Contributions to Psycho-Analysis*, London, 1952, Chap. VIII.]

(1917) 'Träume der Ahnungslosen', *Int. Z. Psychoanal.*, **4**, 208. (214)
[*Trans.*: 'Dreams of the Unsuspecting', *Further Contributions to the Theory and Technique of Psycho-Analysis*, London, 1926, Chap. LVI.]

(1923) 'Zur Symbolik des Medusenhauptes', *Int. Z. Psychoanal.*, **9**, 69. (274)
[*Trans.*: 'On the Symbolism of the Head of Medusa', *Further Contributions to the Theory and Technique of Psycho-Analysis*, London, 1926, Chap. LXVI.]

FLIESS, W. (1906) *Der Ablauf des Lebens*, Vienna. (45)

FREUD, S. (1888-9) Übersetzung mit Vorrede und Fussnoten zu Bernheim *De la suggestion et ses applications à la thérapeutique*, Paris, 1886, unter dem Titel *Die Suggestion und ihre Heilwirkung*, Vienna. (128)
[*Trans.*: Preface to Bernheim's *Die Suggestion und ihre Heilwirkung*, *C.P.*, **5**, 11; *Standard Ed.*, **1**.]

(1893*a*) With BREUER, J., 'Über den psychischen Mechanismus hysterischer Phänomene: Vorläufige Mitteilung', *G.S.*, **1**, 7; *G.W.*, **1**, 81. (13, 235)
[*Trans.*: 'On the Psychical Mechanism of Hysterical Phenomena: Preliminary Communication', *C.P.*, **1**, 24; *Standard Ed.*, **2**.]

(1895*b*) 'Über die Berechtigung, von der Neurasthenie einen bestimmten Symptomenkomplex als "Angstneurose" abzutrennen', *G.S.*, **1**, 306; *G.W.*, **1**, 313. (255)
[*Trans.*: 'On the Grounds for Detaching a Particular Syndrome from Neurasthenia under the Description "Anxiety Neurosis"', *C.P.*, **1**, 76; *Standard Ed.*, **3**.]

(1895*d*) With BREUER, J., *Studien über Hysterie*, Vienna. *G.S.*, **1**; *G.W.*, **1**, 75. Omitting Breuer's contributions. (9, 25, 27, 34, 126, 146, 235-7)
[*Trans.*: *Studies on Hysteria*, *Standard Ed.*, **2**. Including Breuer's contributions.]

(1899*a*) 'Über Deckerinnerungen', *G.S.*, **1**, 465; *G.W.*, **1**, 529. (215)
[*Trans.*: 'Screen Memories', *C.P.*, **5**, 47; *Standard Ed.*, **3**.]

(1900*a*) *Die Traumdeutung*, Vienna. *G.S.*, **2-3**; *G.W.*, **2-3**. (4, 14-15, 24-5, 32, 34, 78, 104, 165, 176, 197-8, 207-8, 212, 216, 220, 241, 264)
[*Trans.*: *The Interpretation of Dreams*, London and New York, 1955; *Standard Ed.*, **4-5**.]

FREUD, S. (cont.)
    (1901b) Zur Psychopathologie des Alltagslebens, Berlin, 1904. G.S., 4;
        G.W., 4. (193, 215)
        [Trans.: The Psychopathology of Everyday Life, Standard Ed., 6.]
    (1905b) 'Psychische Behandlung (Seelenbehandlung)', G.W., 5,
        289. (114)
        [Trans.: 'Psychical (or Mental) Treatment', Standard Ed., 7,
        283.]
    (1905c) Der Witz und seine Beziehung zum Unbewussten, Vienna. G.S.,
        9, 5; G.W., 6. (35, 126, 188)
        [Trans.: Jokes and their Relation to the Unconscious, Standard Ed.,
        8.]
    (1905d) Drei Abhandlungen zur Sexualtheorie, Vienna. G.S., 5, 3; G.W.,
        5, 29. (33, 53–4, 58, 80, 92, 103, 105, 111, 114, 137, 143, 154,
        171–2)
        [Trans.: Three Essays on the Theory of Sexuality, London, 1949;
        Standard Ed., 7, 125.]
    (1905e) 'Bruchstück einer Hysterie-Analyse', G.S., 8, 3; G.W., 5,
        163. (106, 146, 213)
        [Trans.: 'Fragment of an Analysis of a Case of Hysteria', C.P.,
        3, 13; Standard Ed., 7, 3.]
    (1909b) 'Analyse der Phobie eines fünfjährigen Knaben', G.S., 8,
        129; G.W., 7, 243. (89)
        [Trans.: 'Analysis of a Phobia in a Five-Year-Old Boy', C.P., 3,
        149; Standard Ed., 10, 3.]
    (1909d) 'Bemerkungen über einen Fall von Zwangsneurose', G.S.,
        8, 269; G.W., 7, 381. (218)
        [Trans.: 'Notes upon a Case of Obsessional Neurosis', C.P., 3,
        293; Standard Ed., 10, 155.]
    (1910c) Eine Kindheitserinnerung des Leonardo da Vinci, Vienna. G.S.,
        9, 371; G.W., 8, 128. (108, 230)
        [Trans.: Leonardo da Vinci and a Memory of his Childhood, Standard
        Ed., 11.]
    (1910d) 'Die zukünftigen Chancen der psychoanalytischen Thera-
        pie', G.S., 6, 25; G.W., 8, 104. (142)
        [Trans.: 'The Future Prospects of Psycho-Analytic Therapy',
        C.P., 2, 285; Standard Ed., 11.]
    (1910h) 'Über einen besonderen Typus der Objektwahl beim
        Manne', G.S., 5, 186; G.W., 8, 66. (160)
        [Trans.: 'A Special Type of Choice of Object made by Men',
        C.P. 4, 192; Standard Ed., 11.]
    (1910i) 'Die psychogene Sehstörung in psychoanalytischer Auf-
        fassung', G.S., 5, 301; G.W., 8, 94. (51)
        [Trans.: 'The Psycho-Analytic View of Psychogenic Disturb-
        ance of Vision', C.P., 2, 105; Standard Ed., 11.]
    (1911b) 'Formulierungen über die zwei Prinzipien des psychischen
        Geschehens', G.S., 5, 409; G.W., 8, 230. (5, 10)
        [Trans.: 'Formulations on the Two Principles of Mental Func-
        tioning', C.P., 4, 13; Standard Ed., 12.]

FREUD, S. (*cont.*)

(1911*c*) 'Psychoanalytische Bemerkungen über einen autobiographisch beschriebenen Fall von Paranoia (Dementia Paranoides)', *G.S.*, 8, 355; *G.W.*, 8, 240. (225)
[*Trans.*: 'Psycho-Analytic Notes on an Autobiographical Account of a Case of Paranoia (Dementia Paranoides)', *C.P.*, 3, 387; *Standard Ed.*, 12.]

(1912*d*) 'Über die allgemeinste Erniedrigung des Liebeslebens', *G.S.*, 5, 198; *G.W.*, 8, 78. (112, 141)
[*Trans.*: 'On the Universal Tendency to Debasement in the Sphere of Love', *C.P.*, 4, 203; *Standard Ed.*, 11.]

(1912–13) *Totem und Tabu*, Vienna, 1913. *G.S.*, 10, 3; *G.W.*, 9. (68, 77, 80, 110, 122, 124–5, 128, 131, 135, 142)
[*Trans.*: *Totem and Taboo*, London, 1950; New York, 1952; *Standard Ed.*, 13, 1.]

(1914*c*) 'Zur Einführung des Narzissmus', *G.S.*, 6, 155; *G.W.*, 10, 138. (6, 33, 51–2, 68, 102, 105, 109–110, 112, 130–1)
[*Trans.*: 'On Narcissism: an Introduction', *C.P.*, 4, 30; *Standard Ed.*, 14.]

(1914*g*) 'Weitere Ratschläge zur Technik der Psychoanalyse: II Erinnern, Wiederholen und Durcharbeiten', *G.S.*, 6, 109; *G.W.*, 10, 126. (18, 152)
[*Trans.*: 'Recollecting, Repeating and Working Through (Further Recommendations on the Technique of Psycho-Analysis, II)', *C.P.*, 2, 366; *Standard Ed.*, 12.]

(1915*b*) 'Zeitgemässes über Krieg und Tod', *G.S.*, 10, 315; *G.W.*, 10, 324. (163)
[*Trans.*: 'Thoughts for the Times on War and Death', *C.P.*, 4, 288; *Standard Ed.*, 14.]

(1915*c*) 'Triebe und Triebschicksale', *G.S.*, 5, 443; *G.W.*, 10, 210. (6, 30, 54)
[*Trans.*: 'Instincts and their Vicissitudes', *C.P.*, 4, 60; *Standard Ed.*, 14.]

(1915*e*) 'Das Unbewusste', *G.S.*, 5, 480; *G.W.*, 10, 264. (7, 24, 28)
[*Trans.*: 'The Unconscious', *C.P.*, 4, 98; *Standard Ed.*, 14.]

(1916–17) *Vorlesungen zur Einführung in die Psychoanalyse*, Vienna. *G.S.*, 7; *G.W.*, 11. (20, 97, 119, 208)
[*Trans.*: *Introductory Lectures on Psycho-Analysis*, revised ed., London, 1929 (*A General Introduction to Psychoanalysis*, New York, 1935); *Standard Ed.*, 15–16.]

(1917*b*) 'Eine Kindheitserinnerung aus *Dichtung und Wahrheit*', *G.S.*, 10, 357; *G.W.*, 12, 15. (16)
[*Trans.*: 'A Childhood Recollection from *Dichtung und Wahrheit*', *C.P.*, 4, 357; *Standard Ed.*, 17.]

(1917*d*) 'Metapsychologische Ergänzung zur Traumlehre', *G.S.*, 5, 520; *G.W.*, 10, 412. (24, 30, 114)
[*Trans.*: 'A Metapsychological Supplement to the Theory of Dreams', *C.P.*, 4, 137; *Standard Ed.*, 14.]

FREUD, S. (*cont.*)

(1917*e*) 'Trauer und Melancholie', *G.S.*, **5**, 535; *G.W.*, **10**, 428. (68, 104, 109, 130)

   [*Trans.*: 'Mourning and Melancholia', *C.P.*, **4**, 152; *Standard Ed.*, **14**.]

(1918*a*) 'Das Tabu der Virginität', *G.S.*, **5**, 212; *G.W.*, **12**, 161. (113)

   [*Trans.*: 'The Taboo of Virginity', *C.P.*, **4**, 217; *Standard Ed.*, **11**.]

(1919*b*) 'James J. Putnam', *G.S.*, **11**, 276; *G.W.*, **12**, 315. (269)

   [*Trans.*: 'James J. Putnam', *Standard Ed.*, **17**.]

(1919*c*) 'Internationaler psychoanalytischer Verlag und Preis-zuteilungen für psychoanalytische Arbeiten', *G.W.*, **12**, 333. (268)

   [*Trans.*: 'A Note on Psycho-Analytic Publications and Prizes', *Standard Ed.*, **17**.]

(1919*d*) Einleitung zu *Zur Psychoanalyse der Kriegsneurosen*, Vienna. *G.S.*, **11**, 252; *G.W.*, **12**, 321. (12, 33)

   [*Trans.*: Introduction to *Psycho-Analysis and the War Neuroses*, London and New York, 1921. *C.P.*, **5**, 83; *Standard Ed.*, **17**.]

(1919*h*) 'Das Unheimliche', *G.S.*, **10**, 369; *G.W.*, **12**, 229. (3, 125, 273)

   [*Trans.*: 'The Uncanny', *C.P.*, **4**, 368; *Standard Ed.*, **17**.]

(1920*g*) *Jenseits des Lustprinzips*, Vienna. *G.S.*, **6**, 191; *G.W.*, **13**, 3. (67–8, 102, 118)

   [*Trans.*: *Beyond the Pleasure Principle*, London, 1950; *Standard Ed.*, **18**, 7.]

(1921*c*) *Massenpsychologie und Ich-Analyse*, Vienna. *G.S.*, **6**, 261; *G.W.*, **13**, 73. (232)

   [*Trans.*: *Group Psychology and the Analysis of the Ego*, London, 1922; New York, 1940; *Standard Ed.*, **18**, 69.]

(1922*a*) 'Traum und Telepathie', *G.S.*, **3**, 278; *G.W.*, **13**, 165. (176)

   [*Trans.*: 'Dreams and Telepathy', *C.P.*, **4**, 408; *Standard Ed.*, **18**, 197.]

(1922*b*) 'Über einige neurotische Mechanismen bei Eifersucht, Paranoia und Homosexualität', *G.S.*, **5**, 387; *G.W.*, **13**, 195. (172)

   [*Trans.*: 'Some Neurotic Mechanisms in Jealousy, Paranoia and Homosexuality', *C.P.*, **2**, 232; *Standard Ed.*, **18**, 223.]

(1923*b*) *Das Ich und das Es*, Vienna. *G.S.*, **6**, 353; *G.W.*, **13**, 237. (5, 19, 51, 54, 68, 106, 114, 133, 234, 258)

   [*Trans.*: *The Ego and the Id*, London, 1927; *Standard Ed.*, **1**.]

(1923*c*) 'Bemerkungen zur Theorie und Praxis der Traumdeutung', *G.S.*, **3**, 305; *G.W.*, **13**, 301. (20, 32, 166)

   [*Trans.*: 'Remarks on the Theory and Practice of Dream-Interpretation', *C.P.*, **5**, 136; *Standard Ed.*, **19**.]

(1923*e*) 'Die infantile Genitalorganisation', *G.S.*, **5**, 232; *G.W.*, **13**, 293. (274)

FREUD, S. (*cont.*)

[*Trans.*: 'The Infantile Genital Organization of the Libido'
C.P., **2**, 244; *Standard Ed.*, **19**.]

(1924c) 'Das ökonomische Problem des Masochismus', *G.S.*, **5**, 374,
G.W., **13**, 371. (8, 56)
[*Trans.*: 'The Economic Problem of Masochism', *C.P.*, **2**, 255;
Standard Ed., **19**.]

(1924f) ' "Psychoanalysis: Exploring the Hidden Recesses of the
Mind" ', Chap. 73, Vol. 2 of *These Eventful Years*, London and
New York; *Standard Ed.*, **19**. (234)
German original first appeared in 1928. 'Kurzer Abriss der
Psychoanalyse', *G.S.*, **11**, 183; *G.W.*, **13**, 405.

(1925a) 'Notiz über den "Wunderblock" ', *G.S.*, **6**, 415; *G.W.*, **14**,
3. (25, 28)
[*Trans.*: 'A Note upon the "Mystic Writing-Pad" ', *C.P.*, **5**,
175; *Standard Ed.*, **19**.]

(1925i) 'Einige Nachträge zum Ganzen der Traumdeutung', *G.S.*,
3, 172; *G.W.*, **1**, 559. (176, 185)
[*Trans.*: 'Some Additional Notes upon Dream-Interpretation as
a Whole', *C.P.*, **5**, 150; *Standard Ed.*, **19**.]

(1925j) 'Einige psychische Folgen des anatomischen Geschlechts-
unterschieds', *G.S.*, **11**, 8; *G.W.*, **14**, 19. (146)
[*Trans.*: 'Some Psychological Consequences of the Anatomical
Distinction between the Sexes', *C.P.*, **5**, 186; *Standard Ed.*, **19**.]

(1926d) *Hemmung, Symptom und Angst*, Vienna. *G.S.*, **11**, 23; *G.W.*,
14, 113. (13, 20, 97)
[*Trans.*: *Inhibitions, Symptom and Anxiety*, London, 1936 (*The
Problem of Anxiety*, New York, 1936); *Standard Ed.*, **20**.]

(1930a) *Das Unbehagen in der Kultur*, Vienna. *G.S.*, **12**, 29; *G.W.*,
14, 421. (55, 101)
[*Trans.*: *Civilization and its Discontents*, London and New York,
1930; *Standard Ed.*, **21**.]

(1931b) 'Über die weibliche Sexualität', *G.S.*, **12**, 120; *G.W.*, **14**,
517. (146)
[*Trans.*: 'Female Sexuality', *C.P.*, **5**, 252; *Standard Ed.*, **21**.]

(1933a) *Neue Folge der Vorlesungen zur Einführung in die Psychoanalyse*,
Vienna. *G.S.*, **12**, 151; *G.W.*, **15**, 207. (146, 175-6, 181, 183, 185,
191, 200)
[*Trans.*: *New Introductory Lectures on Psycho-Analysis*, London and
New York, 1933; *Standard Ed.*, **22**.]

(1940d) With BREUER, J., 'Zur Theorie des hysterischen Anfalls',
G.W., **17**, 9. (9)
[*Trans.*: 'On the Theory of Hysterical Attacks', *C.P.*, **5**, 27;
Standard Ed., **1**.]

(1941a) Brief an Josef Breuer, *G.W.*, **17**, 5. (9)
[*Trans.*: A Letter to Josef Breuer, *C.P.*, **5**, 25; *Standard Ed.*, **1**.]

(1941c) 'Eine erfüllte Traumahnung', *G.W.*, **17**, 21. (185)
[*Trans.*: 'A Premonitory Dream Fulfilled', *C.P.*, **5**, 70; *Standard
Ed.*, **5**, 623.]

FREUD, S. (cont.)

(1942a) 'Psychopathic Characters on the Stage', Standard Ed., 7, 305. Translation of 'Psychopathische Personen auf der Bühne', which has not been published in German. (17)

(1950a) Aus den Anfängen der Psychoanalyse, London. [Includes 'Entwurf einer Psychologie' (1895).] (6, 8–9, 19, 25–6, 28–30, 63–4, 104, 229, 255)

[Trans.: The Origins of Psycho-Analysis, London and New York, 1954. (Partly, including 'A Project for a Scientific Psychology', in Standard Ed., 1.)]

(1955c) 'Gutachten über die elektrische Behandlung der Kriegs-neurotiker'; German text unpublished. (12)

[Trans.: 'Memorandum on the Electrical Treatment of War Neuroses', Standard Ed., 17.]

FREUD, S., FERENCZI, S., and others. (1919) Zur Psychoanalyse der Kriegs-neurosen, Vienna. (12)

[Trans.: Psycho-Analysis and the War Neuroses, London and New York, 1921.]

GOETTE, A. (1883) Über den Ursprung des Todes, Hamburg. (47)

HARTMANN, M. (1906) Tod und Fortpflanzung, Munich. (47)

JUNG, C. G. (1909) 'Die Bedeutung des Vaters für das Schicksal des Einzelnen', Jb. psychoanal. psychopath. Forsch., 1, 155. (22)

[Trans.: 'The Significance of the Father in the Destiny of the Individual', Collected Papers on Analytical Psychology, London, 1916, 156.]

KELSEN, H. (1922) 'Der Begriff des Staates und die Sozialpsychologie', Imago, 8, 97. (87)

KRAŠKOVIČ, B. (1915) Die Psychologie der Kollektivitäten, Vukovar. (82)

LE BON, G. (1895) Psychologie des foules, Paris. (72–82)

[Trans.: The Crowd: a Study of the Popular Mind, London, 1920.]

LIPSCHÜTZ, A. (1914) Warum wir sterben, Stuttgart. (47, 55)

(1919) Die Pubertätsdrüse und ihre Wirkungen, Berne. (171)

LOW, B. (1920) Psycho-Analysis, London. (56)

McDOUGALL, W. (1920a) The Group Mind, Cambridge. (83–5, 96–7)

(1920b) 'A Note on Suggestion', J. Neurol. Psychopath., 1, 1. (90)

MARCINOWSKI, J. (1918) 'Die erotischen Quellen der Minderwertig-keitsgefühle', Z. Sexualwiss., 4, 313. (20)

MARCUSZEWICZ, R. (1920) 'Beitrag zum autistischen Denken bei Kindern', Int. Z. Psychoanal., 6, 248. (109)

MOEDE, W. (1915) 'Die Massen- und Sozialpsychologie im kritischen Überblick', Z. pädag. Psychol. 16, 385. (82)

MOLL, A. (1898) Untersuchungen über die Libido sexualis, Vol. 1, Berlin. (255)

NACHMANSOHN, M. (1915) 'Freuds Libidotheorie verglichen mit der Eroslehre Platos', Int. Z. Psychoanal., 3, 65. (91)

PFEIFER, S. (1919) 'Äusserungen infantil-erotischer Triebe im Spiele', Imago, 5, 243. (14)

PFISTER, O. (1910) Die Frömmigkeit des Grafen Ludwig von Zinzendorf, Vienna. (139)

(1921) 'Plato als Vorläufer der Psychoanalyse', *Int. Z. Psychoanal.*, **7**, 264. (91)

RANK, O. (1907) *Der Künstler*, Vienna. (55)

(1922) 'Die Don Juan-Gestalt', *Imago*, **8**, 142. (135)

RICKMAN, J. (ed.) (1937) *A General Selection from the Works of Sigmund Freud*, London. (6, 68)

SACHS, H. (1920) 'Gemeinsame Tagträume', *Int. Z. Psychoanal.*, **6**, 395. (137)

SADGER, I. (1914) 'Jahresbericht über sexuelle Perversionen', *Jb. psychoanal. psychopath. Forsch.*, **6**, 296. (157)

SCHOPENHAUER, A. (1851) 'Über die anscheinende Absichtlichkeit im Schicksale des Einzelnen', *Parerga und Paralipomena*, 1 (*Sämtliche Werke*, ed. Hübscher, Leipzig, 1938, **5**, 213). (50)

SIMMEL, E. (1918) *Kriegsneurosen und Psychisches Trauma*', Munich. (95)

SMITH, W. ROBERTSON (1885) *Kinship and Marriage*, London. (110)

SPIELREIN, S. (1912) 'Die Destruktion als Ursache des Werdens', *Jb. psychoanal. psychopath. Forsch.*, **4**, 465. (55)

STÄRCKE, A. (1914) Introduction to Dutch translation of Freud's ' "Civilized" Sexual Ethics and Modern Nervous Illness', Leyden. (55)

STEKEL, W. (1911a) *Die Sprache des Traumes*, Wiesbaden. 2nd edition, 1922. (197, 199)

(1911b) 'Zur Psychologie des Exhibitionismus', *Zbl. psychoanal.*, **1**, 494. (274)

(No Date) [1920] *Der telepathische Traum*, Berlin. (199)

TARDE, G. (1890) *Les lois de l'imitation*, Paris. (88)

TROTTER, W. (1916) *Instincts of the Herd in Peace and War*, London. (87, 118)

WEISMANN, A. (1882) *Über die Dauer des Lebens*, Jena. (45)

(1884) *Über Leben und Tod*, Jena. (45–7)

(1892) *Das Keimplasma*, Jena. (45–6, 56)

[*Trans.: The Germ-Plasm*, London, 1893.]

ZIEGLER, K. (1913) 'Menschen- und Weltenwerden', *Neue Jb. klass. Altert.*, **31**, 529. (58)

LIST OF ABBREVIATIONS

G.S.   = Freud, *Gesammelte Schriften* (12 vols.), Vienna, 1924–34

G.W.   = Freud, *Gesammelte Werke* (18 vols.), London, from 1940

C.P.   = Freud, *Collected Papers* (5 vols.), London, 1924–50

Standard Ed. = Freud, *Standard Edition* (24 vols.), London, from 1953

S.K.S.N.   = Freud, *Sammlung kleiner Schriften zur Neurosenlehre* (5 vols.), Vienna, 1906-22

Neurosenlehre und Technik = Freud, *Schriften zur Neurosenlehre und zur psychoanalytischen Technik (1913–1926)*, Vienna, 1931

Psychoanalyse der Neurosen = Freud, *Studien zur Psychoanalyse der Neurosen aus den Jahren 1913–1925*, Vienna, 1926

Sexualtheorie und Traumlehre = Freud, *Kleine Schriften zur Sexualtheorie und zur Traumlehre*, Vienna, 1931

Technik und Metapsychol. = Freud, *Zur Technik der Psychoanalyse und zur Metapsychologie*, Vienna, 1924

Theoretische Schriften = Freud, *Theoretische Schriften (1911–1925)*, Vienna, 1931

Traumlehre = Freud, *Kleine Beiträge zur Traumlehre*, Vienna, 1925

GENERAL INDEX

This index includes the names of non-technical authors. It also includes the names of technical authors where no reference is made in the text to specific works. For references to specific technical works, the Bibliography should be consulted.—The compilation of the index was undertaken by Mrs. R. S. Partridge.

THE COMPLETE PSYCHOLOGICAL WORKS OF SIGMUND FREUD
ALSO AVAILABLE FROM VINTAGE

☐ Volume I	0099426528	£11.99
☐ Volume II	0099426536	£10.99
☐ Volume III	0099426544	£9.99
☐ Volume IV	0099426552	£11.99
☐ Volume V	0099426560	£11.99
☐ Volume VI	0099426579	£12.99
☐ Volume VII	0099426587	£10.99
☐ Volume VIII	0099426595	£10.99
☐ Volume IX	0099426625	£9.99
☐ Volume X	0099426633	£10.99
☐ Volume XI	0099426641	£9.99
☐ Volume XII	009942665X	£10.99
☐ Volume XIII	0099426668	£10.99
☐ Volume XIV	0099426676	£10.99
☐ Volume XV	0099426684	£11.99
☐ Volume XVI	0099426692	£10.99
☐ Volume XVII	0099426722	£10.99
☐ Volume XIX	0099426749	£10.99
☐ Volume XX	0099426757	£9.99
☐ Volume XXI	0099426765	£10.99
☐ Volume XXII	0099426773	£9.99
☐ Volume XXIII	0099426781	£9.99
☐ Volume XXIV	009942679X	£9.99